The Balogun in Yoruba land
The Changing Fortunes of a Military Institution

Essays in Honour of Chief Lanre Razak
The Balogun of Epe land

edited by
Mufutau Oluwasegun Jimoh
and
Philip Oloruntola

BookBuilders • Editions Africa

© 2016 Oluwasegun Mufutau Jimoh
and Philip Oloruntola

ISBN: 978 978 921 125 8 cased
ISBN   978 978 921 126 5 soft

No part of this publication may be reproduced,
stored in a retrieval system or transmitted
by any form or by any means, electronic,
mechanical, photocopying , recording, or otherwise
without the expressed written consent of the
the copyright owners

Published in Nigeria by
BookBuilders • Editions Africa
2 Awosika Avenue, Bodija, Ibadan
email: bookbuildersafrica@yahoo.com
mobile: 0805 662 9266; 0809 920 9106

Printed in Ibadan
Oluben Printers, Oke-Ado
mobile: 0805 522 0209

Dedicated to the Memory of

Alhaja Amudalat Abegbe Rasak-Ajayi nee Muhammed Oloto

CONTENTS

Foreword
    Asiwaju Bola Tinubu. vii

Preface. ii

Acknowledgments. xiv

List of Contributors. xvi

Introduction. xix

Chapter One
Through the Changing Scenes: The Balogun in Yoruba-land from Pre-colonial to Post-19th Century
    Gabriel Oguntomisin. 1

Chapter Two
The Balogun in Ijebuland
    Taiwo Olatunde, Philip Oloruntola and
    Mufutau Oluwasegun Jimoh. 15

Chapter Three
Balogun Chieftaincy in Ogbomoso
    Rasheed Oyewole Olaniyi. 55

Chapter Four
The Balogun Institution in Ibadan, 1830-1955
    Mutiat Titilope Oladejo. 81

Chapter Five
The Balogun Institution in Epe
    Philip Oloruntola 103

Chapter Six
The Balogun Institution in Egbaland
    Lanre Davies. 139

Contents continued . . .

Chapter Seven
The Changing Status of Military Chiefs in Ijeshaland
Monsuru Muritala............................... 187

Chapter Eight
The Balogun Institution in the Akoko Area of Northeastern Yorubaland
Olusanya Faboyede.............................. 205

Chapter Nine
The Balogun Institution in Ilorin Emirate since 1823
Saad' Yusuf Omoiya............................. 219

APPENDICES
Appendix one: Biographical sketch of Baolgun General Lanre Rasak... 251
Appendix two: A commentary on the institution of the Balogun in Yorubaland, with special reference to Owu Chief Olusegun Obasanjo......................... 254

Index... 261

List of Illustrations
Map 1   Places in Yorubaland mentioned in the text.....

Figure 1.   Balogun Gbadamosi Kuku................... 36
Figure 2.   Balogun Akadiri Somori Kuku............... 39
Figure 3.   Balogun Fasasi Adesoye..................... 41
Figure 4.   Balogun Jinadu Alaba Alatishe.............. 45
Figure 5.   Balogun Shote.............................. 49
Figure 6.   Balogun J.A.B.Odunnuga.................... 51

FOREWORD

The Balogun in Yorubaland: The changing fortunes of a military institution: Essays in Honour of Chief Lanre Razak—The Balogun of Epe Land" is one book that must be described as phenomenal.

This outstanding volume edited by the duo of Mufutau Oluwasegun Jimoh and Philip Oloruntola did not only enrich my understanding of the Yoruba historical tradition, but also espouses the governance order as established by the founding founders of the Yoruba race.

The book also did well in establishing that before the needless modification of the Yoruba identity, Yorubas had military formations; pseudo military units and diplomatic outposts *cum* foreign relations; hierarchical and executive organogram; judicial and arbitration institutions and much more.

The security of lives and property was taken for granted in ancient Yoruba nation, and the authors were deft enough in enlightening deep thinkers to understand that this tranquillity was partly synonymous to the personality occupying the traditional Balogun— head/leader of military—chieftaincy title. In short, life in Yoruba nation-state marshalled by the Balogun was well placed; well-ordered and richly defined. Nonetheless, what is most fundamental is that students of history now have history and facts to affix to their knowledge of pan-Yoruba history.

Foreword

Without gainsaying, the authors should be specially commended for adding to the body of academic knowledge and deepening our collective intellectual calculus on the Yoruba cultural and political epicentre, with special focus on the chieftaincy title of Balogun—the uncrowned ruler in Yoruba states.

From chapter one all through to chapter nine, the foray into the Balogun institution converges at the same juncture—that the Blowgun title is only a notch below royalty! Put simply, through the ages, from Ijebuland to Ogbomoso, to Ibadan, to Epe, to Egbaland, to Akoko area and Ilorin, the Balogun is *primus inter pares*.

Hence, in modern day Yoruba state, irrespective of one's economic endowment, the Balogun chieftaincy title is only bestowed on deserving personality gifted with courage; candour; charisma; gusto and such spiritual wherewithal needed as *mien* to satisfy the heroics synonymous with Balogun's of old.

I will continue to speak about his book in glowing terms because it has created historical wealth for historians and guardians of history alike. With pictorial evidences to buttress their submissions, the authors have upped the *ante* of historical science. The book is, therefore, highly recommended as must read and a must have for all and sundry.

Asiwaju Bola Tinubu
Lagos, Nigeria

PREFACE

The *Balogun* institution is part of an elaborate chieftaincy tradition among the Yoruba of south western Nigeria, whose antiquity predates modern times.[1] The institution is, arguably, one of few traditional institutions of the people with a history across their homesteads.[2] Literally, it is synonymous with the head or leader of a military group - *Baba ni ogun* - whose warlike virtues, courage, charms and military prowess the title extols. But, it is also a

---

1 For historical and ethnographic data on Yoruba sub-ethnic groups, see: S. Johnson, 1921, *History of the Yoruba from the earliest times to the beginning of the British Protectorate*, Lagos: CMS Bookshop; D. Forde, 1954, *The Yoruba-Speaking Peoples of South-Western Nigeria*: London, International African Institute; U. Beier. 1957. "Before Oduduwa." *Odu* No. 3, pp. 25-32; S.O, Biobaku, 1956, *The Origin of the Yorubas*, Lugard Lectures, Lagos: Government Printer; H.U. Beier, 'Before Oduduwa', *Odu* No 3; R.W. Westcott, 'Did the Yorubas Come from Egypt', *Odu* No 4; B. Fage and F. Millet, 1960, 'Ancient Ife: An Ethnographic Summary', *Odu* No 8; J.A Atanda, 1980, *An Introduction to Yoruba History*, Ibadan: Ibadan University Press; J.A. Atanda, 1997. "Who are the Yorubas?" *The News*, 26th May 1997. W. Bascom. 1980. The Yoruba of South-western Nigeria. London: Holt Rinehart and Winston Inc.

2 The homesteads of Yoruba–speaking people in south western Nigeria encompasses present-day Ogun, Oyo, Ondo, Ekiti, Lagos and Osun States, as well as nearly a half of Kwara and Kogi states in north central part of the country.

Preface

designation that is socially and politically loaded, signifying Yoruba warlords not just as a class of military aristocrat who are saddled with guaranteeing security of lives and property in their domains, but also as traditional chiefs with considerable political influence. This book examines histories of origin and significance of the chieftaincy, as well as various contexts of its evolution into a formidable traditional institution in Yoruba land. In doing so, the peculiar traits and experiences of various holders of the title in select Yoruba communities are examined within specific historical contexts, drawing attention to the exploits of heroes and villains in their collective history.

Yet, this book is not so much about eulogising the heroes and condemning the villains, as it is about drawing attention to effects of change and continuity on power structure in Yoruba communities. Indeed, the study is situated within larger history of traditional institutions, particularly with regards to remarkable modifications these institutions have undergone, on which there is a large body of pioneer studies that have provided a general background.[3] Two major general agreements are noticeable in the literature. The one is

---

3 Not the least is the following works: T. Falola and G. Oguntomisin, 2001. *Yoruba Warlords of the Nineteenth Century*, Trenton: Africa World Press Inc; T. Falola, 1984. *The Military in Nineteenth Century Yoruba Politics*, Oyo: University of Ife Press.

Preface

that traditional institutions exhibit prevailing societal features and constantly adapt to new realities across space and time.[4] In other words, their overriding values are subject to dictates of dominant ideologies of the society. The other, more specifically about military institutions, is that title holders have a high tendency to wield both political and military authorities by virtue of ascription, than by right of succession. This was true of great exploits of military elites (*Basorun, Are Ona Kakanfo, Balogun, Olorogun* etc.) who, within the contexts of Yoruba internecine wars in the nineteenth century, were instrumental in forging power alliances across the length and breadth of Yoruba land.[5]

The present volume is not intended to replicate this line of thinking. Rather, it explores new perspectives, x-raying the effects of vagaries of colonialism, western

---

4 O. Vaughan, editor, *Indigenous Political Structures and Governance in Africa*, (Ibadan: Bookcraft, 2004). M. Crowder and O. Ikime, *West African Chiefs: Their changing status under colonial rule and independence*: (Ife: University of Ife Press, 1970).

5 J.F.A, Ajayi, 1974, 'The Aftermath of the Collapse of Old Oyo', in J.F.A, Ajayi and Michael Crowther (eds.) *History of West Africa*, Volume 2, London: Longman; J.F.A Ajayi and R. Smith, 1964, *Yoruba Warfare in the 19th Century*, Cambridge; O.O Ayantuga, 1965, 'Ijebu and Its Neighbours, 1851-1914', Ph.D. Thesis, London; S.O. Biobaku, 1957, *The Egba and their Neighbours, 1842-1872*, London; B. Awe, 1964, 'The Rise of Ibadan as a Yoruba Powers, 1851-1893', D.Phil. Thesis, Oxford.

Preface

legal system, party politics, bureaucracy reforms and, even, oriental and occidental religious ideologies (Christianity and Islam), to name a few, on Yoruba elite military institutions. It discourses effects and courses rather than just causes, which is a slight departure from earlier treatises on the subject. The underlying assumption for this approach is that human societies are in constant flux. Thus, it adopts an approach that focuses on adaptability and resilience factors in the evolution of *Balogun* institution across time and space. To accomplish this, the following posers are raised and addressed. Has a situation in which *Balogun* and other traditional military title holders held near absolute power in pre-colonial Yoruba societies changed? How much change has taken place, particularly in the light of tremendous alterations that traditional institutions have witnessed in colonial and post-colonial times? What were the drivers and circumstances that guided the direction of the change? What is the implication of the change for power arrangement in post nineteenth century Yoruba communities?

The case study approach is adopted in exploring the posers. In other words, each chapter in the book dwells on the intricate and fluid history of the institution in specific Yoruba societies. The intent was to generate context-based data and avoid drawing generalisations. The contextual approach served the purpose of ensuring that they are not trite repetitions of the old wisdom,

Preface

even though their positions are built on existing ideas and assumptions on traditional politics. Whereas drawing general patterns was not a primary motive, one observation that is common to all the sites that are brought under spotlight is that *Balogun* chieftaincy comes across as an institution of leadership, whose functionality bears relevance not only in public safety and defence, but also in political and diplomatic matters. Put differently, holders of the title manifests commitment that goes beyond safeguarding the sovereignty of their communities and protection of the people from both internal and external aggressions.

ACKNOWLEDGMENTS

First, we wish to thank all the contributors for responding to this project and bearing with our numerous editorial demands. In particular, we appreciate Professor Gabriel Oguntomisin, for being a bridge builder between old and new history scholars. Even in retirement from active academic engagements, he did not refuse our invitation to contribute to the book. His introductory chapter helped set the tone of the book.

We also wish to express our gratitude to Dr. Babatunde Oduntan of Towson University, Maryland, USA as well as Dr. Saheed Aderinto of Western Carolina University, also of USA; and Mr. Muyiwa Kalejaiye, News Editor, Radio Lagos/Eko FM, for reading the manuscript and for making useful and valuable suggestions.

We are most grateful to the late Professor Olakunle Lawal, our teacher, mentor, friend and benefactor, formerly of the Department of History, University of Ibadan and former Commissioner of Education in Lagos State.

We also want to thank Dr. Victor Osaro Edo, of the Department of History, University of Ibadan, for his encouraging remarks and for helping us establish contacts with some of the contributors. Dr. Kunbi Olasope, Department of Classics, University of Ibadan, also deserves much appreciation for her constant nudges and

Acknowledgments

hospitality on those extended afternoons, when the manuscripts were being prepared.

Prince Delano Adepoju-Conde and Chief Wole Ojikutu deserve special appreciation for their invaluable interventions at a very critical stage in the production of the publication.

We would be remiss if we did not acknowledge that the financial burden of this publication (from research to production) was borne exclusively by one individual, Chief Lanre Razak, whose passion for history and historical scholarship, goes beyond partisan patronage, despite his reputation for being active in party politics. His commitment to undistorted history is in short supply among people of his political hue and stature, which makes him come across as an individual who deserves honour. It was on the merit of this exemplary benevolence that this volume was published in his honour. Coincidentally, his mother passed on while the manuscripts were being prepared for press. The volume was therefore dedicated to her memory. It is our expectation that this project will serve as worthy example and stimulate similar gestures from members of the public.

Our appreciation also goes to the staff of Silver Lining Consults, the project coordinators, and BookBuilders, the publishers, for accommodating our requests with professional aplomb.

Above all, we thank Almighty God, the ultimate source of our inspiration.

Mufutau Oluwasegun Jimoh
Philip Oloruntola

LIST OF CONTRIBUTORS

Gabriel Oguntomisin is a retired Professor of History and former head of the History Department, University of Ibadan. He has researched and written extensively on Yoruba traditional institutions, warfare and diplomacy in Yoruba land in the 19th century.

Lanre Davies, PhD is a Senior Lecturer in Department of History and Diplomatic Studies, Olabisi Onabanjo University, Ago Iwoye, Nigeria.

Monsuru Muritala, PhD is a lecturer in Department of History, University of Ibadan, Ibadan, Nigeria.

Mutiat Titilope Oladejo, PhD is a lecturer in Department of History, University of Ibadan.

Philip Oloruntola is a holder of Bachelor and Master's Degrees in History and Anthropology respectively. He is of Department of Archaeology and Anthropology, University of Ibadan. Nigeria.

Olatunde Taiwo is a lecturer in Department of History and Diplomatic Studies, Olabisi Onabanjo University, Ago Iwoye, Nigeria.

Olusanya Faboyede, PhD, is a Senior Lecturer in Department, of History and International Studies, Adekunle Ajasin University, Akungba-Akoko, Nigeria.

Oluwasegun Mufutau Jimoh is a lecturer in the Department of History and International Studies, Federal University, Birnin-Kebbi, Kebbi State, Nigeria. He is a member of Society of Social History, USA, and a research fellow with French Institute for Research in Africa.

List of Contributors

Rasheed Oyewole Olaniyi, PhD is an Associate Professor of History, in the Department of History, University of Ibadan, Nigeria.

Saad' Yusuf Omoiya, PhD is a Senior Lecturer in Department of History and International Studies, University of Ilorin, Ilorin, Nigeria.

INTRODUCTION

Initially, this volume was meant to be an all-encompassing study of the Balogun institution across Yoruba societies. But the pursuit of such an agenda in a single volume would have been too ambitious, if not impossible. For instance, determining the Yoruba communities whose narratives should be incorporated into the volume posed a great challenge; particularly so because the Yorubaland that we know today, is remarkably different from what it used to be. Culturally speaking, the area occupied by the people is a transnational territory. Besides their homesteads in southwestern Nigeria, the Yoruba occupy an 'internationally partitioned culture area'[6] which embraces West Africa and the Atlantic World.[7] According to Samuel Johnson,[8] an early historian of the

---

1 The phrase is borrowed from A.I. Asiwaju, "From the Mono to the Niger: Dahomey, Yorubaland, Borgu and Benin" in *West African Transformations: Comparative Impacts of French and British Colonialism*, (Lagos: Malthouse Press, 2001) p. 2.

2 The cultural influence of the Yoruba in the Atlantic World reaches as far as Cuba, Brazil, Trinidad, Bahamas, Haiti, Costa Rica, USA, etc. For comprehensive studies on Yoruba Diaspora in the Atlantic World, read: T. Falola and M.D. Childs, editors, *The Yoruba Diaspora in the Atlantic World*, (Bloomington: Indiana University Press, 2004)

3 S. Johnson, *History of the Yoruba from the earliest times to the beginning of the British Protectorate*, (Lagos: CMS Bookshop, 1921); J.A Atanda, *An Introduction to Yoruba History*, (Ibadan: Ibadan University Press, 1980); J.A. Atanda, 1997. "Who are the Yoruba?"

The Balogun in Yorubaland

Yoruba, the territories 'occupied' by the people before the middle of the nineteenth century embraced areas north of the Bight of Benin, west of the River Niger below its confluence with River Benue, south of the western tributary of the Niger above the confluence, as well as the adjacent parts of eastern Dahomey (now Benin Republic) and central Togo further west. These expansive frontiers of various Yoruba societies were, however, never united politically.

In the same vein, it was really not convenient to speak of 'the Yoruba' as a collective identity until the 1880s, when a mission-educated intelligentsia and clergies began to create a pan-Yoruba cultural nationalism. Prior to the 1880s, Yoruba sub-ethnic groups existed and related as semi-autonomous monarchical states with distinct ethnological identities. [9] Of these the principal ones were the Oyo, Egba, Egbado, Ijebu, Ijesha, Ekiti, Ondo, Akoko, Awori and Owo. Intense and dramatic changes characterised by internal dislocations associated with the turbulent ethnic wars of the nineteenth century and the attendant

---

The News, 26th May 1997. W. Bascom. 1980. *The Yoruba of Southwestern Nigeria*. (London: Holt Rinehart and Winston 1980).

4 For details on the evolution of Yoruba Nationalism, see: A. S, Ajala, 2009, 'Yoruba Nationalist Movements, Ethnic Politics and Violence: A Creation from Historical Consciousness and Socio-Political Space in South Western Nigeria', Department of Anthropology and African Studies, Johannes Guttenberg Universitat, Mainz, Working Paper, No 105.

Introduction

population mix further induced new identities, such as the emergence of refugee settlements and towns such as Ibadan, Ijaye and Abeokuta, as well as survivalist and defensive coalitions, especially the Ekiti-Parapo confederacy, forged among the Ijesha and Ekiti, primarily against powerful common threats. These already complex identities were accentuated by external pressures exerted by colonial rule and boundary delimitations.[10]

For analytical convenience, it was not unusual for scholars to treat Yoruba societies as clusters, employing linguistic affinities, historical similarities and

---

5 For details on the impact of the 19th Century Yoruba Civil War and Colonialism on the demographic and political map of Yoruba land see: J.F.A, Ajayi, 1974, 'The Aftermath of the Collapse of Old Oyo', in J.F.A, Ajayi and Michael Crowther (eds.) *History of West Africa*, Volume 2, London: Longman; J.F.A Ajayi and R. Smith, 1964, *Yoruba Warfare in the 19th Century*, Cambridge; O.O Ayantuga, 1965, 'Ijebu and Its Neighbours, 1851-1914', Ph.D. Thesis, London; S.O. Biobaku, 1957, *The Egba and their Neighbours, 1842-1872*, London; B. Awe, 1964, 'The Rise of Ibadan as a Yoruba Powers, 1851-1893', D.Phil. Thesis, Oxford.; J.F.A Ajayi, 1965, *Christian Missions in Nigeria, 1841-1891*, Longman; A.B Aderibigbe, 1958, 'The Expansion of the Lagos Protectorates, 1868-1902', Ph.D. Thesis, London; A.I. Asiwaju, 1976, *Western Yorubaland Under European Rule, 1889-1945: A Comparative Analysis of French and British Colonialism*, London: Longman; I.A. Akinjogbin, 1967, *Dahomey and Its Neighbours, 1793-1878*, Cambridge: Cambridge University Press; A.I. Asiwaju, 2001, 'From the Mono to the Niger: Dahomey, Yoruba land, Borgu and Benin in the Nineteen Century', pp.10-31, A.I. Asiwaju, 2001, in *West African Transformations: Comparative Impacts of French and British Colonialism*, Lagos: Malthouse Press Limited.

geographical contiguity as yardsticks for analysing similarities and dissimilarities among them. For example, scholars are fond of delineating Yoruba territories of the post-nineteenth century internecine wars into coordinates such as central, western and eastern Yorubaland in their analysis.[11] Central Yoruba land contained the cultural core around Ife and Ilesha. Western Yorubaland included Ibadan, Abeokuta, Ijebu, Lagos, and the western sector of Oyo. Eastern Yoruba land contained Ondo, Ekiti, Owo, Akoko, Ikare. Both the western and eastern Yoruba were further divided into northern and southern clusters. This included towns beyond Ondo's northeastern boundary such as Kabba and Igbomina (in Kwara and Kogi states) which are sometimes called the 'Okun' people from their form of greeting.[12]

One of the ways the challenge posed by identity proliferation has been resolved was through a claim of common descent from an ancestor called *Oduduwa*, a

---

6 S. A, Akintoye, , 1971, *Revolution and Power Politics in Yoruba land 1840-1893: Ibadan Expansion and the Rise of Ekiti Parapo*, Ibadan: Longman; A. Akinjogbin, "Wars in Yorubaland, 1793-1893: An Analytical Categorisation", in A. Akinjogbin (ed.), 1998. *War and Peace in Yorubaland, 1783-1893*, Ibadan: Heinemann Educational Books Nigeria Limited, pp. 33-51.

7 For a review of the creation of Kwara State, see D.J. Murray, 1968, 'Kwara State and its Administration', *Administration*, The Quarterly Review of the Institute of Administration, Vol. II, No 3, University of Ife, pp.130-139

Introduction

semi-mythical figure, who is believed to have established the Ife dynasty in Ile-Ife, their cultural source.[13] This common descent myth is reinforced by the fact that they all speak a mutually intelligible language. They have been further inspired by group survival within the context of ethnic politics in colonial and post-colonial periods in Nigeria to evolve a pan-Yoruba identity across and beyond sub-ethnic and interstate divides, such that it is now convenient to speak of a Yoruba nation.[14]

In deciding the Yoruba communities that should be included in this volume, therefore, we felt it was reasonable to yield to current realities. Since all of them have one viable military institution or the other, especially that of *Balogun,* we had to cast our nets wide

---

8 Ground breaking works on Yoruba ethno genesis include: S. Johnson, 1921, *History of the Yoruba from the earliest times to the beginning of the British Protectorate*, Lagos: CMS Bookshop; U. Beier. 1957. "Before Oduduwa." *Odu* No. 3, pp. 25-32; S.O, Biobaku, 1956, *The Origin of the Yorubas*, Lugard Lectures, Lagos: Government Printer; H.U. Beier, 'Before Oduduwa', *Odu* No 3; R.W. Westcott, 'Did the Yorubas Come from Egypt', *Odu* No 4; B. Fage and F. Millet, 1960, 'Ancient Ife: An Ethnographic Summary', *Odu* No 8.

9 For recent ethnographic data on Yoruba Nationalism in colonial and post-colonial Nigeria, see: A.S Ajala, *Yoruba Nationalism: Politics, Culture and Violence in Southwestern Nigeria (1900-2012)*, (Koln: Rudiger Koppe Verlag 2013); T. Falola and A. Genova, 'The Yoruba Nation' in *Yoruba Identity and Power Politics*, T. Falola and A. Genova, editors, (Woodbridge, Rochester University, 2006) pp. 29-48.

and ensure that, at least, one community in each of the various sub-cultural coordinates in Yoruba land—central, western, eastern and northern—are fairly represented. Narrowing the scope this way did not only help to spread data generated, it also made more in-depth studies possible and reduced bias. This approach is, however, not without its own imperfections. We realised that the communities whose narratives are not integrated into this volume, even though they are by no means less significant, are more than those that are examined. This constitutes a major limitation to the study. Nevertheless, it is envisaged that the towns and areas that are covered would have mirrored a general pattern in Yoruba societies.

Organisation of the Book

This book is organised into nine chapters. In Chapter 1, Gabriel Oguntomisin presents a panoramic view of the roles and changing authority of the Balogun in the politics of Yoruba towns. He examines the status of a *Balogun* in Yorubaland through changing scenes, from pre-colonial to post-nineteenth century, drawing attention to different connotations of the *Balogun* title such as: *Baba ni Ogun* (chief warrior/military commander) and *Oloye/Ijoye Ilu* (town chiefs) with or without active military responsibilities. He posits that the numerous honorary and compensatory *Balogun* titles now usually conferred by the *Oba* (king) on distinguished individuals, as well as the purely

Introduction

religious *Balogun* titles conferred in churches and mosques are modern day adaptations of traditional institutions to new socio-political realities in Yoruba societies. Alluding to relevant instances across Yorubaland, he concluded that the trend represents a gradual mutation of the Balogun title from a purely traditional office to a socio-political and religious title, thereby reinforcing the perception that traditional title holders, including prospective holders of the Balogun title, no longer have to wield military prowess as a *sine qua non*.

In chapter 2, Taiwo Olatunde, Philip Oloruntola and Mufutau Oluwasegun Jimoh situate the argument within socio-political realities of Ijebuland. They argued that the ascendency of the Balogun institution in pre-colonial Ijebuland fostered the disappearance of pre-existing traditional military offices. They demonstrated that some pre-twentieth century Baloguns in Ijebu-Ode, for instance, wielded formidable influence to the extent of being accessories to the disposition and enthronement of a new Awujale, the paramount king in Ijebu-Ode. Even though the decision about the choice of who occupied the office of the Balogun was initially subject to the endorsement of the Awujale, they argued (within the contexts of the life and times of some prominent Ijebu Balogun title holders) that the interplay of wealth, religious affiliation (particularly of Islam), rotational policies and political patronage, rather than kingly ratification, have been the predominant yardsticks for producing Balogun title holders in Ijebu-Ode and in several other Ijebu towns, in the post-colonial period; hence, the power and influence of Balogun chieftains within the religious, cultural and political circles in Ijebu-Ode.

In chapter 3, Rasheed Olaniyi argues that the Balogun institution was a creation of the nineteenth century, when internecine warfare was rife in Yoruba land. Premising his position on the Balogun chieftaincy in Ogbomoso, he argues that 'at the onset, the Balogun was purely a military chieftain; later when there was no more war, the Balogun became redundant'. Olaniyi holds the position that in order to ensure that the Balogun title holder was relevant in contemporary Ogbomoso, the office had to be modified to suit changing realities. In the new order, the *Balogun*became

> a prominent chieftain among the Ilu (town chiefs) and a member of the advisory council of the town...[that] plays important roles in ensuring law and order in the town through collaboration with vigilante groups, night guards, police and other security agencies.

The discourse on the *Balogun* institution in Ibadan (c.1830-1955) in chapter 4 presents a vivid illustration of its changing status and re-adaptation towards meeting the requirement of statehood. In spite of the eccentricities of 'power, diplomacy and autocracy of the *Balogun*institution' in Ibadan, MutiatTitilopeOladejo painstakingly established how a 'state and an economy that was sustained by the military aristocratic system of

Introduction

government' were carefully engineered to suit new socio-political realities. For instance, she argued that Anglo-Ibadan relations, epitomised by colonial administrative re-arrangements, which is embodied by the politics of Ibadan Town Council, and a drive for politics of inclusion and social order within 'traditional power struggles and modern party politics', necessitated new roles for *Balogun* title holders in an increasingly demilitarised Ibadan.

In chapter 5 Philip Oloruntola examines changing fortunes of the Balogun in Epe within the context of the composite nature of the town. The nineteenth century witnessed far-reaching political changes in Yorubaland, one of the fallouts of which was an upsurge of refugees and proliferation of host and refuge towns. Epe, a small Ijebu town on the northern estuaries of Lagos, experienced an influx of migrants from Awori Kingdom of Lagos, who eventually settled there and developed distinct socio-political identities and institutions, including a Balogun chieftaincy structure, which rivalled their Ijebu host. From a comparative perspective, the chapter presents a survey of dynamics of the Balogun institution among the two Yoruba sub-ethnic groups with emphasis on how it evolved and adapted to changing scenes in the town.

The evolution of the Balogun class from Olorogun society/council among the Egba, according to Lanre Davies in chapter 6, presupposes that the former was a nineteenth century necessity to unite the various Egba communities viz., Egba Alake, EgbaGbagura, EgbaOke-Ona and Owu, around a central commander-in-chief. Despite the compromise, which became an instrument of political cohesion in Egbaland, the various Egba groups still maintained independent military hierarchies under varying degrees of autonomy from the federal force. The implications of this loose arrangement for the post nineteenth century military fortunes of the Egba, as well as its twentieth century corollary, are well documented in chapter 6.

In chapter 7, Monsuru Muritala discusses the changing status of military chiefs in Ijeshaland. All the Yoruba communities spotlighted in this volume have a Balogun institution, except Ijeshaland. This was as a result of the nature of the allied communities of the Ekiti-parapo and the implications of the military structure of the Elegbe war leaders at Kiriji war camp. The fact that the military order of the confederacy existed as a convolution of parallel authorities hindered the adoption of, say, an Ibadan type title (Balogun) for war leaders in Ilesha. Even the great Ogedengbe of Ilesha, 'in spite of the enormous influence and power' that he wielded was unable to appropriate the position of Balogun. Thus, rather than the title of 'Balogun', he was given the exclusive title of *'Obanla'*, while other traditional chieftaincy titles in the Elegbe military/ war chieftaincy group, such as *Lejoka, Lejofi, Lokiran, Lodifi, Rinsinkin, Losare* and *Lokoyi*, are conferred on deserving Ijesha indigenes in both traditional and modern times.

Introduction

Chapter 8 highlights the Balogun institution in the Akoko area of northeastern Yorubaland. Olusanya Faborede affirms that 'the Balogun emerged in Akokoland as the most powerful war chief whose military acumen and political power advanced the growth of diplomatic relations among the Akoko communities'.

The resilience and adaptability of the Balogun institution across cultural settings is demonstrated in chapter 9. Saad' Yusuf Omoiya locates the founding of the Balogun institution in Ilorin, in the aftermath of the rivalry between Alaafin Aole of the Old Oyo Empire and his Aare Ona Kakanfo (generalissimo) Afonja, and argues that the death of Afonja left a political vacuum that was seized by forces that were loyal to the Hausa/Fulani interests in Ilorin, where Afonja had sought refuge. He asserts that, in relation to the political structure of the Ilorin Emirate Council, the Baloguns (who are not necessarily direct descendants of Aare Afonja) exist as dominant members in the emirate administration of the town, rather than just mere commanders in the military. Omoiya, however, paints a picture of a Balogun institution that has, since the colonial period, been relegated to a mere ethnic representation in the traditional emirate system in Ilorin. The book winds up with a postscript from Chief Olusegun Obasanjo (the Balogun of Owu, and a former president of the Federal Republic of Nigeria). He discusses the nature and general background on the

The Balogun in Yorubaland

Balogun institution in Yorubaland— and focusses on the evolution, roles and changing circumstances within the institution among the Owu, as well as the positive impacts expected of holders of the title across Yoruba societies.

* * * *

This volume is not a conclusive discourse on Balogun chieftaincy in Yorubaland. For instance, in deciding the Yoruba communities that should be included in this volume, we felt it was reasonable to yield to historical realities, namely that almost all Yoruba communities have one viable military institution or the other, especially that of *Balogun*. As a result, we had to cast our nets wide and ensure that, at least, one community in each of the various sub-cultural coordinates in Yoruba land—central, western, eastern and northern—are fairly represented. Narrowing the scope this way did not only help to spread data generated, it also made more in-depth studies possible and reduced biases.

The approach is, however, not without its own imperfections. We realised that the communities whose narratives are not integrated into the volume, even though are by no means less significant, are more than those that are examined. This constitutes a gap that similar studies of the Yoruba in future could build on, although it is envisaged that the towns and areas that

Introduction

are covered would have mirrored a general pattern in Yorubaland.

Moreso, history is an ongoing discourse and an unending dialogue and a diachronic exchange between the past and the present. Every publication that is worth any merit should stimulate new enquiries that will extend the frontiers of knowledge beyond the present scope. Therefore, we are hopeful that each of the chapters in this volume will not only give readers fresh perspectives on the subject matter, but also serve as an invaluable secondary source for similar studies of the Yoruba in future. In the meantime, we invite our readers to join in reflecting on the effect of the forces of modernity on power structures in Yoruba communities.

Mufutau Oluwasegun Jimoh
Philip Oloruntola

1

Through the Changing Scenes:
The Balogun in Yorubaland from pre-Colonial to the Post -19th Century

Gabriel Oguntomisin

Introduction

The institution of the *Balogun* can be traced to the evolution of mini-states and the inception of warfare in Yorubaland.[1] This period witnessed inter-state squabbles, not only over the acquisition of scarce resources, the occupation of geographically suitable places for settlement but also the pursuit of ambitious leaders for territorial aggrandizement. Initially, struggle among the mini-states featured wrestling bouts among their leaders. The defeat of a mini-state leader meant the surrender of his state.[2] However, as sedentary

---

1 For the development of mini and mega states in Yorubaland see G.O. Oguntomisin, in J.A Atanda, editor, *A Comprehensive History of the Yoruba People up to 1800* (Ibadan: John Archers (2007) p. 16-23; J.F.A. Ajayi, and M. Crowder, *History of West Africa*, volume one (London:Longman, 1977 repr) p. 201-263.

2 G.O. Oguntomisin, "Warfare in Pre-colonial Yorubaland: Development and Changes in Weapons, Strategy and Tactics"in *Nigerian Warfare through the Ages*, A.S. Ekoko, and S.D. Agbi, editor,

communities increased in population and resources, wrestling bouts began to develop into wars, and the organization of people either in the form of volunteers or levies became the vogue. In some states or kingdoms such as the Old Oyo, standing military officers called the *eso* (royal guards) were organized as state militia.[3] In this process intrepid fighters adroit in the art of war, were appointed by the civil authority as the war leaders.

The war leader was called various names such as *Balogun, Jagun/Jagunna, Gbonka, Olori Ogun,* etc. in different Yoruba states, kingdoms and communities. Thus, the Balogun (*Baba ni Ogun*) that is, chief warrior or war commander was an *oye ilu* (town chief) responsible for leading warriors to war.[4] He was also responsible for organizing able-bodied men in his community, state or kingdom for defensive and offensive purposes.

Before the 19th century, the Balogun was responsible to the civil authority. He was appointed by the king. In some Ekiti towns, he was from the grade of

---

Lagos, National War museum Committee, p. 45; T.O. Ogunkoya describes the wrestling contest between Obante and Oluigbo the head of the Idoko. *Journal, of the Historical Society of Nigeria,* 1(1) 1956 p. 50.

3 S.O. Johnson, *The History of the Yorubas* (Lagos: C.S.S. Bookshops, 1973, reprt), p.3.

4 Ibid, p. 133 - 135.

elegbe (war-chiefs) or *egiri* (age grade of warriors)[5]. In Old Oyo, he was initially the *Gbonka*, the first among the sixteen senior *Eso*.[6] By 1689, when Alaafin Obalokun reorganized the Oyo military and created the title of the *Aare-Ona-Kakanfo* (commander-in-chief),[7] the appointment of the Balogun in Oyo became formalized. He was officially appointed by the Alaafin and posted to a vulnerable area of the kingdom.

The duty of the Balogun during this period was mainly military, particularly in times of war. In the absence of war, he engaged in his vocation either as a farmer or a hunter. He did not determine the cause or the course of war. These were within the purview of the civil authority who was responsible for the conduct of the foreign and internal affairs of his kingdom or state. The Balogun did not fight his own personal war, as all wars were declared by the king and fought in his name. Johnson says:

> Every expedition is supposed to be sent out by the king (Alaafin). It is in his name war was generally declared, and his permission or at any rate his assent must be obtained before any army can march out.[8]

---

5 For Ekiti, see Revd Father, Oguntuyi. *History of Ekiti from the Beginning to 1900*. (Ibadan: Bisi Books, 1979).

6 Johnson, p. 73.

7 Ibid, p. 74.

8 Johnson, p. 135; see also S. Robert. "Yoruba Warfare and Weapons," in S.O. Biobaku, editor, *Sources of Yoruba History*, (Oxford: Clarendon Press, 1973), p. 227.

Indeed the Alaafin determined the period for the termination of war. It was the convention in Oyo that a military expedition must not exceed three months. An are-ona-kakanfo (commander-in-chief) was expected to win a war within three months or, on the contrary, be carried home a dead man.[9]

The Balogun in the nineteenth century

The 19th century was a period of endemic warfare in Yorubaland. Wars were frequent and revolutionary in nature. The major wars can be categorized as (a) the wars that attended the decline and fall of the Old Oyo Empire (b) the Owu and Egba wars (c) Ibadan imperial wars (d) the Ekiti-Parapo wars.[10]

Apart from these internecine wars, the Yoruba had to defend themselves against invasions from the Edo Kingdom of Benin in the North-East and the Kingdom of Dahomey from the West.

The consequences of these wars were far-reaching. First, there was large-scale destruction of life and property. Many towns in the northern part of the Yorubaland were destroyed. Prominent among these were Old Oyo (Oyo- Ile) Ikoyi, Esiele, Wonworo and in the south, Owu and many Egba towns.

---

9 Johnson, p. 74.

10 For these wars, see T. Falola and G.O. Oguntomisin, *Yoruba Warlords of the 19th century* ,(Trenton: African World Press, 2010) p. 3–8.

Second, there was an upsurge of refugees and a proliferation of refugee centres and towns such as Ibadan, Ijaye, Abeokuta, Aiyede-Ekiti and Oke-Odan where non-civil authorities held the reins of power. Third, there was the emergence of professional soldiers, that is, a cadre of warlords who took warfare as a serious occupation.[11] These warlords had new ideas of war and they were no longer willing to subordinate themselves to traditional authorities. Prominent among them were Oluyole, Ibikunle, Ogunmola and many others from Ibadan; Ogedengbe and Arimoro of Ilesa; Fabunmi of Okemesi; Adeyale of Ila and Ekiti warlords such as Faboro, and Aduluju.[12] Fourth, warfare itself became revolutionized with attendant change in tactics, strategy and weaponry. Total warfare involving long sieges, greater casualties and large deployment of troops was introduced.[13]

In these new circumstances, traditional authorities could no longer cope with contemporary political chaos and insecurities. Thus, the Balogun acquired greater power and status than hitherto. First, they organized and trained their own armies comprising their war-boys who were either their slaves, members of their own families, their retainers and others who came under

---

[11] J.F.A. Ajayi, "Professional warriors in nineteenth century Yoruba politics" *Tarikh*, 1(1) 1968: p. 72–81; for details on the activities of these warriors, see Falola and Oguntomisin, op.cit.

[12] Falola and Oguntomisin, op.cit

[13] Oguntomisin, p. 56-59.

their banners for protection. Second, they could lead their own private army freely on military expeditions for the purpose of booty and acquisition of political power. Third, they could determine the cause and dictate the course, direction and dimension of wars without recourse to any civil or traditional authority. Wars were declared and fought in their names.[14] Fourth, some of them acquired political power and assumed rulership in some towns where they established military-oriented governments. Examples of such warlords were Esubiyi of Aiyede-Ekiti, Kurunmi of Ijaye, the Ibadan and Egba military rulers.[15] Fifth, the warlords relegated the civil authority to the background in political affairs, including the determination of policy, internal and external affairs. In Ibadan for instance, decisions on important matters affecting the state were made in the war front.

The Ekiti and Ijesa warlords that congregated at the war camp in Okemesi usurped the position of the Ekiti and Ijesa traditional heads in the peace negotiation that ended the Ekiti-Parapo wars[16]. In Ilorin, the Balogun became pre-eminent in political and economic matters. Banwo states:

---

14 Falola and Oguntomisin, p. 17- 18.

15 Ibid; O. Olaoba Bamigboyega, "The Ata Dynasty in Aiyede Kingdom–1850–1880: An experiment in traditional political culture," *African Notes*, xiv, 1 & 2, (1990) p. 62 - 69.

16 Johnson, op cit.; C.M.S. I/1/9, Phillips Diary and letter books, 1877–1886, entry for 1886.

The Balogun: pre-Colonial to post-19th Century

> The emirate was divided into four wards, each headed by a Balogun (war commander) who represented a major interest-cum-ethnic group. For instance Balogun *Gambari*, which traced its origin to Katsina area, controlled the Hausa. The Fulani who originally came from Sokoto lived in the ward governed by *Balogun Fulani*. The Yoruba from Kuwo and Reke were under the *Balogun Ananamu* while those from Iseyin were under the *Balogun Ajikobi*.[17]

He writes further:

> Every Balogun was at the same time in control of the economic sector or group. The Balogun Gambari supervised Hausa traders, artisans warriors, and immigrants. The Balogun Fulani was the 'lord' of the Fulani cattle dealers and caravan traders. Similarly Yoruba traders and artisans fell under the authority of Balogun Ananamu and Ajikobi.[18]

It can be surmised from the foregoing that the 19th century was the era of the supremacy of the Balogun in the politics of many Yoruba towns. Their appointments were, unlike hitherto, based not on ascription but on ability and prowess. Some were self-made, having risen

---

17 See O.A. Banwo, "Notes on Warfare and the Ilorin Aristocracy" in Toyin Falola and Robin Law, p. 60 – 63, for the roles played by the Balogun in Ilorin politics.

18 Ibid, p. 61.

to the position by dint of courage, charisma and adroitness in the art of soldiery. The Balogun in their various societies reached the peak of their power and influence.

By the last quarter of the 19th century, the Balogun had started to decline in power and influence. The main factors responsible for this were the advent of the Christian missionaries and the intervention of the British colonial administration in the wars in Yorubaland.

By 1842, Christian missionaries had reached Badagry. They got to Abeokuta, which they regarded as "sunrise within the tropics", in 1846.[19] The missionaries detested the wars in the hinterlands of the Yoruba and the slave trade which it encouraged.

They were also unfamiliar with the military cadre (the *olorogun*) which had pushed the civil authority (the *ogboni*) to the background. They were not at ease with the lack of civil authority in Abeokuta. Thus in 1854, through the influence of Henry Townsend, the Christian missionary persuaded the Egba to install the first *Alake* (king) in Abeokuta.[20] This was followed by the installation of the first Olowu in 1855, the first Agura in 1870 and the first Osile in 1897.[21] With the installation of

---

19 Ajisafe, p. 85; G.O. Ogunremi, M.O. Opeyemi, O. Siyan, editor, Badagry: *A Case Study in History Culture and Tradition of an African City*, (Ibadan: Rex Charles Publications, 1994), p.192.

20 Ajisafe, p. 102.

21 Ibid.

these traditional rulers, the Egba returned to civil rule. The *olorogun* (war society) ceased to be predominant in Egba politics. Although the institution of the Balogun in various Egba townships in Abeokuta still existed, the Balogun were responsible to the civil authorities.

The second factor was the intervention in the wars in the hinterlands of Yorubaland, which is the Ekiti-Parapo wars.[22] Following the British bombardment of Lagos in 1851, and the subsequent cession of the island kingdom to the British in 1861,[23] the latter's interest in Yorubaland continued to grow. They were interested in the extension of "legitimate" trade to the hinterland areas of Lagos. They wanted to stop the wars in Yorubaland, which hindered peaceful trade and jeopardized commerce in the British Colony of Lagos between 1886 and 1893.

The Church Missionary Society (the CMS) and the British government in Lagos consequently made peace arrangement between the warring factions in Yorubaland. A peace treaty was signed in 1886 and in 1893, the British supervised the final disengagement of troops and the burning of the Ekiti-Parapo and the

---

22 For the Ekiti–Parapo wars, see S.A. Akintoye, *Revolution and Power Politics in Yorubaland 1840 – 1893*. (London: Longman Group, 1971).

23 For the British bombardment and the cession of Lagos, see J.F.A. Ajayi, "The British Occupation of Lagos 1851–1861: A critical review" *Nigeria Magazine*, Volume 69, 1961, p. 96 – 105

Ibadan war camps. Thereafter, Yorubaland was declared a British Protectorate.[24]

The implication of the *Pax Britania* and its attendant subjection of Yorubaland to British rule was that the Balogun and other war lords had to adjust their activities and adapt themselves to peaceful life under their civil authorities. In Ibadan, which had instituted four lines of chieftaincy viz: the *Olubadan*, the *Balogun*, the *Seriki* and the *Iyalode* lines, adjustment was, to a large extent, not very difficult.[25] As the rulership of the town rotated between the Olubadan and the Balogun lines, a holder of the Balogun title had the chance of becoming the Olubadan.

In Abeokuta, which had reverted to the civil rule since 1854, adaptation of the Balogun to the changed socio-political situation was not problematic. After the death of the old warlords such as Somoye, Sokenu, Ogundipe, and many others, towards the end of the 19th century, Egba townships and sections appointed their respective Balogun or Jagunna including the Balogun of Owu. However, these were the Balogun belonging to the oye ilu (town chiefs). They were *ipso facto* responsible to the civil authority. In Ijebuland, the British invasion of Ijebu-Ode leading to the defeat of

---

24 For the details of these events, see S.O Johnson, Ibid. p. 547–642.

25 S. Biobaku, *Olubadan Succession Formula*, (Ibadan: John Archers Publishers) See also, T. Falola, *The Political Economy of a pre-Colonial African State: Ibadan, 1830–900*. (Ile–Ife: University of Ife Press, 1984) p.64–70.

Ijebu warriors at Magbon in 1892,[26] resulted in the acquiescence of Ijebu war lords like Balogun Kuku and Ogunsigun to civil life.

Unlike in Abeokuta and Ibadan, the warlords in Ijesaland and Ekiti kingdoms could not easily adapt themselves to civil life. For instance, Ogedengbe of Ilesa could not immediately disband his war boys, after leaving the war camp in 1893. His warriors continued to raid adjoining Ilesa towns and villages. He was arrested by the British in August 1895. He spent sixteen months in prison before he was released after the Owa of Ilesa (Oba Hastrup) paid a sum of £2000 to guarantee his good behaviour. His war boys were disbanded. Although he was highly respected in Ilesa and given the title of the *Obanla* next in rank to the *Owa*, he died in June 1910.[27]

Similarly, *Aduloju* of Ado-Ekiti who had labelled himself as *Osoko Ekiti Soko Akoko* (the Lord of Ekiti and Akoko) because of his successes in these areas, could not adjust to peaceful and civil life. With his base at Imesi-Lasigidi (now Imesi–Ekiti in Gbonyin Local Government of Ekiti State), his war boys continued to raid the surrounding settlements. He was arrested in 1898 by Captain Bower, the first British resident in Yorubaland. His slaves and war boys abandoned him, and he returned to his home town, Ado-Ekiti. He refused an offer of a chieftaincy title, perhaps because of

---

26 For the Magbon War, see Johnson, p. 618–622.

27 Falola and Oguntomisin, p. 105–107.

his unwillingness to adjust to civil life. He died in 1902.[28]

Their opposition to the Emirs' reassertion of political influence in Ilorin threatened political stability in the emirate. They were checkmated by the British and the Royal Niger Company invasion of Ilorin in 1896.[29]

The post-19th century period

The British subjugation of the warlords opened a new era in the institution of the Balogun in Yorubaland in the post-19th century period. Since there were no more wars to be fought, the role of the Balogun as warlords and military commanders was no longer relevant. Consequently, the Balogun title-holders reverted to playing civilian roles as the *oye ilu* (town chiefs or civil chiefs). The Balogun title was encapsulated in the socio-political hierarchy of administration in Yoruba towns. Ibadan provided a spectacular example. Because of the peculiar structure of its political organization, the Balogun title was (and still is) non-hereditary. It was/is possible for a man to rise to the position through a system of promotion from the lowest echelon of the chieftaincy line. Thus it was easy in Ibadan for the warlords to convert to civilian duties.[30]

In other Yoruba towns, however, the title of the Balogun was hereditary. The oba (paramount ruler)

---

28 Ibid p. 88 – 89.

29 Ibid. p. 170.

30 See: Falola, p. 64-70.

reverted to the traditional modes of appointing the Balogun as town chiefs, playing civilian roles. Thus because of the circumstances of the post-19th century period, the Baloguns have come to adapt themselves to the new socio-political situations in Yorubaland.

The post-19th century period also witnessed the proliferation of the Balogun as religious and social titles. The advent of Islam and Christianity contributed largely to the entrenchment of this phenomenon. In the process of legitimizing and consolidating their religions, the votaries resorted to drawing inspiration from the intrepidity with which the 19th century Balogun fought for the courses of the communities. Thus, the Christian churches as well as the Muslims resorted to appointing people of indomitable character who could spend their time and resources for evangelism as the Baloguns did for war. Consequently, in the Christian churches, the title of *Balogun Ijo* (the *Balogun* of the congregation) was instituted along with other titles such as *Baba Egbe* (father of the Christian societies), the *Iya Egbe* (mother of the societies), the *Baba Isale* (father in residence), and so on. In the same vein, various Muslim groups appointed *Balogun Musulumi* (Muslim *Balogun*) or *Balogun Adini*. This practice is prominent in Abeokuta, where there were (and still are) parallel *Baloguns* viz: the *Balogun Ilu*, the Muslim *Balogun,* and the *Balogun* Onigbagbo, that is, the town *Balogun*, the Muslim *Balogun*, and the Christian *Balogun* respectively.[31]

Apart from the institutionalized religious *Balogun* titles, it is now fashionable to appoint articulate individuals as *Balogun honoraris causa* in communities and convivial associations. For instance, obas (kings) give the title to honour articulate and vocal individuals who make valuable contributions to the development of their communities in particular and the larger society in general. Civil rights crusaders are similarly rewarded. It has been demonstrated that in the ancient period of Yoruba history, individuals identified by virtue of their prowess, fortitude, intrepidity and patriotism were chosen to lead their primary communities. As these communities developed into states there arose the need for organized defensive and offensive operations. The positions occupied by such individuals saddled with such important duties became institutionalized in a title known variously as *Balogun, Jagun, Jagunna, Oloriogun*, etc. The endemic wars of the 19th century presented ample opportunities for these warlords to acquire power and influence in their various states. Once there were no more wars, the power and influence of the warlords ebbed in the post-war-period, however, the institution of the Balogun survived in its transformed nature and it is still relevant in the Yoruba society today.

---

31 This practice, which probably began as Christianity or Islam, entrenched itself in Abeokuta, and has become conventional in the town today.

2

The Balogun Institution in Ijebuland

Olatunde Taiwo, Philip Oloruntola
and Mufutau Oluwasegun Jimoh

Introduction

The territories that constitute Ijebuland have shifted at different times in pre-colonial, colonial, and post-colonial periods. Prior to colonialism, the western boundary of 'Ijebuland extended to several Ijebu–speaking people in towns and settlements to the eastern frontiers of Lagos, from Langbasa, Ejinrin, Palma, Lekki, Okun Ode to Itsekiri', and on the south, 'from Ijebu-Ode, Ikorodu to Iro'.[1] Presently, the bulk of Ijebuland embraces the towns and settlements within Ijebu East, Ijebu North, Ijebu North East, Ijebu-Ode, Odogbolu, Ogun Waterside local governments and Remo in parts of Ogun State, Epe and Ikorodu in Lagos State, Nigeria. These areas saw the *Balogun* title originate, evolve, flourish, castigated and ultimately, entrenched. The Balogun title was indeed a towering feature in virtually

---

1 NAI, Ije Prof.2 file No. C.55/1: Intelligence Report of Ijebu-Ode, and Ije Prof.3/7 No. C5/1921: Petition From Awujale Ademolu and his council to Lt. Governor, Southern Province, 5 March 1925 on the colony boundary, Ijebu-Ondo and Ijebu-Ibadan boundaries.

all the principal polities of Yorubaland, before, during, and after the colonial period, but in Ijebuland, it was (and remains) understood in the following light.

Among the *Ijebu*, the Balogun is conventionally one of the most important offices in the traditional administrative arrangement of their major communities. The earliest recollection of the office is its holders' valour in terms of courage, use of weaponry and somewhat invincibility in terms of the deployment of charms in wars that involved the pre-literate societies in Ijebuland.[2] Such a titleholder, in addition, had to be armed at all times with unassailable evidence of his ancestry in a chain of legendary military generals of the land. This, for many, is the reason why the traditions and early literature of the Ijebu continue to be littered with names of warlords like: Sikakerewe, Kalejaiye, Meleki, Osunlalu, Amoibo, Onayelu, Ogunade, Olisa Dipe, Olisa, Arowosanle, Omolanre, Adde Sounlou, Otuo-Nouyo, Ogborangan, Ajebu, Olode, Obaruwa, Yemule, Osodehinde, Adebote, Otunsemade, Osinuga Opaso, Ogunnupebi, Osiogbe, Osulalu Kuyoro, Kuyagba, and Ogunshigun.[3]

---

2 Chief Adebisi Adara, the Ogbeni Odi of Ijebuland, 70 years, interviewed at the Palace of the Awujale of Ijebulaland on 10 December 2012; Chief J.A.B Odunnuga, the Paramount Balogun of Ijebuland, 80 years, interviewed at Imoru Ijebu-Ode on 15 February 2013.

5 D. Oguntomisin, " Military Alliances in Yorubaland in the 19th Century" in I.A. Akinjogbin (ed) *War and Peace in Yorubaland, 1783-1893* (Ibadan: Heinemann Educational Books Nigeria, 1998), 106; O.

Even then, in Ijebuland today, totally contemporary and significant forces of modernity, some of which include economic standing, Western-style education, political pedigree, communal acceptance, popularity, and status in a *Regberegbe*, have come to overtake martial-ancestral links and, in fact, completely replaced bravery in war, as qualifications for anyone wanting to assume the Balogun office[4] Remarkably still, these forces have also not left the office's earliest functions — law enforcement, defence, territorial expansion, coordinating the high command of the army, trade dominance, protection of trade caravans, — unaffected.[5]

Ojo, *Ancient Ijebu* (Ibadan: Abiodun Printing Works, 1968), 26; T. Oduwobi, "Oral Tradition and Political Integration in Ijebu" *History in Africa*, Vol 27, 2000, 249; S. Johnson, *The History of the Yoruba: from 4 Earliest Times to the Beginning of the British Protectorate* (Lagos: CMS Nigeria Bookshops, 1921),166; S. Sofela, *Egba-Ijebu Relations* (Ibadan: John Archers Publishers, 2000), 20-31; P.C. Lloyd, " Osifekunde of Ijebu" in P. Curtin, editor, *Africa Remembered. Narratives by West African from the Era of the Slave Trade* (Madison: The University of Wisconsin Press, 1967), 285.

5 Chief J.A.B Odunnuga, interview; Mr. Gbenga Aroyewun, Publisher *Obanta Newsday*, 49 years, interviewed at Abasi Street, Ita Osu Ijebu-Ode on 19 February 2013.

6 O. Olubomehin, " A Survey of Inter-Group Relations in Ijebuland in the Nineteenth Century" in O. Olubomehin, editor, *The Ijebu of Western Nigeria. A Historical and Socio- Cultural Study* (Ibadan: Bamon Publishing Company, 2001),10-22; A. Atanda, "Government of Yorubaland in the Pre-Colonial Period" *Tarik,* Vol. 14, No. 2,1973: D. Oguntomisin, " Military Alliances in Yorubaland in the 19th Century", 108-109; T. Falola, *The Military in Nineteenth Century Yoruba Politics* (University of Ife Press, 1984), 98-99;

Before we examine how these unfolded, it is imperative to acceptably identify the *Baloguns'* moment of evolution in Ijebuland. Unlike the unanimity which the basic meaning of the Balogun title seems to enjoy in Ijebuland, the precise period it emerged is a matter of varying conclusions. To Olusola, for example, the Balogun institution is as ancient as Ijebuland. The reason being because Ijebu oral traditions identify the first Balogun as Ogunfeyibo—a pre-Obanta settler, and acknowledged founder of (Italapo) one of the twenty-five original quarters of Ijebu-Ode.[6] On the other hand, there is the position spearheaded by Oduwobi, Okubote, Oguntomisin, Chief J.A.B. Odunnuga, Aroyewun, Otunba Payne, and Adara. This position ascribes the mid-nineteenth for the onset of the Ijebu Balogun institution.[7] Its proof is Onafowokan, known popularly as Otutunibon, and verifiable in many parts of Ijebu-Ode today as the first holder of the Balogun title. Otutunibon is considered to have lived between the

---

7 O.Ojo, *Ancient Ijebu*, 27; T. Falola and A. Genova, editors, *Yoruba Identity and Power Politics* (New York: University of Rochester Press, 2006), 9.

8 T. Oduwobi, "A Historical Study of Administrative and Political Developments in Ijebu, 1892-1960" Ph.D Thesis, 1995, University of Lagos, 32; M. Okubote, *Iwe Itan Ijebu* (Ibadan: Third World Information Services,1930), 48-161; A. Payne, *Table of Principal Events in Yoruba History with Certain Other Matters of General Interest* (Lagos: Andrew M. Thomas, 1893), 40; Oguntomisin,, " Military Alliances in Yorubaland . . . , 104-109.

reign of Awujale Fidipote and Awujale Adeona Fusigboye.

Another conclusion is that held by Falola. Here, to the extent that the Balogun institution was an invention of the republican military state of Ibadan, its evolution in Ijebuland, could not have been before 1829, the year the Ibadan military republic was founded.[8] Rather than confusion, considerable light is what all of the above introduces to any future examination of the remotest roots of the Balogun structure in Ijebuland. To be sure, it establishes that the onset of the Balogun title in Ijebuland could not have been outside the third quarter of the nineteenth century. Second, it suggests that, even if the Ogunfehinbo approach is prone to instant dismissal,[9] the *Ijebuness* of the Balogun is still not in question. The record is clear, the Ibadan military state was founded by the Ijebu, Ife, and Oyo warriors (and refugees). The Ijebu were actively involved in the nascent administration of Ibadan, and by consequence must have contributed to the evolution of the Balogun title there.[10]

---

9 T. Falola, "From Hospitality to Hostility: Ibadan and Strangers, 1830-1904" *Journal of African* History, 35(1) 1985: 51-62; T. Falola, *The Military in Nineteenth Century Yoruba Politics*, 44-59.

10 Vaughan, *Nigerian Chiefs. Traditional Power in Modern Politics, 1890s-1900s*, 17.

Going by the description of the Balogun that was earlier presented, it is probable that some of the warrior-forebears of Onafowokan partook in the Owu War of the 1820s; and the creation of Ibadan thereafter. Falola instructively identified the random return of a significant number of these warriors to Ijebuland, beginning from 1830.[11] These ancestors of Onafowokan might have been among this throng of returnees. In the event, Onafowokan, who was already Balogun of Ijebuland by 1862, certainly had a fertile tradition from which to spring forth.

Who was Otutunibon Onafowokan?

Otutunibon was succeeded by some subordinate, albeit provincial bloguns; and in fact eight paramount Baloguns of Ijebuland. Who are these personalities relatedly, what imprints, vis-à-vis the unique socio-cultural, political and economic forces of their times, did these Baloguns impress on Ijebuland? It is to these that we now turn.

The Balogun in pre-colonial Ijebuland:
The incubation of the generalissimo

The pre-colonial period for Ijebuland effectively ended in 1892. An idea of the overarching political structures in this area before then is required, if the consequences of these, are to be sufficiently understood. Thankfully,

---

11 T. Falola, " From Hospitality to Hostility..., 51-63.

this subject—19th century socio-political Ijebuland—has ben a major preoccupation of many of the eminent historians of the twentieth century. In their analyses, Ijebuland, which then extended to Epe, Ikorodu, Ibeju Lekki, and the entire Remo settlements, had evolved into a kingdom.[12]

At the centre of that kngdom was Ijebu-Ode— the capital, metropolis, abode of the pre-eminent ruler of Ijebuland, and seat of the kingdom's military high command, that included its military commander-in-chief.[13] Other sections of the Ijebu Kingdom included over 600 towns and villages of different sizes.[14] These sections or provinces equally had sovereigns, and they

---

12 E. Ayandele, "Ijebuland 1800-1891: Era of Splendid Isolation"in G. Olusanya, editor, *Studies in Yoruba History and Culture: Essays in Honour of Professor S.O.* Biobaku (Ibadan: University Press Limited, 1983), 90; A.Akinjogbin, "Wars in Yorubaland, 1793-1893: An Analytical Categorisation" in A.Akinjogbin, editor, *War and Peace in Yorubaland, 1783-1893* (Ibadan: Heinemann Educational Books Nigeria , 1998), 33; T. Oduwobi, "Early Ijebu History: An Analysis on Demographic Evolution and State Formation" in T. Falola and A. Genova 2006, 165-166; D. Oguntomisin, *A Comprehensive History of the Yoruba People Up to 1800* (Ibadan: John Archers Publishers, 2007), 59-62; R. Smith, *Kingdoms of the Yoruba* (London: James Currey Limited, 1969) , 63; . Oduwobi, "A Historical Study . . . Political Developments in Ijebu, 1892-1960", 28-32; T. Falola and A. Genova, *Historical Dictionary of Nigeria* (Toronto: The Scarecrow Press, 2009), 166.

13 Falola and Genova, 2009, 166; E. Ayandele, *The Ijebu of Yorubaland 1850-1950. Politics, Economy and Society* (Ibadan: Heinemann Educational Books Nigeria, 1992), 3-7.

14 Ayandele, 1992, p.1.

were in several respects autonomous—even if only to the extent of their unending inviolability of the paramountcy of the ruler at Ijebu-Ode.[15] The towns or provinces also usually maintained a military, to which compliance to the inviolability principle apparently devolved. These provincial armies instructively had to avail soldiers to the military high command, whenever they were needed at the centre, predictably to safeguard of the territorial, economic and cultural sovereignty of the Ijebu Kingdom. Oguntomisin and Falola came within a hair's breadth of mentioning this all-Ijebu army, when they located the army's first experience of discord in the 1880s.[16]

Biobaku, his contemporaries, and some recent literature mention the title of the pre-Balogun metropolitan military officials and commanders-in-chief of the Ijebu kingdom. Whereas the *Olisa* office and occupant contained the spirit and functions of the

---

15 O. Olubomehin, "The Quest for Political Autonomy: Remo and Ijebu Relations, 1892-1938" in O.Olubomehin, editor, *Themes in the History of Ijebu and Remo of Western Nigeria* (Ibadan: Bamon Publishing Company, 2010), p. 55-70; E. Ayandele, "The Changing Position of the Awujales of Ijebuland under Colonial Rule," in M. Crowder and O.Ikime editors, *West Africa Chiefs. Their Changing Status under Colonial Rule and Independence* (Ile-Ife: University of Ife Press, 1970), 231.

16 T. Falola and D. Oguntomisin, *Yoruba Warlords of the Nineteenth Century* (Trenton: Africa World Press, 2001), 137-138; Ayandele, "The Changing Position of the Awujales . . ."; 233 ; Oduwobi, "A Historical Study of Political Developments in Ijebu, 1892-1960". . . , 37-38.

commander-in-chief, that of the *Olorogun, Olukongbon, Ade Kola, Adechegou (Adesegun)* embodied the functions of the captain, commanding general, general, and divisional general, respectively. Remarkably, the *Agbon, Kakanfo,* and *Lapoekun* military offices of pre- *Balogun* Ijebuland only ceased to exercise military functions from the third quarter of the nineteenth century. Yet, related military positions like those identified by Oguntomisin and Falola—namely, the *Kakanfo, Sibeluwo* and *Mayungbe*—probably have evolved around the 1850s.[17] To be sure, *Olisa* Dipe is on record to having led the all-Ijebu armed forces in the Owu War of the 1820s, in much the same manner as Olisa Adebote would lead the Ijebu military in the Eleduwe War of the 1830s.[18]

Whoever the holder of the *Olisa* title was in 1862, he was no match for Onafowokan, in terms of requisite martial qualities and other relevant tools of warfare. For "If ever there was a bedlam", to use the exact words of

---

17 T. Falola and D. Oguntomisin, 127-138; O. Ojo, *Ancient Ijebu*, 30-33; M. Okubote, *Iwe Itan Ijebu*, 161-166; R .Smith, "Yoruba Warfare and Weapons" in S.O. Biobaku, *Sources of Yoruba History* (London: Oxford University Press, 1973), 229; P. Talbot, *The Peoples of Southern Nigeria. A Sketch of their History, Ethnology and Languages with an Abstract of the 1873 Census* (London: Frank Cass and Company, 1926), 219-225; P.C. Lloyd, "Osifekunde of Ijebu", 284-287; S.K. Adetona, *Plea: Confirmation of Oloriogun Title as Hereditary Title of Balogun Kuku Family*, 1993; Ayandele, "The Changing Position of the Awujales. . . ", 235.

18 M. Okubote, *Iwe Itan Ijebub*, 161-169; R. Law, "The Chronology of the Yoruba Wars of the Early Nineteenth Century: A Reconsideration," 211-222.

Ayandele, "then Yorubaland . . . of the nineteenth century, outside the area occupied by Ijebu, was one".[19] Indeed, nineteenth century Yorubaland was notable for many reasons, including that almost everything was to be settled on the battlefield. As a polity, you were respected or taken seriously, depending on the strength of your military and its commander-in-chief. This fact was probably more fundamental to the Ijebu than any of the empire-seeking states of Yorubaland in that period.[20]

According to tradition, when the Onafowokan demonstrated his overwhelming gallantry in leading the Ijebu military campaign to douse Iperu's insurrection, (aftermath of the Ijaye War), it became inevitable, upon his return, that he assumed the leadership of the Ijebu military.[21] The Olisa chieftancy title was, however, hereditary![22] A new office necessarily had to be created. It was the Balogun title; and the pioneer Balogun was Onafowokan Otutunibon. The era of the Baloguns in Ijebuland had begun!

---

19 E. Ayandele, *The Ijebu of Yorubaland 1850-1950. Politics, Economy and Society*, 5.

20 Falola and Oguntomisin, *Yoruba Warlords of the Nineteenth Century*, 129.

21 Olubomehin, " A Survey of Inter-Group Relations in Ijebuland in the Nineteenth Century", 10-13; Oduwobi,"A Historical Study . . . of Political Developments in Ijebu, 1892-1960", 32.

22 Ayandele, *The Ijebu of Yorubaland 1850-1950. Politics, Economy and Society*, p. 3.

The emergent Balogun Onafowokan must have been so powerful in subsequent internal political arrangement of the Ijebu Kingdom, so much so, that some of the traditional military titles had to beat a permanent retreat, particularly as Otutunibon grew in prominence. Nearly no trace, for instance, remained of the, Olukongbon, Ade Kola, and Adechegou institutions by the eight decade of the nineteenth century.[23] The inverse connection between the ascendency of Balogun Onafowokan and the cessation of military functions in the (still existing) *Agbon* and *Lapoekun*, which are institutions, is equally significant.[24] Akinjogbin asserted that the Ijebu Kingdom was illustrative of uncommon peace between 1865 and 1877.[25] To no other personality but the Balogun, could this have stemmed from, especially at a time when the Balogun and his war-boys had completely replaced the *omodowa* (the police force) and its head in law enforcement at Ijebu-Ode.[26] How much Onafowokan, and the Balogun structure had grown in terms of economic and socio-political

---

23 R .Smith, " Yoruba Warfare and Weapons" . . . p. 224-247.

24 S.Alatishe, editor, *Ojude Oba Official Brochure*, 2012, 16-20; Idem, *Ojude Oba Official Brochure*, 2009, 21-25; Idem, *Ojude Oba Official Brochure*, 2008, 20-25; Idem, *Ojude Oba Official Brochure*, 2007, 16-20.

25 A. Akinjogbin, "Wars in Yorubaland, 1793-1893: An Analytical Categorisation" in A. Akinjogbin, p. 46-47.

26 P. Talbot, *The Peoples of Southern Nigeria.* . . p. 40; P.C. Lloyd, "Osifekunde of Ijebu" in P. Curtin editor, *AfricaRemembered*, p. 284.

influence is captured by the unique episode of 1882-3 in Ijebuland.

The year of 1882 dawned with the premier Ijebu monarch (Awujale Fidipote) and the army still involved in the Kiriji War. While the Ijebu army remained on the side of the Egba-Ilorin-Oyo-Ife-Ekiti alliance, it faced an equally ably constituted Ibadan, throughout the sixteen-year Kiriji War.[27] Interestingly, by 1882, some of the provincial Ijebu towns, for reasons Olubomehin and Oguntomisin rightly identified as economic, had begun to manifest visible objections and insubordination due to ongoing Ijebu participation in the war.[28] Their argument was economic in the sense that they longed to resume their lucrative trade in the interior, and notably Ibadan. The war, they reasoned aloud, promised little benefit for Ijebuland. Moreover, the Egba, who supposedly were on the side of the Ijebu, had secretly, resumed trade with Ibadan.[29]

This sentiment soon intensified in the capital of the Ijebu Kingdom. Before long, mercantile interests (symbolized by the Ijebu-Ode commercial class) had

---

27 T. Falola and M.Heaton, *A History of Nigeria* (Cambridge: Cambridge University Press, 2008) 76; Falola and Oguntomisin, *Yoruba Warlords of the Nineteenth Century*, 138.

28 Oguntomisin, "Military Alliances in Yorubaland in the 19th Century",108;Olubomehin,"A Survey of Inter-Group Relations in Ijebuland in the Nineteenth Century", 12-19.

29.Falola and Oguntomisin, *Yoruba Warlords of the Nineteenth Century*, 135-138.

found a willing handmaiden in the Ijebu military high command, now led by Balogun Onafowokan.[30] What happened next is easy to reconstruct: a notice to Fidipote to withdraw Ijebu support for the Ekiti Parapo —and resume trade with the interior or total insurrection. Fidipote, for whatever reasons, failed to properly discern the militaristic spirit of the times. He dismissed the notice. Onafowokan and the battalion he commanded would have nothing of such nonsense. The Awujale was promptly banished to Epe in 1883;[31] he would be there for another two years before his death, some say from small pox, in 1885.

That Fidipote was forcibly removed from the Awujale stool by the formidable Balogun Otutunibon is however, not the primary significance of that incident. For the next three years, Ijebu-Ode and by implication virtually all of Ijebuland was under the influence of Balogun Otutunibon.[32] So powerful did Otutunibon become that no one was able to stop him from installing his "puppet" as Fidipote's successor.[33]

This new profile of the Balogun would appear to have changed little even towards the end of the pre-colonial period in Ijebuland. When Samuel Johnson visited Ijebu-Ode in 1886, for example, he was quick to

---

30 Ibid. p. 137-138.

31 Ayandele, op cit.

32 Olubomehin, p. 14-15; Falola and Oguntomisin, op cit.

33 Falola and Oguntomisin, op. cit.

discover that he could secure access to the Awujale, only after the express intervention of Onafowokan.³⁴ Johnson also noted that all the administrative structures of Ijebu-Ode, including the office of the Awujale, was under the influence of Balogun Onafowokan.³⁵ According to Johnson, the ultimate judicial functions in the kingdom were similarly being discharged by Balogun Otutunibon, in the sense that "the only court to which appeal lay was to Balogun Onafowokan".³⁶

Before the 1892 colonization of Ijebuland, the Balogun institution in the Ijebu metropolis had an outstanding impact in other parts of the kingdom. This was in the evolution of Balogun titles in some of the provincial towns of the Ijebu Kingdom. Kehere of Ipara, Atambala and Jasinmi of Ikorodu, Sosinmi of Makun, Rosanwo, Ogoji, and Sarunmi of Idomonwon are the notable baloguns observable in the records to have been active in the other parts of the Ijebu Kingdom between the 1860s and 1880s.³⁷ Curiously, while they exercised military and law-enforcement functions, by no means did the performance of such functions extend beyond

---

34 Johnson, p. 587.

35 Ibid.

36 Ibid. p. 612; G. Aroyewun, "Balogun Odueyungbo Bello Kuku: From Mustard Seed to Giant Oak", *Obanta Newsday*, November-December, 2007, p. 1-2.

37 Ayandele, p. 16; Payne, p. 40; Olubomehin, p. 12-13; Okubote, p. 184-187; G. Aroyewun, "The Early Ijebu Muslim Converts", *Obanta Newsday*, January, 2010, 30-31.

their individual towns. In other words, except in very rare situations they complied with the inviolability principle of the Awujale at Ijebu-Ode, and supported the Balogun of the Ijebu–Ode military high command any time contingents were needed to safeguard the territorial integrity of the Ijebu kingdom. Very much in the same way that virtually all the political and cultural structures in these integral towns, mirrored that of the capital.[38]

Colonisation and the changing fortunes of the Ijebu Balogun institution

Between 1885-1892, the British in Lagos attempted to make the Ijebu Kingdom and Ijebu-Ode in particular, not only travelable, but also habitable for all previously unauthorized and abominable influences and persons.[39] With the superior British military capacity always dangling over their heads, those years very soon saw the Awujale, Balogun and other Ijebu chiefs reluctantly endorsing the entry of missionaries, Christianity, *Saros*, abolition of human sacrifice, military aid, coloured foreigners, Western-style literacy, free trade, and irregular immigration into Ijebuland.[40] One of the salient, though unfortunate, consequences of this policy

---

38 Ojo, p. 30-34.

39 Falola and Heaton, p. 89-126; Talbot, p. 226; Falola, and Oguntomisin, p. 136.

40 Ayandele, p. 16-25; Ojo, p. 64-65.

was a decline in the popular appeal and acceptance of Awujale Aboki and Balogun Onafowokan. The Ijebu were never known to cower to any outside force—let alone one external to Yorubaland—many, particularly, the rank and file of the military protested.[41]

In 1892, situations came to a head. Partly, in an attempt to reverse the abominable concessions, Balogun Otutunibon with the endorsement of the Awujale sent out a force to crush that of the British, whose mission was to maintain the British toehold in Ijebu Kingdom. The resultant Imagbon War is famous for signaling the termination of Ijebu independence and its colonization by the British. But, for the Balogun institution it was perhaps more telling. Notably, never again will ANY Balogun of Ijebuland preside over a high command, brigade, or contingents of combatants. Gone also were the days when superior mastery and use of native charms and the provisioning of other implements of war provided direct access to the Balogun office.

However, in the years that immediately followed the conquest of Ijebuland, the person of the Balogun was also to suffer one humiliation or the other. So subdued was Balogun Onafowokan, that at a point, he had to plead with a mere officer of the new British colonial overlords of Ijebuland for respite.[42]

---

41 Ayandele; Ojo, p. 44.

42 Johnson, p. 622.

Cooper recently underlined the element of divide and rule in the application of the theory of colonialism by British officers.[43] This was greatly applied on what remained of the traditional administrative structures of the Ijebu Kingdom. In this regard, three persons were recognized by the British conquerors of Ijebuland, at the capital. These were the Awujale, Seriki Odueyungbo Kuku (a former general in Otutunibon's high command), and Balogun Onafowokan. Specifically, they were— on condition of their unflagging loyalty to the new British managers of Ijebuland—placed on stipends of 200, 100, and 50 pounds, respectively. Not only did the introduction of cash remuneration permanently substitute for "war-booty" as the conventional reward for the Balogun, it more instructively provided the much needed confidence for Seriki Odueyungbo Kuku to eventually supplant Balogun Onafowokan shortly thereafter.

Four paramount baloguns, in actual fact, defined colonial Ijebuland. They included, Chief Bello Odueyungbo Kuku (1899-1907), Chief Gbadamosi Tayo Kuku (1907-1927), Chief Akadiri Somori Adefuye Kuku (1927-1950), and Chief S. E. Adesoye (1951-1961). Indeed, all but one of them came from the same ancestral tree. Odueyungbo, Gbadamosi and Akadiri in fact represent three generations of the Kuku family. And successively they—thanks, particularly, to the

---

43 F. Cooper, *Colonialism. Theory, Knowledge and History*, (Los Angeles: University of California Press, 2005),p. 1-25.

dexterity of Odueyungbo—presided, virtually throughout the colonial period, over what became of the Balogun institution. The rise and reign of Balogun Odueyungbo is critical in appreciating how the interplay of wealth, religion and (to a declining extent) intrepidity produced future Baloguns in Ijebuland.

Traditions establish that Odueyungbo was the only son to a mother (Detimoku) who died shortly after his birth in 1845.[44] Odueyungbo was given the alias, "Kuku", that is 'survivor' in the Ijebu linguistic tradition of the time. Commenting on the immensely lucrative caravan trade of the nineteenth century Yorubaland, Falola remarks that, "...the Ijebu traders were groomed for this job from an early age".[45] Nobody perhaps personified such preparation in Ijebuland in the 1860s like Odueyungbo Kuku. At the age of fifteen, Odueyungbo is reported to have joined his first trading caravan—to markets like Ode Ondo, Apomu, Ketu, Ilorin, Ibadan, Ikosi ,and Lagos.[46] In the process, Odueyungbo recorded unprecedented profit in form of slaves, firearms, and cowries.[47] Understandably, subsequent years saw Odueyungbo repeating this enterprise.

---

44 Aroyewun, p. 4.

45 T. Falola,"The Yoruba Caravan System of the Nineteenth Century" *The International Journal of African Historical Studies*, 24 (1) 1991: 118.

46 Ibid.

47 Aroyewun, p.111-127; Falola, and Oguntomisin, p. 137.

To the extent that Odueyungbo would have become so notable to be appointed Seriki (the only office next to the Balogun in terms of military power) in the 1880s, it is presumed that he must have supplied both personal and military aid to the Onafowokan led all-Ijebu army of that decade.[48]

Nothing, however, could have sealed Odueyungbo's rapid ascendency than the previously mentioned entrepreneurial success. The conventional economic base of the warlords were bribes, tributes, war booty, fines, market dues and gifts from professionals. Kuku combined all these with the immense revenue from his far-reaching trading activities and network.[49]

By 1890, Odueyungbo Kuku was probably the wealthiest man in Ijebuland, illustrated amply by his harem of over forty wives.[50] He must have been so invincible, that it was to him Onafowokan and the Awujale Tunwashe turned, to crush the intractable insurrection at Ijebu Igbo that was being led by another aggrieved general—Ogusigun—of the Ijebu high command.[51] Moreover, the reported mutual estrangement and attendant contest for political supremacy between the Awujale, Balogun Onafowokan, the *Pampa*, the *Owa* on one hand, and Seriki

---

48 Oduwobi, p. 32.

49 Falola, p. 52-53; Aroyewun, p. 4-9.

50 Aroyewun, p. 4-7.

51 Johnson, p. 607.

Odueyungbo (in 1891 Ijebu-Ode) cannot but constitute another explanation of Odueyungbo's rising preeminence.[52]

Three other factors prior to 1899 foreshadowed the accession of Odueyungbo Kuku to the office of Balogun. First was Odueyungbo's refusal to be involved in the planned military response against the imminent British expedition force in 1892. In return for which he, in fact, received the offer of the Awujaleship from Captain Robert Lister Bower, the leader of the expedition.[53] Second was the sublime negotiation that Odueyungbo midwifed between the British agents of occupation and the conquered Ijebu capital. Such that, whereas the British got what they wanted, the complete obliteration of the traditional administrative structures of the Ijebu capital was avoided. The third was Odueyungbo's conversion (and emergence as principal patron) to Christainity—which, like Islam, was winning Ijebu converts in droves.[54]

In addition to the measured British recognition earlier mentioned, these foregoing forces, more than other things, properly paved the way when, around 1899, very old Onafowokan voluntarily ceded the Balogun office to Odueyungbo. That is Bello

---

52 Aroyewun, p. 4-10.

53 Ibid.

54 A. Aroyewun, "115 Years of Christianity in Ijebuland. The Genesis", *Obanta Newsday*, January (2012), p.12-13;. Ayandele.

Odueyungbo Kuku, a man whose father and forefathers, radically, had no manifest evidence of heroic military exploits! Apparently, the cross-section of Ijebu citizens had little continued use for a commander-in-chief who could not muster the necessary courage to prevent their subjugation, and that of their heartland.

Wealthy, a war veteran, a beacon of enlightenment;[55] guarantor of law and order in Ijebu-Ode, principal retainer of the new British lord of Ijebuland, and savior,[56] Odueyungbo's accession to the office of Balogun, between 1899 to 1906, would be inexorably entrenched when he became the quintessential magnate in timber—the principal source of revenue with which the British financed the Native Admin-istrative Structure it imposed on colonised Ijebu-land.[57]

---

55 Being a Christian and later a Muslim in 1902.

56 Ijebu-Ode civilians set for massacre in1892.

57 J. Odutola, " Balogun Kuku: 100 Years. What People Say", *Obanta Newsday*, November-December, (2007), p. 19-20; Ayandele, op cit.

During this period (1899-1906), the Balogun institution received a bureaucratic facelift in the Ijebu-Ode Town Council; and later the District Council, the Judicial Council, and Advisory Board that constituted the major machinery of British political governance in Ijebuland.[58] Odueyungbo Kuku, by spearheading the replacement of the Odela Festival with the Ojude Oba Festival (initially *Ita Oba* Festival), not only had he incorporated the Balogun institution into the Ojude Oba Festival, it also placed the office at the centre of what has become the most important annual event in contemporary Ijebuland.[59]

Balogun Gbadamosi Kuku

The transformation of some other outstanding generals that fought side-by-side with Onafowokan and

---

58 Ibid. p.159-160.

59 Odutola, p. 20; G. Aroyewun,"Islam in Ijebu-Ode and the Balogun Kuku", *Obanta Newsday*, p. 17; S. Alatishe, editor, *Ojude Oba Official Brochure*, (2012), p. 45.

Odueyungbo in to baloguns, even if of subordinate status, is equally an element associated with the tenure of Balogun Odueyungbo. Balogun Odejaiyi, Balogun Saromi, and Balogun Odunuga, belong this category. In the future, eldest scions of these families would come to use these subordinate Balogun titles, and be accordingly decorated.[60]

Balogun Odueyungbo Kuku died in November 1907. At his death, not only had he become the acknowledged leader of the adherents of Islam in Ijebuland, he was in fact the 'uncrowned ruler' and most powerful native in Ijebu-Ode.[61] Indeed, on several occasions, fines were levied against the awujales, sequel to the British officials' mediation of altercations between this principal Ijebu monarch and Balogun Odueyungbo Kuku.[62]

The foregoing support indices, rather than acting as the coordination of any army high command, provided the pillars for the tenure of Chief Gbadamosi Kuku and Chief Akadiri Somori Kuku as paramount Balogun of colonial Ijebuland.

Balogun Akadiri Somori Kuku

---

60 Kabiatu Anike Odejayi, wife of the grandson of the first Balogun Odejayi, 70 years, interviewed at Balogun Odejayi Street Ijebu-Ode on 5 March, 2013; Aroyewun, p. 2.

61 Ayandele, op. cit.

62 Ibid, 100,161

In an era where the existential threat of invasion by neighbouring villages had ceased, and where a war-invested baloguns mattered little, these colonial baloguns cleverly reinforced their material inheritance with the considerable followership among the Ijebu Islamic faithful, patronage of Western-style education, positioning as access and conduits of the colonists' exploitation of the economic resources of Ijebuland, martial re-enactment activities at the yearly Ojude Oba ceremony, personal friendship with British residents and officers on the ground, and bureaucratic roles in the British-designed political structures for Ijebuland. Remarkably, their tenures were, as early as 1926, characterized by the evolution and infusion of two subordinate offices, the *Otun Balogun* and the *Osi Balogun*, into the balogun line.[63]

When Balogun Akadiri Somori Kuku died in 1950, very few individuals in the new Ijebu Province were a match for

Balogun Akadiri Somori Kuku

---

63 Ibid. p. 86; Chief Adebisi Adara.

Chief Timothy Adeola Odutola and Alhaji Fasasi Adesoye in terms of charisma, influence, and wealth.[64] In the stiff competition that accompanied the search for Balogun Akadiri Kuku's successor, it was charity and wealth that arguably clinched the title for Fasasi, ahead of the other eminent contenders for the office.[65] After all, no Ijebu man was as successful as Fasasi, to whom some employees owed a debt of gratitude for the construction of their houses.[66] Nor was there anyone that was the frequent toast of the eminent Yoruba musicians of the time.[67]

Unlike his predecessors, no martial ancestry, interestingly, can be produced for Fasasi. Neither was he a warlord by any means. But then Balogun Adesoye was obviously a business warlord, and one who was very liberal in the deployment of its gains; two indices that increasingly appeared to be the most important factors in choosing a Balogun in Ijebuland then.

---

64 Mr. Gbenga Aroyewun, Publisher *Obanta Newsday*, 49 years, interviewed at Abasi Street, Ita Osu Ijebu-Ode on 20 March 2013.

65 Chief J.A.B Odunnuga, the Paramount Balogun of Ijebuland, 80 years.

66 G. Olorode, "The Life and Times of Alhaji Fasasi Balogun Soye and How He Reincarnated Fifty Years after His Death", *Obanta Newsday*, April–May, 2011, p. 33; Mr. Gbenga Aroyewun, Publisher *Obanta Newsday*, 49 years, interviewed at Abasi Street, Ita Osu Ijebu-Ode on 20 March, 2013.

67 Ibid.

40   The Balogun in Yorubaland...

Balogun Fasasi Adesoye is known to have kept thirty-eight wives,[68] which, for the time, is a vivid index of his immense means. Unsurprisingly, at the heart of Fasasi's fortune was one of the instructive forces of the colonialism: road transportation.[69]

Born in 1900, Balogun Adesoye started off as a produce dealer in two commodities—cocoa and kolanut—whose cultivation was vigorously pursued by the British.

As observed by Oyemakinde, "... in the late twenties the upward spiral of vehicle efficiency, traffic density, and road construction engulfed Yorubaland, Fasasi was one of the few Ijebu who took

Balogun Fasasi Adesoye

---

68 Ibid.

69 Ayandele; Olorode, fn 66.

advantage of the then concealed opportunity".[70] From just one lorry, Adesoye's evolving Shoye Transport Services had, by the 1940s, developed into a fleet of lorries, trucks and buses.[71] His vehicles dominated in the movement of passengers, goods and produce to the northern part of Nigeria, Lagos, Shagamu, Ikorodu, and Abeokuta throughout the 40s and 50s.[72] From the surplus profit from the booming transport business Balogun Adesoye invested in properties and cash crop plantations at Ososa, Ajebandele and Odedeyo.

Chief Odunnuga, father of the presiding paramount Balogun of Ijebuland, and one of the major contenders against Adesoye in 1950, apparently did not come close to the latter in terms of business success. Similarly there appeared to be no question as to who was the most philanthropic, and the most popular Muslim, between the two.[73] Besides, another contender, and the scion of Balogun Odejayi, who believed he deserved the main office had spurned the Awujale, by rejecting the monarch's offer of the Otun Balogun office.[74]

---

70 R. Gavin, and W. Oyemakinde, "Economic Developments in Nigeria Since 1800" in O. Ikime, editor, *Groundwork of Nigerian History*. (Ibadan: Heinemann Educational Books, 1980), p. 507

71 Olorode, p. 33.

72 Ayandele, p. 165; Olorode op.cit, fn 66.

73 Olorode, p. 32- 33.

74 Mr. Olatunde Shote, 56 years, interviewed at Ijebu-Ode, on 19 February, 2013; Mr Adekitan Alatishe, 50 years, interviewed at Obalende Ijebu-Ode on 22 March, 2013.

Consequently, it was a conveniently positioned Fasasi Adesoye who was made the paramount Balogun by Awujale Gbelegbuwa II in 1951.

Though Balogun Adesoye's tenure is remarkable for many of the same factors that bolstered the reign of his three immediate predecessors, it is, even more so, for the blow it dealt one (and reinforcement it gave another) of the unwritten rules of accession to the Balogun, Otun Balogun, and the Osi Balogun offices in post-Akadiri Kuku's Ijebuland.

It is uncertain when it became customary that the Balogun office must be rotated among the three traditional constituent wards—Porogun, Ijasi, and Iwade Oke (of Ijebu-Ode). Similarly, No one can say exactly when it became mandatory that any of the three balogun offices must be occupied by at least a member of each of the wards. That this must be the case, was, however, already current in 1951, particularly to the Awujale and his inner court. Given that Otutunibon, and the Baloguns from the Kuku family were respectively from Ijasi and Iwade Oke, the Odejayi family from Porogun, naturally felt it was its turn to produce the paramount Balogun. As earlier mentioned, the Awujale, who gives final endorsement in such matters, ended up giving the title to Adesoye, from Ijasi. And when the eldest son of Balogun Odejayi rejected the monarch's Otun Balogun offer, the Awujale was quick to find a worthy Porogun man, Chief Juniad Alatishe, to take the Otun Balogun title.[75]

Any discussion of Balogun Adesoye's tenure will be incomplete without a mention that it was he that pioneered the pomp, fanfare, and feasting that would, henceforth, be a definite characteristic of the Balogun titleholders, especially during the Ojude Oba festival.[76]

Post-independence and the Balogun instution in Ijebuland

> Independence brought a bitter experience for the chiefs… Whatever status the chiefs had since 1960, is owed…rather… to business connections, the ability to align their interests with that of the leading members of their towns.
>
> The chiefs… traditional legitimacy is being questioned… they lack coercive powers…a person could sue a chief and show him no courtesy. Those among them who … wield influence do so on account of wealth, connections, and charisma.[77]

That was the evaluation of the post-colonial Yoruba chieftaincy structure, by one of the most accomplished

---

75 Ibid.

76 Olorode, op cit.

77 T. Falola, "The Yoruba Nation" in Falola and Genova, 2006, p. 171-173.

Yoruba historians of the last century. More or less the same description can be extracted from the personalities and tenures of post-colonial Ijebuland baloguns, and the Balogun institution itself. To recall an apt example, independence in fact dawned with the paramount Balogun institution in Ijebuland embroiled in what became a protracted litigation among vested stakeholders, so much so that between 1961-1971, the Balogun seat in Ijebu-Ode stood visibly vacant.[78]

The problem started with the sudden death of Balogun Adesoye in 1961, and with it the now characteristic tussle for the vacant office.[79] Beginning from 1962, Ijebu-Ode witnessed the vigorous aspirations of the Odejayi family for the office of the paramount Balogun. To the Awujale and his inner court, however,

Balogun Jinadu Alaba Alatishe

---

78 Mr Adekitan Alatishe.

79 Mr. Olatunde Shote

the custom whereby the paramount Balogun is succeeded by the Otun Balogun was to be applied. This provided all the incentive that the Odejayi family needed to institute a suit against the Awujale and Chief Junaid Alatishe.[80] The demand of the Odejayi family was predictable: the office of the paramount Balogun or nothing. The case would be in the courts until 1970, when judgement was given in favour of Chief Junaid Alaba Alatishe and the Awujale.[81] Little time was subsequently wasted in the latter's decoration of the former, as the sixth paramount Balogun of Ijebuland.

There is reason to believe that a few other critical factors were instrumental to the Awujale's final endorsement of Chief Junaid Alaba Alatishe. Like Adesoye, Alatishe was a man of immense means.[82] His mosques, wshich resembled sprawl-ing estates at Italapo and other parts of Ijebu-Ode, provide evidence of this, besides revealing his instructive religious subscription. Alatishe had made his wealth as a produce agent through his company (CWS Company Limited) which had omnipresent tentacles across the Western Region in Nigeria.[83]

---

80 Mr Adekitan Alatishe

81 Ibid.

82 Mr. Gbenga Aroyewun, Publisher *Obanta Newsday*; Chief Adebisi Adara, the Ogbe Odi of Ijebuland.

83 Ibid.

The key components in Balogun Junaid Alatishe's cognomen goes thus:

Balogun Dondodawa,

Omo anihun toyinbo oni...

omo...tingba igba powun losu...

Ajifowowe baba...kare o.

Translated:

Balogun, first among equals, envy of the white man. One whose monthly income never went below 200 pounds. At all times, bathing with money.

Indeed, for he was the only Ijebu man who could afford to send some of his children to private primary schools in the Great Britain, as early as the fifties.[84] He was educated at Ijebu-Ode until 1922; three of his thirty children became medical doctors and one, Hairat, was the first female Attorney General of Lagos State as well as a Supreme Court judge.[85] Remarkably, the Awujale and Balogun Alatishe's interests would additionally appear to have converged at the juncture of royalty. Explicitly underlining this, is the fact that one of Chief Junaid Alatishe's sons is the present *Gbegande of Ososa*. This was made possible because Balogun Alatishe's

---

84 B. Nwannekamma, 'Hairat Balogun: A Woman Lawyer of Many Firsts" www.guardiannewsngr.com.

85 Ibid.

grandfather was, in fact, the first Gbegande of Ijebu Ososa.[86] Further, future stability must have been cleverly introduced into Balogun Alatishe's tenure when the Awujale ensured that, whereas the office of the paramount Balogun was in the hands of a Porogun man, that of the Otun Balogun and Osi Balogun were accordingly in the hands of Ijasi men (Chief Shote) and (Chief J.A.B. Odunnuga) an Iwade Oke man.

Shortly before the demise of Balogun Alaba Alatishe, two developments took on special significance in in Ijebu-Ode. The first was the popular appeal and imposing social charisma of Otun Balogun Shote. The second was the dominant influence of the outstanding implications of business connections on whoever became Balogun in Ijebu-Ode.[87] As it were, no one reinforced the first attribute more successfully than the Yoruba Juju musician, King Sunny Ade. Eulogising Shote, sang:

> Otun Balogun ana Osi Balogun, geshin keshe,bode -nu baba won bi o dokan won geshin keshe. Asote maru omo towobola, patako eshin, ki jeshin o shubu shubu, Iru eshin, ki we mo eshin lorun…baba eni iya eni…chief executive … Shokas…Otunba….Shote….
>
> [from the album: *Let Them Say*]

---

86 Kabiyesi Toye Alatishe, Gbegande of Ijebu Ososa, 60 years +, interviewed at Ijebu-Ode, on 22 March, 2013.

87 Chief J.A.B Odunnuga, the Paramount Balogun of Ijebuland, 80 years, interviewed at Imoru Ijebu-Ode on 15 February, 2013.

Translated:

> Otun Balogun the in-law of the Osi Balogun. On princely horse, throttle on. Whoever is offended, that is his own headache and his father's. On princely horse, throttle on. Shote, one for whom fuss is additional elevation. Shote whose hands are permanently in wealth. You can never fall off the horse. Never. Never... Shote Chief executive Director at Shokas Industry.

Sunny Ade in fact devoted a whole track in the album *Let Them Say* to the praises of Chief M.O. Shote when Shote was only a subordinate Balogun. Very few personalities in Ijebu-Ode as at the time could boast of such a praiseworthy eulogy. But if Sunny Ade described Shote in the way he did, to the ordinary Ijebu man who heard of, and came in direct contact with him, Chief Shote was simply, *Baba Alaanu* ("The Compassionate").[88]

---

88 Mr. Lasisi, Former employee at Shokas Industries; now of the Library Department of the Olabisi Onabanjo University, 50 Years+, interviewed at O.O.U Ago Iwoye, on the 25 March, 2013.

Balogun M.O. Shote

In the early 90s, it was evident that Shote was one of the wealthi-est and most philanthropic individuals in Ijebu-Ode.⁸⁹ His business later expanded to include the

---

89 Chief Adebisi Adara, the Ogbe Odi of Ijebuland, 70 years; Chief J.A.B Odunnuga, the Paramount Balogun of Ijebuland, 80 years.

manufacture of textiles and embroidered textile fabrics (lace). So successful was this enterprise, that his factory, Shokas Industry Limited, ranked number one, among the retail sellers of the product in the major markets at Lagos, Ibadan and other parts of Western Nigeria in the late eighties and nineties.[90] It is amidst the foregoing that Balogun Juniad Alatishe died in 1995. Otun Balogun M.O. Shote's roots in Jadiyara, the twenty-fifth Awujale, and his membership in the same *Regberegbe*, Mafowoku, as Awujale Adetona, arguably made the ambition of any other person for the Balogun office unattractive to the Awujale. In 1996, Chief M.O. Shote consequently became the paramount Balogun of Ijebuland. The Otun Balogun office was accordingly filled by Chief J.A.B. Odunnuga, whilst that of the Osi Balogun office went to Alhaji Agboola Alausa (from Porogun).

Although Balogun Shote's reign was very short, nevertheless it heralded the deepening of the Balogun institution, as a mechanism for maintaining peaceful co-existence among residents of Ijebu-Ode, as a major feature in the Awujale's itinerary, and as a deliberate tool for cultural renaissance, particularly as captured in

---

90 Mr. Olatunde Shote; Mr. Lasisi, former employee at Shokas Industries; now of the Library Department of the Olabisi Onabanjo University, 50 years +, interviewed at O.O.U Ago Iwoye, on the 25 March, 2013.

its increasing elaborateness of the re-enactments during the Ojude-Oba Festivals.[91]

The Balogun institution would appear to have come full circle upon the death of Balogun (Alhaji) M.O. Shote in 2001, and the accession to the office Balogun (Alhaji) J.A.B. Odunnuga, whose martial descent, interfaced with the rotation policy, to produce the paramount Balogun titleholder.

Balogun J.A.B. Odunnuga

An assessment of Chief Odunnuga's tenure, so far, reveals the relevance of the rotational system of the Balogun office among the three traditional sections in

---

91 Chief Adebisi Adara, the Ogbe Odi of Ijebuland, 70 years, interviewed at the Palace of the Awujale of Ijebulaland on 10 December, 2012; Chief J.A.B Odunnuga, the Paramount Balogun of Ijebuland, 80 years, interviewed at Imoru Ijebu-Ode on 15 February 2013; Mr. Olatunde Shote.

Ijebu-Ode, its considerable following among the Islamic faithful in Ijebu-Ode, Western-style education, and annual celebration of the Balogun-inspired Ojude-Oba festival to record the methodical pursuit and achievement of novel ideas. That is, the formal demand and movement for the creation of an Ijebu state. Much the same way, the motion to build a one billion naira cultural pavilion (including a royal arcade, museum and library) for the hosting of Ojude-Oba festival was adopted in one of the pre-2008 Ojude-Oba festivals, and realized tree years later.[92]

Conclusion

This study has established the origins and meaning of the Balogun title in Ijebuland. While tracing the evolution of the title, it exposes its implications to the socio-political and economic aspects of Ijebuland from the pre-colonial period to the twenty-first century. The essay argues that there is a direct connection between the disappearance of such traditional military offices like the *Olukongbon, Ade Kola*, and *Adechegou* in precolonial Ijebu-Ode and the subsequent evolution of the non military Balogun titleholders in colonial and post-colonial Ijebuland. Similarly, this chapter links the retreat of military functions in such offices as the Agbon and the Lapoekun to the ascendency of the Balogun institution as a civic-oriented office.

---

92 S. Alatishe.

The change in the customary leadership of the all-Ijebu military high command, from the Olisa to the Balogun in the pre-colonial period is also attributed to this ascendency. During this time, the Balogun institution became so powerful that it deposed some awujales, and appointed some as well.

The study identifies Christianity, Islam, and other dynamics of the colonial economy (the production of cash crops, the use of currency in buying and selling and road construction) as some of the major factors behind the continuity and change observable in the Balogun institution in the colonial and post-independence period. The study submits that these factors combined with such elements as charity and philanthropy gave rise to the prominence of the Balogun institution in Ijebuland.

54   The Balogun in Yorubaland...

3
Balogun Chieftaincy in Ogbomoso
Rasheed Oyewole Olaniyi

Introduction

Ogbomoso had a composite foundation. It was situated almost midway between Igbon and Iresa kingdoms. In the words of Oyerinde, "Ogbomoso was surrounded by four powerful kings of remote antiquity: Aresa to the east; Onikoyi of Ikoyi to the west; Olugbon to the north and Timi of Ede to the south".[1] To survive in the midst of powerful neighbours, Ogbomoso developed a political structure dominated by warlords and military chiefs.

Prior to the 1650s, in the area now known as Ogbomoso, there had existed interspersed mini-states of Igbon, Iresa, Ikoyi, Ile-Oje, Idewure, Ajawa, Masifa, Isoko, Osupa and so on. These mini-states were semi-autonomous, because they had their crown kings and recognised no authority other than that of the Alaafin of Oyo. The Alaafin's authority was exercised in this area through his provincial oba –the Onikoyi of Ikoyi and Olugbon of Igbon. It was not that these two powerful

---

1 NAK/IBA PROF. 3/8: History of Ogbomoso by N.D. Oyerinde, p. 39.

obas had any political superiority over the other obas, rather, they all recognised the political sovereignty of one another. The obas recognised one another's boundaries, and efforts were made to ensure that these boundaries were respected.

Before the arrival of Soun Olabanjo Ogunlola (Aisa Agbe), Aale, a Nupe elephant hunter, settled at Oke-Elerin; Ohunsile from Ota settled at Oke-Ijeru, and Orisatolu from Boyu (Bariba) had settled at Isapa in the area now known as Ogbomoso. Also, Akandie settled at Isale Afon, but overtime his family became extinct. Soun Ogunlola spearheaded the formation of *Egbe Alongo* (Defence Pact League) to promote inter-community relations among the various mini-states and ensure security in Ogbomoso area. The Egbe Alongo served as a unifying banner and a melting pot devised to bring the various groups of mini-states together. EgbeAlongo was a precursor of Ogbomoso town.

At this period, Soun Ogunlola who served as the leader of Egbe Alongo was not an oba, but a brave warrior and hunter. But as events turned out, Ogunlola, who arrived on the scene as a hunter became widely known throughout the Old Oyo Empire.

During the reign of Alaafin Ajagbo, there was a warrior called Elemoso, who vigorously terrorised the Old Oyo Empire and defeated the Oyo army in the *Ogbo-Oro* War. Soun Ogunlola, who had been condemned to death for killing an Ijesha trader, offered to confront Elemeso on behalf of the Alaafin. Soun's victory over Elemeso made him a Yoruba hero who was honoured by the Alaafin with the Sword of Victory (*ogbo*), the symbol of authority. His settlement, hitherto known as Abule Soun (Soun's homestead) became Ogbomoso (derived from *Eni-ti-o-gbori-Elemeso*), that is, "the one who has slain Elemeso". Thus, the various settlements of Oke-Elerin, Isapa, Akandie and so on, came under his direct control, but, of course, excluding the mini-states of Igbon, Iresa, Ikoyi, Ile-Oje, Ajawa and Idewure.

Soun, the brave hunter, became *primus inter pares* in his new town of Ogbomoso and he was recognised as such by the neigbouring obas. The Egbe Alongo continued to thrive in promoting inter-community relations. Following the establishment of the *Sounship*, Ogbomoso became a mini-state and interacted with Iresa, Igbon, Ile-Oje and Ajawa as such. Subsequently, as war became inevitable, the Egbe Alongo transformed into *Egbe Ogun* (Warriors Defence League).

As noted by Adeleye, the wars fought by Ogbomoso could be viewed from three different perspectives —cooperative, aggressive and defensive.[2] The wars of the 18th and 19th centuries were fought either to repel the Fulani from Ilorin or to subjugate Ijesha and Ekiti people in cooperation with its allies, especially, Ibadan.

Although similar, the administrative structure of the new Ogbomoso could not be compared with the ancient

---

94 A. Adeleye, *Ogbomoso in the Centuries of Conflict and Development*. (Lagos: Loladis Nig. 1999), p. 1.

Ile-Ife, the Old Oyo Empire, Ikoyi or Iresa. At its infancy, the administrative structure was not elaborate. Two brave warriors supported the Soun in defending the Ogbomoso town from the aggression of existing powerful towns or states. The courageous deeds of Lafinjin and Aolu protected Ogbomoso against external invasion. Lafinjin became the *Jagun*, a war title equivalent to war general in the Old Oyo Empire. Lafinji led Ogbomoso in battles against Ile-Keke and Ile-Ola, the two powerful settlements that threatened Ogbomoso's growth. Lafinjin killed an Oyo masquerader, called Akere who often terrorised inhabitants of Ogbomoso by extorting money (200 cowries) from each compound.

The second powerful warrior and notable councilor of Soun Ogunlola was Aolu Agoro. He migrated to Ogbomoso from Ajase'Po when the town was under the Aresa. He became the first Areago in Ogbomoso. However, having lost a battle, he demoted himself from Areago to the title of Ikolaba in order to demonstrate his diminishing military prowess.

To assure his subjects of their safety and security, Soun further invited other warriors such as Yaku from Ajagusi (beyond Aasa River), Olufa from Ifon and Agbooye from Ogbin. Before the 18th century, the palace chiefs (*Ilu* chiefs) were composed entirely of titleholders of the small original town who descended from the first settlers, before the various surrounding villages took refuge and formed large quarters in the town during the 19th century wars.

Making of a Balogun chieftaincy

At inception, the Balogun chieftaincy institution did not constitute part of the administrative structure of Ogbomoso. Its introduction was part of the political innovations to cope with the exigencies of wars, power and diplomacy in 19th century Yorubaland. Ogbomoso was founded by brave warriors, hunters and herbalists. The rulers were warriors, and therefore, the Balogun chieftaincy did not gain political importance until the growth and expansion of the town in the 19th century. Indeed, Ogbomoso superseded other Yoruba towns in producing several *Aare Ona Kakanfos* (war generalissimo) for the old and new Oyo Empires. The introduction of the Balogun chieftaincy signified a change in power politics and administrative arrangements needed to strengthen the security of the town against external aggression and to maintain internal political stability.

The palace chiefs (*Ilu* chiefs) under the Baale or Soun of Ogbomoso was originally composed of the following.

Aareago: He was the war chief and head of Soun's bodyguards. Specifically, he was responsible for the defence of the Ilorin gate known as *Odi Idi Araba*, towards Aguodo area in the past. The Aareago had his own troops that he led to the war. Before the emergence of the Balogun, it was the Aareago who used to lead

Ogbomoso troops. Today, the Aareago is the chairman of the ilu chiefs and kingmakers (*afobaje*). The Aareago is the second in command as well as an adviser to the Soun. He is also a customary court judge.

Jagun: He was the controller of the market and hunters, and also protected traders and strangers. He acted as the treasurer of the ilu chiefs. Today, he is a customary court judge.

Bara: He looked after the farmers. In the past, bara was a warrior and used to lead his own troops to wars involving Ogbomoso. Today, he is one of the kingmakers, an adviser to the Soun, and a member of the customary court.

Ikolaba: He was responsible for the Baale's food whenever he was on an outing. He played important roles during the Oro festival. He also opened the gate of the palace to allow women go out in the morning. Today, he is a customary court judge.

Abese: In the past, Abese served as the Soun's messenger. Abese was a warrior and used to lead his own troops to wars involving Ogbomoso. The first Balogun of Ogbomoso, Odufopo, was formerly an Abese who was installed in the 1860s by Baale Ojo Olanipa (Aburumaku). Today, the Abese is one of the kingmakers, an adviser to the Soun and a member of customary court.

Alapo: He was responsible for carrying quivers, arrows and spears. He was in charge of the armoury. Now, he is a customary court judge.

In Ogbomoso, the Aareago had always been the most senior member of the palace chiefs. In other Yoruba towns, Aareago was a minor title usually under the Balogun line. In Ogbomoso, there appears to be no definite explanation why the Aareago was the most senior chief next in rank to the baale. There is a theory that in the past, one Aareago was a powerful man and assumed the right to be considered next to the baale (soun). This position has been jealously guarded and retained by subsequent Aareago up to contemporary times. It should be noted that prominent Yoruba towns often had the military title of Jagun while small settlements or city-states had Balogun. Powerful warriors and courageous people were made Jagun to assist the Aare Ona Kakanfo (The Yoruba war generalissimo). Baloguns were dispatched to guard the city gates and small settlements. This implies that the Aare Ona Kakanfo led the wars, followed by the Jagun of prominent towns or kingdoms, his warriors and the Balogun. Samuel Johnson is of the view that Jagun and Balogun were military titles that are interchanged in different towns.³ They performed the same function as the leader of the military of these towns. However, it seems that the Jagun title is more ancient than Balogun in most of the Oyo Yoruba towns that used Balogun. The use of Balogun was possibly a later development. Areago and Jagun were the older military titles. This paper posits that at different periods in the history of Ogbomoso, the Balogun co-existed with Jagun and Aare Ona Kakanfo.

The imperative of seeking a new political structure for the building of a formidable fortress in the face of mounting aggression became more pronounced when towns such as Ibadan, Abeokuta and Ijaye became more determined to subjugate other Yoruba towns. This was more so, towards Ogbomoso, when Toyeje became the Aare Ona Kakanfo (1797-1825).

The implication of this was that the composite groups in Ogbomoso (including the hosts and the settler communities) were as a matter of necessity, forced to map out strategies for the joint defence of their new community. The people of Ogbomoso considered the aggressive forces of Ilorin, Ibadan, Abeokuta and Ijaiye as common enemies, which they were prepared to repel at all cost. According to Oyerinde, Ogbomoso was serious about its warfare, as Ibadan was overwhelmed with wars, so was Ogbomoso.⁴ Indeed, Ogbomoso

---

95 S. Johnson, *History of the Yorubas* (Lagos: CMS, 2001), p. 77

96 N.D. Oyerinde, *Iwe Itan Ogbomoso* (Jos, 1934), p. 123

fought alongside Ibadan in Kiriji, Offa and Modakeke in defence of Yorubaland.

According to Oyerinde, Ilorin did everything in its power to conquer Ogbomoso. However, Mallam Alimi from Sokoto had visited Ogbomoso and prophesied that the town would be enlarged and enemies would not prevail against her.[5] Nevertheless, Malam Alimi's sons tried to subdue and depopulate the town.

Baale Toyeje Akanni (Alebiosu), an Aare Ona Kakanfo, who was also the Soun of Ogbomoso between 1797 and 1825 built a wall around the town at a period when many towns had been sacked by the Fulani and there was great division among the Yoruba. After Afonja's death, rivalry prevented the Yoruba from cooperating among themselves to confront the Fulani in Ilorin.

As stated by Oyerinde, Ogbomoso was not a big town when Toyeje died.[6] The wall of defence that Toyeje built passed behind Oluntan's compound near Oloko, behind Olukuewe's compound near Laka, and behind Oniyirokun's compound at Oke Ogede. The pit where mud was dug for the walls on the road to Masifa later became the Oloko stream. This has helped in determining the size of the town when Baale OluwusiAremu (Olusi) reigned between 1826 and 1840.

N.D. Oyerinde, (NAK/IBA PROF. 3/8...) p. 22.

Ibid, p. 26.

During Baale Oluwusi's reign, there were prominent warriors and military chiefs. The most famous were Lasinmiran, Lasemi, Oluya, Ogunrunbi, Bammeke and Lagbedu. Bammeke was invited by Oluwusi from Sukuru when the town was destroyed. He was a brave warrior who had many horses. Bammeke constructed the town wall from Oloko to Gbira gate. He also built Ora gate, known as Ora Alase. He had a firm grip on Isale Ora and the quarter was called Isale Bammeke. Bammeke sold people into slavery, irrespective of whether they were Ogbomoso natives or non-natives.[7]

Unlike Toyeje, Oluwusi did not bother to repel the Fulani; his primary objective was to make Ogbomoso an independent town. Before the town became strong enough to resist external aggression, the Fulani at Ilorin commanded Oluwusi to Ilorin to pay homage. In his absence, Oyelekan, his close relative, usurped power.

Lasinmiran, a powerful warrior who belonged to the Onpetu family had felt betrayed, after he had assisted Oluwusi to win a war against the invading Fulani. Lasinmiran conspired with the Fulani to invade Ogbomoso. Ogbomoso soldiers camped at the city gate on the Ikoyi road. Lamisinmiran ensured that his political enemies, the Areago Lanlewu and Jagun Olukuewu were killed in the battle called *Igba Aladorin* (seventy locust tree).

Ibid, p. 27.

Ogbomoso became a safe haven for about 143 neighbouring settlements that sought refuge in the town. In turn, the new arrivals in Ogbomoso made it a strong Yoruba city. Adeagbo, Akinsanmi and Onitilo commanded Oluwusi troops against Ilorin. Ogbomoso continues to cherish the memory of Odebi, the son of Olakoso, Bammeke, Lagbedu (*Eiye Agannangannan*) "the swift footed" and Oluya for their courage and military exploits during the conflicts between Ogbomoso and Ilorin.

Oyerinde opined that five or six subordinate chiefs controlled the town (they served as the judiciary). Their chieftaincies were not hereditary, but the holders included those who were serviceable to the Baale and the town. For example, the Aareagos (the war chiefs) were selected from nine different and unrelated families; the Jaguns from seven families, and the Ikolabas from six different and unrelated families. It should be noted that six different families were given the title of Aareago once each but remained in obscurity. These were Arolu, Olufa, Labosin, Oluronbi, Oniyirokun and Ori Oro.

In effect, the administrative arrangement of the town was changed to cater for the component parts of the federal structure that had evolved. It became the responsibility of the Alapo, to herald the Soun to the battle fields, emergencies or the forest, for the annual hunting expedition. Arolu was appointed the Aareago (the war chief).

The Onpetu and the Soun agreed that the two towns of Ogbomoso and Ile-Oje should merge and the two obas, as well as others, agreed to live together peacefully and respect each other's rights. Thus, the Onpetu as well as other settler obas in Ogbomoso became full-time members of the Ilu Chiefs.

As part of the new security arrangements, the defence of the gates of the town became a shared responsibility. In this way, the Gbira gate was defended by the Areago; the Igbon gate by the Olugbon; the Ola gate by the Balogun; the Ora gate by the Jagun; the Alokomaro gate by the Onpetu and Ilorin gate by the Soun. The Soun's war leader was the Balogun while the Onpetu's was Seriki, and it was agreed that one would not go to war without the other.

In the 19th century, the role of Ogbomoso became more apparent as a frontier Yoruba town in close proximity to the Fulani in Ilorin. From the 1850s, the tension and discord, as well as external aggression and general insecurity of lives and properties, drove Ogbomoso to seek ways of ensuring political stability.

The Balogun of Ogbomoso, the Iyalode and the Otun Baale were admitted to the palace chiefs (Ilu chiefs) after the conclusion of the Ilesha War in the 19th century. In 1865, Ojo Aburumaku, the Aare Ona Kakanfo, became the Baale of Ogbomoso. However, he was not a fighter or a warrior like his predecessors. Aburumaku adopted the Ibadan administrative system by choosing the Balogun and his assistants. For instance, Ajai Olubao was delegated by the Aare to the Ijebu War in 1866, where he was killed.[8]

Odufopo became the Balogun of Ogbomoso; Ayoola Ajibowoje, the Otun; Ilori, the Osi; and Popoola, the Bada. It was during the reign of Ojo Aburumaku that the Balogun assumed the responsibility of leading the Ogbomoso troops to war, which means that the Baale or Soun no longer led troops into battle. It appears that other members of the Ilu chiefs also went to war, but the Balogun took the custody of the war staff (*opagun*). The Balogun chieftaincy was, therefore, part of the political dynamism of Ogbomoso during the period.

More importantly, Aburumaku made them war chiefs with the hope that they might perish in the Ilesha War of 1867 and he could reign peacefully. However, Aburumaku died in 1869, two years after the departure of Ogbomoso troops to Ilesha. Therefore, Ogbomoso was left without valiant warriors.

Aburumaku was succeeded by his son, Otunla, who imposed himself as the Baale in 1869. During this period, Akinfenwa, the Aareago; Odelotan, the Abese; and Abelepo, the Balogun were away on the battle field. Omoniyi, the Jagun; Ojo Otalekun, the Ikolaba; and Okonu, the Bara were the only important chiefs in the town but they were not brave enough to challenge Otunla.

As stated by Oyerinde in *Iwe Itan Ogbomoso*, it is likely that Apapa, Lasinminran and Olubao were Baloguns before Odufopo p. 77.

In 1877 when Olaoye (Orumogege) became the Baale, Ogbomoso, like Ibadan had turned war into a major preoccupation. According to Oyerinde, "The foolishness of Ibadan, has spread to and is stamped on Ogbomoso."[9] Thus, Ogbomoso took war very seriously for their survival and the corporate existence of the Yoruba. Ogbomoso fought alongside Ibadan. Ibadan considered Ogbomoso as a free and independent town and not as a tributary town. The war chiefs when Olaoye became the Soun were: Ilori Yemoru, Balogun; Oduntan Sekengbede, Otun Balogun; Lala Isale Alasa, Osi Balogun; Akinsinde, Seriki; Balogun Popoola, Bada and Tanimoma Ajadi, Agbon Ekerin.

Ilori Yemoru of Agodi compound, Masifa, was the first known core Ogbomoso indigene to be made a Balogun by Soun Olaoye Orumogege. All members of the Ilu Chiefs were from the cores of the town (Oja Igbo, Oja Ajagun, Isale Afon and Oke Elerin areas). He was a member of the military class and resided within the core of Ogbomoso. Yemoru, the Balogun, and his Otun, Sekengbede were killed during the Offa War. This was a source of great sorrow to the Ogbomoso people. The Balogun vacancy was not filled for a long time. Cognomen of Balogun Ilori Yemoru:

    Ilori Yemoru,
    Aparaogun bi eninpale,
    Opooriniidiigbanitoriomo-olomo,

Oyerinde, p. 102.

awututu bi olosoonu

Iloriosonu

Ojuureloniawo n papa

Denge tutu leyin

Ogbonaninu

Wansari Baba Ogundepo

Baba Banjoko

Eni a koleemu

Olohun laa fi fun

Otoriogun de aburo

Owoogunl'owo re

Ilori di yemoru

O nleogun-un lo

Aruna de gbo

Baba nile Baba logun

Praise Song[10]
Otoriogun de aburo
Owoogunl'owo re
Ilori di yemoru.

Interviews with High Chief Alhaji Shittu Kolade Ilori, Yemoru II, Balogun of Ogbomosoland, interviewed on 18th and 19th Jan. 2013 in Ogbomoso; High Chief Samuel Sobalaje Otolorin, Aareago of Ogbomosoland, interviewed on 26th January, 2013. He was installed as Aareago on December 14th, 1990; Chief Tijani Abioye, Bara of Ogbomosoland interviewed on 29th January, 2013. He was installed as Bara on 22nd May, 1979; and High Chief Amuda Odutona, Abese of Ogbomoso-land, interviewed on 2 February, 2013.

The installation of the Balogun of Ogbomoso

After the death of a balogun, the next lineage would inform the monarch that they were ready for the installation. The monarch would give them the list requirements to be met before the installation. These included items such as: money, bitter kolanut, alligator pepper, cow and wine. The installation day would be fixed by the monarch. At the installation ceremony, the Balogun would prostrate in front of the monarch, the Ilu chiefs and all the people seven times in the open arena of the palace where the installation was taking place. The Ikolaba, whose function was to bring the Balogun to the arena, would pour sand on the prospective Balogun's head. Then, the monarch would order the Ikolaba to place <u>the</u> *Igba Iwa* (Virtue Calabash) containing various fetish materials at a strategic place in the town. That would signify that he had become the Balogun. After this, the monarch, the chiefs and all the people would pray for him. Then the monarch would present him with the certificate and/or staff of office.

The Ilu chiefs, including the Balogun, were usually chosen by the Soun, from among his friends and supporters. The name of the chief to be would be proposed to the council. Members of the family that had hitherto occupied the post could still contest for it. A person from a family that had never occupied the position could also be made the chief. When a selection was made, he would be called before the Soun and the council, and one of the chiefs would be asked to place the "coronation leaves" on his head while the Jagun would give him a charge. Placing the leaves is called *jawe lee lori*. The Soun would then present him with the *ogbo* or cutlass, as an insignia of office. The titles were not inherited as is the case today.

The Balogun and power politics in Ogbomoso

The Balogun headed the warriors. His office was strictly military. The Balogun's war instruments included gun, arrow, cutlass, charms and a war staff (*opagun*). The war staff was like a flag to announce the arrival of the troops at the battle field. It was believed that the war staff had the power to win wars. It represented the power of a town. No town dared go to war without the war staff. It was always kept in the custody of the Balogun. Whenever a town was going to the battlefield, the Balogun would lead the troops with the opagun in his hands. At the battlefield, the war staff would be fixed on the ground, a wrapper would be spread on the ground beside the war staff, and gun powder would be spread on the wrapper. After this, the Balogun would sit on a stool beside the instruments of war with his sword beside him. Then the troops would take turns to load their guns with the gun powder. This process would continue until the gun powder was exhausted.

The opagun would be propitiated when the troops returned from war. Men and women were used as sacrifice to propitiate the opagun. Today however, goats are used to propitiate opagun and this is done in the month of March of every year.

In the past, the Balogun used to appoint his lieutenants: Otun, Osi, Bada, Asipa and Sarumi. Today, the Balogun can only appoint his lieutenants with the consent of the Soun or they are directly installed by the Soun if he so wishes. The Balogun had other lieutenants such as Ekerin, Ekarun, Abese, Maye, Ekefa, Asiwaju, Ayingun, Lagunna, Aare Egbe Omo Balogun, Gbanka, Aare Onibon and Ajiya.

During the Kiriji War and the Eleesun battle, it was Aaeago Akinfenwa (known as *Obembe l'Esu* — small devil) that led Ogbomoso troops. Throughout Soun Laoye Orumogege's reign, there was no record that another Balogun was installed. It was Soun Majengbasan Ajibola Eleepo (1902-1908) who made an effort to install a new Balogun. It should be noted that after the Kiriji and Offa wars, there was relative peace in the land, which may be the reason why no effort was made to fill the vacant position of the Balogun until the reign of Soun Ajibola Eleepo. It was he who made enquiries about the whereabouts of the opagun (war staff) in order to propitiate it. It was Taiwo Gbebi who told the Soun that the staff was in his custody. Because of this, Soun Eleepo decided to make Taiwo Gbebi the Balogun.

Although the war leaders in Ogbomoso preferred a man called Ogbinkun from Masifa, Soun Eleepo, despite Taiwo Gbebi's age, made him the Balogun. He was the third Balogun of Ogbomoso. Ogbinkun was rejected perhaps because he was not from the core of Ogbomoso. Taiwo Gbebi was the Balogun during Atanda Layode's (I) reign as the Soun (1908-1914). He was later removed by Layode (I) who made Popoola the Bada, the Balogun. This was as a result of the intrigue that arose following the succession dispute on the death of Ajibola Eleepo. Taiwo Gbebi had supported Oke, Jagun Lawani's younger brother and son of Soun Gbagun against Layode (I).

Soun Bamgboye (Gbagun or Ondugbe), who reigned between 1870 and 1877, distributed the existing tolls to obas and chiefs, including the Olugbon, Onpetu, Areago, Jagun and Balogun, having allocated one to himself.[11] By the 20th century, the structure of the Ilu chiefs at the time of British colonial rule included: Baale, Areago, Jagun, Bara, Ikolaba, Abese, Balogun, Otun Baale and Onpetu of Ijeru quarters.

The Balogun was considered to be in the same category as other minor titleholders such as Oluode (the head of the hunters), until admitted to the council of Ilu chiefs. The minor title holders who could become the Balogun included: Otun Balogun, Osi Balogun, Seriki Balogun, Ekerin Balogun, Sarumi, Ashipa and Bada.

These minor titleholders under the Balogun would attend the Baale's court if called or, if interested in a matter under consideration, and would usually follow

---

Oyerinde, NAK, p. 7.

the Balogun to the palace. It was customary for these minor title holders and quarter heads to meet at the Baale's house on the last day of every 'month' (29th day according to the Yoruba system of counting). Some of the minor titleholders and personal followers of the chiefs could go to the Baale's palace for the inner council meetings with their seniors but would not actually attend the meeting; they were informed of the decisions by the Jagun, who was the spokesman of the council.

Before the 20th century, the Ilu chiefs functioned as the judicial authority in the town with the Jagun as spokesman. Minor cases were settled, if possible, by the various compound heads in their quarters. Under British colonial rule, the Ogbomoso subordinate Native Authority had the following chiefs: Baale, Areago, Jagun, Bara, Ikolaba, Abese, Balogun and Otun Baale. They held meetings with the other title holders and quarter heads once a month in accordance with local customs. Before arriving at a decision on any important administrative problem, the Ilu chiefs would first consult the title holders and quarter heads. If the problem concerned the district and neigbouring settlements, a district and town council would be convened. The Ilu chiefs formed a town council to meet once a month, with the inclusion of the Onpetu Ijeru Quarters, Baale Opete and the title holders under the Balogun line.

On the judiciary, in addition to the native system, Ogbomoso Court (Grade B) comprised the following members: The Baale or his representative (Dawodu), Areago, Jagun, Bara, Ikolaba, Abese and the Balogun.

From inception, only five royal families existed in Ogbomoso. They were: Toyeje, Oluwusi, Baiyewuwon, Bolanta and Odunaro. The Soun is rotated among the royal families in this order: (1) Laoye, (2) Bolanta, (3) Layode, (4) Itabiyi, (5) Oyewumi (the present ruling house).

Since 1952, there has been an open contest for the Sounship between the descendants of those who had ruled Ogbomoso as Soun in the past. The kingmakers include Aareago, Jagun, Bara, Ikolaba, Abese, Balogun and Iyalode. The Aareago serves as the chairman of the kingmakers.

The Balogun and crime control in Ogbomoso

From the 1870s, Ogbomoso was overrun by criminal elements. Oyerinde states that Soun Orumogege could not tolerate the thieves, incendiaries and murderers.[12] Thus, he commissioned hunters to patrol the streets at night and to protect traders in the town. During the reign of Soun Layode I, the number of thieves and bandits continued to increase in Ogbomoso. He therefore, provided the hunters with two barrels of gunpowder and two bowls of bullets with ten shillings.

Oyerinde, 1934, p. 112.

Yet, the menace of armed bandits continued unabated. Soun Layode I made Popoola the Balogun, not because they were friends but because of power politics. It should also be noted that Popoola actually favoured Itabiyi, another contestant to the throne. The people of Ogbomoso accused Popoola and Itabiyi of being the ring leaders of the armed bandits in the town. Popoola challenged Itabiyi such that both of them would swear at Soun's tomb to confirm the leader of the criminals.

Popoola went to swear but Itabiyi refused to go. Thereafter, Popoola as the Balogun was determined to patrol the streets at night himself. He would sit in the huts built for idols and at blacksmith's workshops. In February 1914, Popoola arrested a gang of armed robbers whose leader rode a horse. Popoola was wounded in the conflict that ensued between him and the robbers and taken to hospital for treatment. Itabiyi (Ojo Aburumako's son) disrupted the government of his younger cousin, Layode I (son of Odunaro), with his intrigues, leading to the deposition of Layode I, who spent two years in Ibadan. The Alaafin then ordered Layode I to return home from Ibadan. When Layode got to Oyo, he sent for Popoola, the Balogun of Ogbomoso.

On May 19, 1914, Itabiyi usurped power and made himself the Soun of Ogbomoso. He wanted Popoola to remain the Balogun, but Popoola refused. He (Itabiyi) subsequently complained to the Alaafin who advised him to pacify the Balogun with valuable gifts. Itabiyi invited Popoola and gave him a big gown, and put over it another gown with a guinea fowl colour pattern. The big gown had been poisoned. It was the hunters from Masifa that gave Popoola the medicine that neutralised the effect of the poison that had entered through his skin from the big gown. When Itabiyi observed that the poison had not killed Popoola, he ordered Popoola to quit the town.

Other chiefs such as Orisafayo the Olugbon, Oyeniyi the Onpetu, Lafimi the Alasa, and Osun the Lagbedu said, "We also are ready to leave the town (*with our people*)...There should be civil war before we leave."[13]

Itabiyi regretted his plan to eject Balogun Popoola from the town. He sent an emissary, Akinbola Owoka, to Popoola asking him not to leave. This prevented civil war from breaking out in Ogbomoso.

Before Itabiyi's death, there were rumours that Layode would return to Ogbomoso. So, Balogun Popoola, his Otun, Ogundeyi and his Osi, Osundeji, Bello Giwa from Agbede quarters and their friends and followers went to Oyo to meet Layode. At Oyo, the Balogun and his entourage realised that Layode had been sent to Saki, apparently by the Alaafin who was an ally of Itabiyi. Popoola was highly disappointed and was barely prevented from committing suicide. Balogun and his men were arrested at Oyo for creating disturbances and were taken to Ibadan as a warning.

Ibid, p. 133.

From the time of Layode (I), Ogbomoso became subject to the authority of the Alaafin of Oyo. Thereafter, there was lawlessness, with thieves and burglars who paraded the streets of Ogbomosho, terrorising people. Itabiyi respected no other king but the Alaafin of Oyo. He once replied to the Christian missionaries who preached to him about the gospel of Christ, "Who is the Lord? There is no Lord but the one I have at Oyo." Itabiyi died a painful death on January 21, 1916.

Conclusion

In conclusion, the Balogun chieftaincy is rotated among three families in Ogbomoso: (1) Ilori Yemoru of Masifa, (2) Popoola of Oke-Agbede, and (3) Taiwo Gbebi of Isale Afon. From the 1870s to the present time, Ogbomoso has had more than eight Baloguns from these families:

1. Odufopo (during Aburumaku's reign);
2. Ilori Yemoru (during Gbagun/Laoye's reign);
3. Taiwo Gbebi (during Ajibola Eleepo's reign);
4. Popoola (during Olayode I);
5. Ogundeji (during Itabiyi);
6. Olaleye (during Layode II);

7 & 8 Sule and Shittu Ilori (during the incumbent Soun Ajagungbade III).

Initially, the Balogun was purely a minor military chieftain and gradually became the chief warrior under

Baale Aburumaku. Later when there was no more war, the office of the Balogun became redundant. Consequently, Soun Layode II (1966-1969) thought it expedient to include the office of the Balogun among the Ilu chiefs. Today, the Balogun is a member of the advisory council of the town. In other words, the Balogun serves as an adviser to the monarch of the town and is one the kingmakers of the town. The Balogun plays an important role in ensuring law and order through collaboration with vigilante groups, night guards, police and other security agencies. The Balogun also offers useful advice in resolving conflicts in the town.

In contemporary times, most of the ancient titles in the Balogun line have become honorary titles that the Soun could bestow on any deserving personality in Ogbomoso or from elsewhere. Between 1973 and 2005, Soun of Ogbomosoland, Oba Jimoh Oyewunmi (Ajagungbade III) has installed honourary chiefs in the Balogun line.

Blank

4

The Balogun Institution in Ibadan 1830-1955

Mutiat Titilope Oladejo

Introduction

From inception, Ibadan's socio-political and economic history was associated with militarism. Accumulation of wealth was based on the ability to engage in war expeditions which thereafter enriched the individual and the state. The relationship between the state and the economy was sustained by the military aristocratic system of government. Between 1830 and 1893, the mode of governance in Ibadan placed the military warlords at the helm of affairs. Vividly, two categories of chieftaincy emerged from the civil and military lines. The civil line developed as an alternative to replace the military when they were out of town on war expedition. The position of *Balogun* emerged out of competence and bravery displayed during wars and in recognition of his efforts in war; he became prestigious in the politics and governance of Ibadan. After the death of a *Baale*, the Balogun was offered the position of Baale based on his achievement and fortune at war. As such, the office of the Balogun was well institution-alized and when the position of the head of state was rejected by a particular Balogun, the post was passed to the second-in-command, that is, the *Otun Balogun* and not the *Otun Baale*. This rejection elongated the Balogun line in Ibadan leadership. It was after 1898 that the first Otun Baale had access to power.[1] This rejection could be described as a diplomatic means of entrenching the Balogun institution and the fact that the revenue generated from constant war expeditions sustained the state made the power status unquestionable. Furthermore, the Baloguns were always at war, so they could not easily combine governance and warfare together. They preferred to acquire more wealth to reinforce their power in the society.

The Balogun and *Seriki* were both military institutions, but the Seriki were junior military warlords. The office of the Balogun was composed of senior military chiefs. The senior cadre formed a decision making group sacrosanct to determine war expeditions. Invariably, they participated in decision making to declare and terminate wars.

In nineteenth century Ibadan, the Balogun institution emerged, as Basorun Oluyole successfully prevented the Fulani invasion of Yorubaland. This achievement entrenched militarism as a basis of power

---

1 From the 1840s to 1890s, about four Balogun rejected the office of the baale (the most superior leadership status in Ibadan). Oderinlo rejected in 1847, Akere in 1867, Osungbekun in 1893, and Akintola did twice in 1895 and 1897.

and access to wealth in Ibadan.[2] The Balogun institution was very significant after the evolution of Ibadan, and it was in vogue for about fifty years. This made twentieth century changes difficult because the 1893 treaty signed with the British curtailed the incidences of war. Hence, the power status of the Baloguns was challenged as the passive baale line struggled to become the Baale (the ultimate leadership position for both the military and civil lines). Despite the challenges encountered by the Baloguns in the protection of their power status, the colonial administration injected the idea of modernity which absolutely changed the factors that determine who gets into the Balogun chieftaincy line in Ibadan.

Power, diplomacy and autocracy in the Balogun institution

All warriors strove to acquire power and gave all that was required to achieve their aspirations. The balance of power was dynamic. This was achieved rigorously through the quest for wealth, prestige and influence. To achieve this, political conflicts were rampant. According to Toyin Falola, the political conflicts revolved around elimination of rivals and opponents, due process in determining competence for promotion,

---

2 See B. Awe, "Militarism and Economic Development in Nineteenth Century Yoruba Country: The Ibadan Example" *Journal of African History* 14, no.1, (1973), p. 65-77.

liquidation of over ambitious men and the relegation of senile leaders.[3] The quest for power fostered rivalries and opposition to the extent that, the ability of each warrior was put to test in the battlefield. Akinyele rightly explained:

> If any man presumed to assume a title that he did not deserve, the man who had the right to the title would challenge the usurper when they got to the battle to come along with him to face the enemy. If the usurper was worsted in the fight, the rightful owner would assume the title in dispute from the very battle field.[4]

Thus, every title holder at each level was cautious about his display of wealth and power as his opponents would seriously plot to eliminate or plan to demote him in the military hierarchy.

Beyond military actions, access to power depended on the ability to maintain popular support. The masses were most important within the socio-economic structure of everyday life in pre-colonial Ibadan. Thus, the warlords maintained large group of followers and this in itself depended on the extent of their wealth. The warlords used their wealth to entice people from various lineages and towns to work on their farmsteads

---

[3] T. Falola, *Ibadan: Foundation, Growth and Change, 1830-1960* (Ibadan: Bookcraft, 2012), p.129.

[4] I.B. Akinyele, *Outline History of Ibadan*. (Ibadan: Caxton Printers, 1946), p. 97.

(*oko-egan*). This was a kind of plantation farming, and the proceeds from the farm were sold by itinerant women traders. This mode of production and reproduction of wealth meant that the followership was a form of investment expected to expand wealth. The fact that migrants to Ibadan aspired to attach themselves to a warrior to seek protection increased the revenue base of the warlords.

It is important to emphasise that the trans Atlantic trade favoured the power of the warlords. They were able to engage in trade because they had the wherewithal to finance coastal trade. As the demand for slaves, palm-oil and palm-kernels increased, they were able to acquire more arms and ammunition which enabled the process of war expeditions. Internal trade networks were controlled by warlords. Even women were expected to assume absolute loyalty to the office of the warlord because space for trading was provided by the warlord and in return proceeds were expected.

In the 1830s, in the bid to rise to power in the internal environment, Oluyole's plot to depose Lakanle gave him the opportunity to become the Basorun. The military achievement in the wars of independence for Yorubaland against the Fulani was as a result of the military efforts of Oluyole and warlords from other towns. For this, he was appointed the *Basorun Oyomesi*. With this new position, he diplomatically attempted autocratic rule in Ibadan.

Autocracy as displayed by Oluyole was a means of ensuring absolute and unquestionable power, which was rare in other towns. His idea of autocracy was to take advantage of the fact that Ibadan, being an emerging town, would be suitable for new politics and government. Diplomatic moves to sustain power as practiced by Oluyole involved the maintenance of a large army and he took advantage of the migrants from northern Yorubaland. He ensured that this category of migrants remained absolutely loyal to him. In this way, he built an army of energetic men.

However, until his death in the late 1840s, his autocratic moves were rarely achieved because the chiefs preferred the principle of collective action and in the process; Balogun Bankole Alesinloye, Lajubu, and Akintuyi were killed, while other chiefs were expelled from Ibadan.[5] While his autocracy was not welcomed in Ibadan politics, his military achievements ensured the protection of the Yoruba from the Fulani. Within Ibadan, his market (Oja-Iba) was meant to maintain the economy and it remained a centre of commercial convergence for traders within and outside of Yorubaland.

Rising through the household of Chief Toki Onibudo in the late 1840s, Balogun Ibikunle became the head of the household after the death of Chief Toki. The

---

5 See K. Morgan, *Akinyele's Outline History of Ibadan Part I*. (Ibadan: Caxton Printers)

wealth and property of Chief Toki was used to finance military-expeditions. His cognomen attested to the fact that he engaged in several war expeditions.[6] The readiness of the holders of Balogun office to fight and head for war is well depicted in *Balogun* Ibikunle's cognomen which goes thus:

> We request that he be not the king of the forest.
>
> The Balogun became the king of the forest
>
> He ruined the forest
>
> We ask he be not the king of savanna, Balogun chose to be king
>
> He destroyed the savanna completely
>
> He who dares the elephant dares death
>
> He who dares the buffalo expects a charge
>
>> He who confronts the wild masquerade prepares to go to heaven
>>
>> There is no god that can excel Ogun, others are just full of mere affront
>>
>> Without his leadership, they cannot have an inch
>>
>> Without his company, they cannot march confidently on
>>
>> If Ibikunle, Lord of his quarters, is no more,

---

[6] The cognomen recorded from his oral biographers showed that his expeditions extended to the following Yoruba towns Ohan, Ikogosi, Igbein, Ijebu, Egba towns, Ilorin, Ede, Ilesa, Efon, Ifon, Ejigbo among others.

> They cannot even challenge the jackal to a duel.
> Arowolo! He who outwits them in the city
> Charger of the trees and of the fields
> A Champion in the battlefield
> Arowolo! Master in the city
> Charger of trees and fields
> Terror in the battlefield.

This, depicts the wealth and power enjoyed and ascribed to wealthy military men in Ibadan society.

Balogun Ibikunle actually reigned from 1851 to 1864 and his reign was relatively legitimate in Ibadan society. Unlike, other Baloguns, he adopted a wealth sharing formula within Ibadan that made him influential, but his autocratic tendencies reflected in the use of military power against other Yoruba towns.

However, despite the wide avenues to acquire wealth and power, the war-lord in the office of the Balogun was not absolutely free from the criticisms of opponents that could shift power out of his control. Wealth became a source of trouble for Balogun Ajobo in the 1870s.[7] Based on the pattern of migration and settlement in Ibadan, Balogun Ajobo had migrated from Ikire in the 1830s and rose through the ranks of the junior military line (Seriki) to the Balogun line. In the 1860s, he was the Seriki. He became Balogun in the

---

7 See K. Morgan, *Akinyele's Outline History of Ibadan, Part II.*

1870s. No doubt, Ajobo's ability to manage the economic system to acquire wealth and his rise to political power was relatively fast in a newly formed town of people with diverse backgrounds. Balogun Ajobo's era in the 1870s did not imply that he was the most experienced, but was favoured by the fact that he strategized to attain success which other warlords and chiefs could not achieve. This created hate and animosity towards him because many young boys and men chose to follow him, as they preferred him as the *Babaogun* and *Babakekere*. A conspiracy to eliminate him arose when the Baale and his colleagues disobeyed the principle of collective action in Ibadan governance system by appointing the *Owa* of Ilesa without consultation with and consent of the chiefs, thus the plot to eliminate him was justified.[8] After a condemnation of his actions, the chiefs gave him an option of suicide or exile. Balogun Ajobo opted for exile and surrendered the staff of war on August 5, 1871 and left for Ijebu Iperu.[9]

Similar to Ibikunle's reign was that of Basorun Ogunmola's tenure which started in 1866.[10] It was obvious that Oluyole's rule was a lesson to other leaders and hence Basorun Ogunmola was more diplomatic and

---

8 Falola, p.132.

9 Ibid.

10 S. Johnson, *The History of Yorubas* (Lagos: CMS Nigeria Bookshops, 1921) p.365.

democratic in the governance of Ibadan. He worked in the interest of the masses and his colleagues. Of specific importance was the fact that non-linear chieftaincy titles were created to reward the masses that contributed significantly at war expeditions. As such, the titles *Foko, Gbonka* and *Owota* were borrowed from Oyo chieftaincy to appreciate efforts. Furthermore, cases of important legal implications were handled with intellectual dexterity during his tenure. He carried out the functions of a judge in Ibadan with a high level of impartiality. There was a case in which a man accidentally killed a goat that had strayed on his corn farm. The owner of the goat demanded a compensation of £3 and refused all pleas for leniency. To guarantee the payment, the owner of the goat bribed Basorun Ogunmola fifteen shillings for a judgment in his favour. To help the defendant (that is, the owner of the corn farm), Ogunmola gave £3 to assist in payment to the plaintiff. Under the local court proceedings, the defendant was summoned immediately and was referred to as stupid, because he could not forward a counter-accusation against the plaintiff for the corn eaten by the goat. The corn eaten, quantified as 40 ears of corn, was multiplied by £3, bringing the total cost to £120. The defendant followed Ogunmola's suggestion and demanded in return money for the corn eaten, based on Ogunmola's advice. The judgment went thus:

> Listen all of you and learn a lesson from this case. As long as I live, and as long as I sit in

judgment over cases, I will always be just and fair to all. Three days ago, the owner of the goat came to offer me a bribe of fifteen shillings so that I may give judgment in his favour. Here is his money. I do not need it. Bribery is not good, it is worse than poison for it destroys in the end. Listen, everyone of you; if anyone of you attempts to bribe me again, I shall punish him severely.[11]

This judgment was meant to promote peace among settlers in Ibadan. Power could be aspired to and achieved, but the judgment preached against exploitation among the citizenry.

However, in the quest to entrench his political status, he displayed dictatorial tendencies and being the head of the Oyomesi, *Alaafin* Adelu could not defy Ibikunle.[12] *Alaafin* Adelu then installed two Bashoruns, Ogunmola for Ibadan and Bashorun Gbenla for Oyo. The latter held the insignia of the office, which the former insisted must be given to him. Alaafin Adelu had to consent because of the power of the Basorun as the head of the Oyomesi. Other autocratic acts of Ogunmola manifested in how he treated the *Aseyin* of Iseyin. Being a punishment for supporting Kurunmi in the Ijaiye war, the Aseyin was mandated to visit

---

11 K. Morgan, *Akinyele's Outline History of Ibadan, Part II*, p.90.

12 Falola, p.146.

Ogunmola and was thus compelled to run backwards and forwards on the street, three times with earth on his head and prostrating each time. Though embarrassed, this act made the Aseyin compose a song for Ogunmola.[13]

Power conflicts revolved around the Baale and Balogun in Ibadan. An analysis of the roles of the Balogun revealed that they ignored the Baale by taking unilateral decisions.

None of the Baloguns, despite the extent of their power, could behave in an autocratic manner without without being questioned. The activities of the Baloguns were checked because the pressure groups, such as long distance traders, and other settlers had attempted to sue for peace in the 1870s, to prevent the warriors from invading their emigrant towns. On the other hand, the fact that migrant settlers were in Ibadan to make a profit influenced the Balogun institution to wage wars against the Egba and Ijebu so that trade routes could be freely accessed. In 1863 and 1877, Ibadan traders called for war against Egba and Ijebu due to the blockade of trade routes to the coast.

Aare Latoosa was interested in the Egba-Ijebu trade routes and he used his wealth to seek power by maintaining the loyalty of other chiefs. To entrench his power status, Aare Latoosa used his wealth to win the favour of junior military officers in the Seriki line. The

---

13 Ibid.

senior chiefs in the Balogun line were paid to lobby against each other. He had been trained in Ogunmola's army and his participation in the Ijaiye war created a landmark achievement, through the conflicts he had with *Iyalode* Efunsetan and against the Serikis.

The problem in Ibadan in the 1860s and 1870s was the fact that each individual, military or not, perceived the potential for acquiring wealth in the Ibadan economy. This reduced the revenue base of the leaders, thus Aare Latoosa had to engage a familial strategy by empowering his son— Sanusi to build a strong private army. He even realized that Seriki Iyapo's (Ogunmola's son) loyalty was a deceit. He only pretended to be in support of Latoosa to gradually acquire wealth. Based on this aggression, Latoosa ensured that his opponents were eliminated and destroyed. Having discovered that loss was imminent in the Kiriji war, Latoosa and his son diplomatically retired to Ibadan and continued to display autocratic tendencies within Ibadan and with Egba and Ijebu to facilitate coastal trade in the 1890s. Shortly before 1893, Aare Latoosa's reign in Ibadan had become cruel and he was accused of all sorts of crimes; as a result he was given the option of suicide to save his family from extinction in Ibadan society. Latoosa's death paved the way for flexibility and compromise in the traditional political system as Balogun Akintola emerged as the successor. Balogun Akintola refused to become the baale based on the assumption that the British stay in Ibadan was temporary. His aversion to the town council was based on the fact that he wanted to prove his mettle in wars which the British residents had suppressed.

Balogun institution and Anglo-Ibadan relations

As at 1862, Ibadan's attitude to trade and the willingness to expand coastal trade was noticed by the British in Lagos. Hence, attempts were made to establish friendly relations with Ibadan. To this end, the missionaries were used to establish friendship ties.[14] However, the traditional chiefs were opposed to the friendship and two opposing groups emerged--the pro-British and anti-British. During the reign of Balogun Ibikunle in the early 1860s, there was an aggressive conquest policy, the institutions of *Ajele* and *Babakekere* were utilised to ensure that all the conquered Yoruba towns paid tribute to Ibadan. Subsequently, he made a concession towards the British, which implied that war would no longer be a means to conflict resolution.

However, the anti-war stance of Balogun Ibikunle generated hostility towards him in Ibadan and also towards other anti-war groups that emerged in the late nineteenth century. Of course, the state apparatus of the Babakekere, Babaogun and Ajele was already a source of livelihood for young men in the society, hence change was resisted.

---

14 T. Falola, "Church, Politics and Society in Ibadan in the Nineteenth Century," *Journal of Religious History* 1(1985), 295-305.

Balogun Ajayi Ogboriefon in a chat with the missionaries in the 1870s emphasised that the Balogun institution was meant to fight wars "If we must give up war, why am I made a Balogun and why were chiefs created".[15] The wars had brought revenue to the Ibadan state and it was divided between the Balogun and the baale. Slaves were an integral part of the economic system as they were needed to work on the farms and for sale to Europeans. During the reign of the baloguns in Ibadan, that is from the 1830s to 1890s, slave raiding was a source of accumulation of wealth and to that extent, Governor Campbell of Lagos estimated that about 10,000 slaves were captured by Ibadan in the 1850s.[16]

Initially, Basorun Ogunmola was anti-British, but it was later realized that some aspects of British civilization were useful for Ibadan, especially their military technology. In the bid to open up access to Lagos, Ibadan had to forge an alliance with the British to fight Egba and Ijebu. The fact that the Baloguns later realized the significance of British friendship marked the beginning of an alliance against Abeokuta.[17] As at 1863, Governor Freeman suggested that Ibadan's support through the Baloguns was necessary for four reasons: to strengthen commercial activities in Lagos; to

---

15 Johnson, p .321.

16 T. Falola, p. 208.

17 Ibid, p. 269.

annexe and put Abeokuta under British control; to control the Ijebu and ultimately to seek an alliance to reduce unfavourable commercial hegemony of Egba-Ijebu.[18]

Through the office of the Balogun, alliances were formed with the British and the attack on the Egba at Ikorodu in 1865 was welcomed in Ibadan because it opened access to trade routes.[19] At the forefront of the attack was Governor Glover and for his actions, he was appreciated by Ibadan war chiefs. In appreciation, he was nicknamed *Afari Ogun* (a person with strong military skills) and gifts were sent to him.[20]

Subsequently, Basorun Ogunmola realized that subtle diplomatic relations with Egba and Ijebu had better opportunities to access trade routes. As it was during Balogun Ibikunle's reign, Ogunmola used conciliation instead of war from 1860-1862.[21] The fact that Lagos changed its opposing stand on Egba-Ijebu had implications for Ibadan. Hence, Ibadan projected its interest by settling conflicts with Egba-Ijebu. However, within Ibadan, Basorun Ogunmola's stance was met with stiff opposition, because, the younger warriors believed in war expeditions as the only solution to

---

[18] Colonial Office CO/147/3, Freeman to Newcastle, December 10, 1863

[19] S. Johnson, p. 360.

[20] Colonial Office CO/147/8, Glover to Cardwell, May 8, 1865.

[21] Falola, p. 271.

Egba-Ijebu blockade of trade routes. In the end, the conciliation strategy worked out as trade routes were reopened in 1867.

After Basorun Ogunmola's reign, other Baloguns were either pro or anti war. The anti-war Baloguns were unlucky to live long. Balogun Orowusi attempted to use diplomacy in 1870 but his successor – Aare Latoosa in 1871 rejected diplomacy and adopted the traditional war system to pursue an expansionist foreign policy. This prolonged the Kiriji war because Latoosa was aggressive in his campaign to increase his wealth and revenue base in Ibadan. In a conversation between Latoosa and Reverend Olubi (an influential indigenous Anglican missionary in Ibadan), the former was of the view that there should be only one dominant force in Yorubaland. Latoosa illustrated that:

> If two calabashes (that is Ibadan and the Egba/Ijebu) appear strong, you cannot be the better judge until you strike one against the other, then you will distinguish better which is stronger and which is not.[22]

The increasing aggression from Ibadan's expansionist policies was considered a threat to British commerce in Yorubaland. This was because of the fear that Ibadan hindered free flow of trade by preventing other states from accessing Lagos. Thus, Governor Carter

---

22 C.M.S CA 2/075, Olubi, Journal Extracts for December, 1877.

intervened in 1893 to negotiate a treaty for free trade movement and the establishment of a military force to promote peace.[23] Being a military state, Carter's proposal to Ibadan was perceived as an affront because a resident was placed in Ibadan and this eventually undermined their autonomy which the office of the Balogun had sustained since the 1830s. British intervention in the Kiriji War was quite diplomatic, the independence agitation of the Ekiti Parapo was absolutely granted, and other Oyo speaking areas were also granted relative autonomy.

Obviously, the chiefs in Ibadan barely understood the implication of the 1893 treaty; therefore, they were eager to continue their war expeditions. The Balogun and the junior rank-seriki were prepared for war. However, the British resident, Captain Robert Bower, asserted that colonialism was not meant to support wars. By this, all chieftaincy institutions opted for trade as source of wealth. Invariably, access to wealth and power became more rigorous and complex.

The traditional military tendencies were suppressed as the Baloguns were disciplined, repri-manded or jailed because the colonial administration had absolute power. For instance, in 1900, Basorun Fajimi was fined for executing two criminals, as he was supposed to have

---

23 Falola, p. 278.

asked for permission before such an execution.[24] The post-1893 reality changed the perception of the Baloguns on sources of livelihood and their engagement in money-making ventures. Hence, many war chiefs in the offices of the Balogun diversified their business interests to trade. Farming and non-farming occupations were taken as an alternative. They focused instead on the farmsteads (*oko egan*) acquired in wartime and the production of foodstuff and cash crops on a large scale.

The status of the Balogun institution in Ibadan Town Council 1897-1917

Five factors changed the status of the Balogun institution in the twentieth century. They were: the end of wars to prove their military prowess and acquire wealth; the influence of the colonial officers; the acquisition of wealth through colonial commerce; the expanding and domineering influence of strangers and the presence of the educated elite.

It was very difficult for the Balogun from a military household to become the Baale in Ibadan because there were no avenues to fight wars and the British government was not ready to encourage violence. In

---

24 C.H. Elgee, *The Evolution of Ibadan,* (Lagos: Government Printer, 1914), p.11.

this regard, Balogun Kongi relentlessly adopted diplomatic means and this materialized in 1914.[25]

While the war chiefs diversified into farming and trade, the colonial administration realized that the process of managing finances of administration required the cooperation and collaboration of the indigenous chiefs. To this end, there were moves to establish a town council in Ibadan. Balogun Akintola resisted the idea of a town council based on the view that the town which comprised brave military men should not be subjected to foreign control. An anti-town council move was made clear to the resident, to the extent that Balogun Akintola and other chiefs boycotted the meeting organized by Resident Fuller.[26] Diplomacy by division and blackmail was used by the resident to gain support of some chiefs while the uncooperating ones were humiliated. Baale Fajimi's cooperation was retained by threatening him with deposition, while Balogun Akintola was popularly downgraded.

The British administration used Baale Fajimi to ensure the inauguration of Ibadan Town Council. Gradually, the British idea of a town council evolved as the indigenous chiefs reconciled and partook in considering the decisions at the meetings. At this point,

---

25 T. Falola, (2009) *From Basorun Oluyole to Hon. Adegoke Adelabu: Ibadan Warrior Traditions and the Anatomy of Success*. Ibadan Foundation Public Lectures, p. 52.

26 Falola, p. 367.

the chiefs in the Balogun and Baale lines were included and recognized at meetings, while the Iyalode and Seriki were ignored.

The recognition of the Balogun line implied that some legacies of its pre-colonial stance were brought into twentieth century modern issues. The council allowed the chiefs to exercise some power. In fact were it not for the town council, the Balogun institution would have become moribund. Therefore, the compromise on the part of the indigenous chiefs actually favoured the existence of the Balogun institution in Ibadan, though with new perspectives.

It was obvious that the chiefs in the Baale line were readily open to British rule, while those in the Balogun line largely resisted. The colonial admin-istration mandated the chiefs not to hold secret meetings, except for those who were members of the town council.

Balogun Ola, however, was not ready to accept this; thus, spies were sent to monitor his activities. Ola used the Oke'badan festival to incite the masses against the colonial administration; Ola also held private meetings at his residence to criticize Grier.[27] As Ola was struggling in the tussle to become the baale, the British perceived him as a threat and they ensured that the traditional politics worked against his ambitions.

The chiefs resented the Alaafin's control over Ibadan. In fact, non-compliance led to the deposition of

---

27 Falola, p. 561

Baale Irefin in 1914.[28] Despite this, Ola continued to resist Oyo's control because Ibadan had had a legacy of independence before being subjected to Oyo. The colonial administrators were threatened by Ola's position because he mobilized the chiefs to stop cooperation and support for the British army during the First World War.[29] For this, he was dealt with and on 18 June, 1917, the resident sent soldiers to surround his house. Further, the chiefs were warned not to visit his house. Anyone who did would be treated as a collaborator. In addition, he was to be removed as a member of the council of chiefs, and he was disqualified from promotion to the office of the Balogun "under any circumstances."[30]

---

28 Akinyele, p. 179.

29 Falola, p. 56.

30 NAI, Correspondence Book, Grier to Bale, 19, June 1917.

5

The Balogun Institution in Epe
Philip Oloruntola

Introduction

Epe is a riverine town on the eastern shores of Lagos, in an area characterized by vast lagoons, creeks and fishing settlements.[1] Oral tradition with respect to the origins of the town revolve around two legendary founders: *Huraka* and *Alara*—the former, a hunter, and the latter, an Ile-Ife prince. Legend has it that the two men and their followers migrated at different times to the town before the nineteenth century. According to the Huraka tradition, a hunter (Huraka), who migrated from Ile-Ife, is recognized as the founder of the town. Oral tradition states that Huraka first arrived in Poka, a small town, a few kilometres northwards, before he finally settled in Epe, on the prompting of the *Ifa* oracle.

The other account favours Alara, an Ife prince, who came with his royal entourage from Ile-Ife to settle in the town. An oral tradition has it that Alara later vacated the town—reasons were not given—leaving behind some of his sons who have continued his lineage. The original

---

1 R.K. Udo, *Geographical Region of Nigeria.* (Heinemann. London and University of Carlifonia Press, 1970), p. 42.

group was also joined by other pioneers such as Lugbasa, Agbaja, Ofuten, Ramepe, Ogunmude and a prince known as Sagbafara from Ijebu-Ode, among other progenitors of the indigenous Ijebu people who presently form the nucleus of the town. [2]

From the middle of the nineteenth century, a group of immigrants from the Awori Kingdom of Lagos came to live among the Ijebu in Epe. The non-indigenous population was later enlarged by other immigrant groups, including the Ilaje of Mahin and the Ijaw, who were attracted to the town due to its strategic physical features, especially its vast shorelines, which held prospects for their livelihoods as fishermen, boat

---

[2] There are contrasting claims about the origins of Epe. While it may be difficult to ascertain which of the versions is more authentic, the assumption that Epe, like most other Lagoon communities around it, evolved as a meeting place for hunters, fishermen and adventurers from Ile-Ife, Ijebu-Ode and other places in Yorubaland long before the 19th century, seems a plausible historical conjecture. For a full account of the traditions of origin of Epe, See, G.O. Oguntomisin, *The Transformation of a Nigerian Lagoon Town of Epe: 1852-1942*, (Ibadan: John Archers Publishers,1999); T.O. Avoseh, *A Short History of Epe*, The Parochial Committee, Saint Michael's Anglican Church Epe, (Lagos: C.M.S, 1960); B. Oluyomi Philips,'Origin, Growth and Development of Epe from earliest times to 1966' (B.A Project, University of Ibadan, 1989); A. Adefuye, Lagoon Communities of Epe Division: Melting Pot of Cultures, History Department Seminar, No 2, 1978/79, University of Lagos.

makers, lumbermen and traders in aquatic and non-aquatic products.³

As the population of the town grew more diverse and its social structures more complex, existing social structures could no longer sustain its new multicultural blend. As a result, new institutions emerged, while some of the older ones were subjected to various degrees of modification, ostensibly, to suit emerging realities.⁴ The sweeping changes were accelerated by colonial rule, but became aggravated as a result of intra-ethnic wrangling among the indigenous Ijebu hosts, and inter-ethnic politics and cut throat rivalries between them and the Awori immigrants. The objective of this chapter is to examine how traditional institutions in Epe have fared under these circumstances over the years. The focus is on the fortunes (or misfortunes) of the *Balogun* institution from pre-colonial to colonial regimes.

The traditional system of government in Epe

The traditional system of government in Epe is strictly hierarchical. At the top of the pyramid is a central council or the Oloja-in-Council, comprised of titled

---

3 A major attraction of immigrants to the littorals of Epe Lagoon was the prospect it holds as means of livelihood. See Adefuye, op. cit.

4 Ref: N.A.I, RG/C5: Report on the Administrative Re-organisation of the Epe District Native Treasury Area of the Colony, by H. Child and E. Gibbons, 1939, p.21 – 23.

chiefs (*oloye ilu*) and presided over by the Oloja (the traditional ruler of Epe). The Oloja-in-Council constitutes the executive arm of government. Key members of the Oloja in Council include: *Olisa, Agbon, Aro, Kakanfo, Obafuwaji, Lapekun, Jagun Oba, Lootu* and the Balogun. The Olisa is accorded the privilege of being the second in command in the realm. Judicial power is exercised by the *Osugbo*, a conclave of traditional elites, who are reputed for their integrity, uprightness and vast knowledge of the culture and customs of the people. They are consulted by the Oloja-in-Council on almost all matters affecting the town. The Oloja confers with key officers of the Osugbo such as the *Oluwo* (head of the Osugbo chiefs), *Akonoran* and *Apena*, for sound advice. Their input into major decisions usually put a stamp of credibility on the activities of the Oloja-in-Council. In theory, the Osugbo acts as a check to the power of the Oloja.

From inception, Epe was comprised of two main Ijebu quarters, namely, *Apakeji* and *Aleke*. The former is located on the left flank of the town, while the latter occupies the right flank. The location of the quarters on either sides of the town was based, perhaps, on where the initial immigrants settled upon arrival. The Apakeji quarter is sub-divided into *Etita, Iberekodo, Ebode* and *Bado Oba*, while the Aleke quarter comprises *Itungbeyin, Ajagonabe, Eyindi,* and *Etitun*.[5] Each of the quarters was

---

5 NAI, F.O/Dispatch No: E.32/1923/27. District Office in Epe to the Administrator of the Colony of Lagos, 19 Oct, 1932.

further divided into wards or sub-quarters known as *itun,* under the headship of an *Olori Itun* (ward head). The Olori Itun represented their respective wards in the central council of the town. They were also responsible for the settlement of minor disputes and the maintenance of law and order in their respective domains.

Traditional titles are structured to ensure fair representation of every quarter and sub-quarter in the central council. For instance, all the titles in the Oloja-in-Council, except the Balogun, are permanently ceded to specific quarters. The office of the Olisa is ceded to Ajagonabe, the Agbon to Ebode, the Aro to Eyindi, the Kakanfo to Iberikodo, the Obafuwaji to Etita, the Lapekun to Itungbeyin, the Jagun Oba to Baado Oba, and the Lootu to Etitun. This way, power does not tilt in favour of any quarter at the expense of another.

The governance of each of the adjoining villages to the southeast and southwest of the main township across the lagoon, where the Epe people spend most of the rainy season in occupations such as fishing, boat making, and farming, was placed under a *baale*—an uncrowned traditional chief. The baale was responsible for the maintenance of law and order in the smaller settlements on behalf of the Oloja. He was, therefore, accountable to the Oloja for all his actions. And because his allegiance was to the Oloja, he paid quarterly and yearly tributes to him on behalf of the village. An erring baale could be punished or even deposed for serious offences, especially for insubordination to the authorities of the Oloja and the Osugbo.

Even though Epe exists as an independent town with its own autonomous institutions, the people recognise the primacy of the *Awujale* in Ijebu-Ode as the overall paramount ruler of Ijebuland. In pre-colonial times, the Awujale treated Epe as his vassal and exerted his authority in the town through the Osugbo and the Agunrin (royal military emissaries). The latter were periodically dispatched to all subordinate towns of Ijebu-Ode to collect tributes and maintain law and order as well as quell uprisings whenever the authority of the Awujale was rebelled against.

Balogun in traditional government in Epe

The office of the Balogun is an important component of the traditional authorities in Epe. The office consists of two titles, namely the Balogun (war captain and chief military officer of the town) and *Otun Balogun* (commander of the right wing of the army). The Otun Balogun usually succeeds the Balogun upon the death of the latter.

Balogun title holders wield enormous political power as Oloye Ilu (town chiefs) and key members of the Oloja-in-Council as military aristocrats. In fact, within the traditional political hierarchy, the office of the Balogun is the only title that is not permanently ceded to any of the eight sub-quarters in the town. Holders of the office of the Balogun are usually selected from the two main quarters in the town namely, Apakeji and Aleke on a rotational basis, but usually not without keen contests among the sub-quarters. It appears that there is an unwritten consensus that whenever the Balogun is chosen from one quarter, the Otun Balogun (assistant to the Balogun) must come from the other.

The responsibility for the initial nomination of candidates for the office of the Balogun is an exclusive prerogative of the quarters, through a selection process that is characterized by a series of intra-quarter consultation. At the nomination stage, leaders of thought and representatives of each of the sub-quarters, led by their respective Olori Itun, usually meet to screen credible candidates from the quarter. Thereafter, nominees that are considered most worthy by consensus are presented to the Oloja and members of his council for ratification. The process reaches a climax with the presentation of the chosen candidate to the general community. The installation ceremony usually takes place amidst fanfare from all the quarters in the town.

The dynamics of the process of selecting the Balogun are rooted in leadership by ascription. It is worthy of note that the distribution of traditional titles and privileges in Epe, that is, who gets what within the traditional context of Epe—and this includes any aspirant to the title of the Balogun—must be an indigene by birth and tradition. Besides being an indigene by birth and culture, the aspirant must be an individual with a good sense of judgment and acceptable social standing within the community. The Balogun nominee must be a bridge builder and an embodiment of the common interests and aspirations of all cultural constituents of the town. He must be a hardworking and enterprising individual who engages in a legitimate livelihood like all other citizens. Such a person must also be found worthy in character and acceptance to the people.[6] Also, because of the sensitive nature of his traditional responsibility as a defender of his people, the holder of the Balogun title was expected to be warlike. This was because the responsibility for both internal and external security of the town was vested in him.

The Balogun in Epe prior to the 19th century

In the pre-colonial period, the Balogun was responsible for controlling the activities pirates on the territorial waters of the town. His influence thus extended outside the main town into the adjoining towns and the fishing villages (*Eyin Osa*) that criss-cross the shores of the lagoons that divide the main town and the narrow strips of land that are adjacent to the Atlantic Ocean (*etikun*), where Epe fishermen and traders spent several days away from their homes.[7] Whenever there were trade

---

6 An interview with Chief Lanre Razak, current Balogun of Ijebu community in Epe, on May 17, 2015 in Lagos.

7 Prominent among such villages were Orimedu, Magbon, Abomiti, Emina, Ilagbo, to mention a few. See B. P. Oluyomi, 'Origin , Growth and Development of Epe from Earliest Times to 1966', op.cit 13

disputes between Epe traders and fishermen and any of their counterparts in neighbouring towns, the Balogun ensures that the disputes did not result into inter-town rivalries. In the event of a war, his obligation was to defend the interests of Epe town and the people. As a result, he was expected to be patriotic, warlike and sometimes bellicose.

Very little evidence is available on the exploits of the holders of the Balogun title prior to the 19th century. However, a popular legend about the career of Balogun Agoro, perhaps one of two most popular Balogun figures in the period, depicts him as an astute defender of the town and its people, who feared no threat to his life in protecting the overall welfare of his people.

For instance, there was once a misunderstanding between Epe and the Makun Omi fishermen and traders in 1850. The case involved a trade dispute between the two over the right of commerce on their respective territorial waters. The Makun people had placed an embargo on Epe traders and fishermen, forbidding them from trading on Makun rivers. However, Balogun Agoro and Sigbekun, two Epe traders, violated the sanction and were murdered by Makun pirates. The murder compelled Epe to impose a retaliatory trade embargo on Makun traders. After being hard-pressed by the prolonged trade embargo, Makun traders implored the then Awujale of Ijebu land, *Oba* Anikilaya, to intervene. The Oba intervened as requested and summoned delegates from both sides to a meeting with his chiefs and the *Agunrin* (royal guards) at Oju Alaro in Epe with a view to broker peace and lift the embargo.

The conciliatory approach of the Awujale displeased Balogun Omuni, a leader of the representa-tives of Epe at the peace meeting. In defiance of the authorities of the Awujale, at whose behest the peace talk had been convened, Balogun Omuni shot at and killed Nobintan, a war chief and leader of the Makun Omi delegates. A legend among the Ijebu people in Epe has it that Nobintan's head was hung on a stake and paraded round the town with much fanfare.

That Balogun Omuni could defy the Awujale says so much about his personality as a principled person, even though he was fully aware that the consequences of his actions could mean that the Awujale might disrupt the whole town. In the Yoruba traditional diplomatic context, such a blatant disregard for the orders of a paramount Oba, especially a powerful ruler with the clout of the Awujale of Ijebuland, was a sacrilegious act that usually attracted capital sentences[8]

As expected, the belligerence of Balogun Omuni elicited a stern reaction from Awujale Anikilaya. The Oba dispatched his Agunrin to Epe to punish the people. In a bid to escape the wrath of the Awujale, the people fled the town and sought refuge in their fishing

---

8 G.O. Oguntomisin, *The Process of Peacekeeping and Peacemaking in Pre-colonial Nigeria, Conflict Resolutions in Pre-Colonial Yoruba land*, (Ibadan: John Archers Publishers Limited, 2004).

and farm villages across the lagoon, deserting their homes, until the anger of the Awujale had subsided.

An account by an Ijebu local historian affirmed that the traditional ruler of Epe then, *Oloja* Olumade, fled to a place called oko oloja (Oloja's farm), somewhere beyond the lagoon[9] The temporary desertion of the town by the people, as will be shown below, marked a turning point in the fortunes of traditional institutions and, indeed, the Balogun institution in Epe.

The changing fortunes of the Balogun institution in Epe, 1851- 1861

The period between 1851 and 1862 was a turning point in the fortunes of traditional institutions in Epe. The occupation of Lagos by the British in 1851 triggered social and political ripples whose impact went far beyond the immediate confines of the town. British anti-slavery campaigns on the Bight of Benin deposed Kosoko, one of the princes of the Kingdom who had seized the throne from Akitoye, his uncle. The British meddled in the bitter succession disputes among members of the royal family of Lagos and deposed Kosoko for his alleged involvement in slave trade and re-installed Akitoye, his pro-British uncle, in his place. The annexation of Lagos and the forceful ouster of Kosoko triggered a massive exodus of pro-Kosoko groups from the town. Kosoko and his loyalists

---

9 Ibid, p. 7, 14, 19.

numbering about 1,500 fled Lagos and journeyed along the eastern estuaries of Lagos until they arrived in Epe in the early days of 1852 in fleets of large canoes with small iron guns.[10]

Kosoko takes refuge in Epe

The advent of Kosoko and his entourage in Epe coincided with the period when the indigenous Ijebu inhabitants had deserted the town. However, the Kosoko-led immigrant Awori did not encroach upon the homes of the fleeing indigenes of Epe. Rather, Kosoko sent a deputation to Awujale Anikilaya, the reigning Awujale in Ijebu-Ode, who was his distant relation, to seek permission to settle. For strategic reasons, they were allowed to settle in small quarters below the hills that overlook the lagoon and along the coastline together with other immigrant groups, where they set up a distinct administrative structure. Kosoko appointed chiefs among his loyal lieutenants to oversee the quarters, while he presided over serious administra-tive

---

10 For general background information on Awori migrations in the 19th century and British intervention in the domestic affairs of their kingdom in Lagos, see I.H. Tijani, "The Lagos Awori Frontiers: 19th Century History of Migrations and Transformations of an African Society", *Ife Journal of History*, 4 (2) March 2007: 1-22; R. Smith, "To the Palaver Island, War and Diplomacy on the Lagos Lagoon in 1852-1854", *J.H.S.N*, 1, 1969: 6; R. Smith, "The Lagos Consulate 1851-1861: An Outline", J.A.H. 15 (3) 1974.

and judicial matters, without interference from their Ijebu host.[11]

Kosoko was said to be content with being a chief in a central administrative council of the entire town, which was then presided over by the *Oloja* of Epe. In fact, in a letter to the governor, John Glover, in 1863, Kosoko introduced himself thus: 'I Kosoko ex-chief of Epe and formerly king of Lagos...'.[12]

However, Kosoko extended his economic influence to the outlying fishing and coastal villages and settlements southeast of Epe, especially Oriba, Igbogun, Orimedu, Leke, Olomowewe and Ibeju through trade relations, which he described as his 'ports of trade by right of [his] former ownership' as ex-king of Lagos.[13]

---

11 The areas occupied by Kosoko's followers included *Oke Oba* (the King's Hill), *Popo Oba* (King's Street), where Kosoko settled with his immediate attendants; *Oke Balogun* (Balogun's Hills) *Oke Iposu* (Iposu's Hill), *Isale Agoro* (Agoro's Plain), *Baado Oke* (Upper Baado), *Baado Isale* (Lower Baado), where war chiefs and their soldiers and retainers settled. It would appear that the settlement of the Kosoko followers on the coastal flank, imposed upon them the burden of being a buffer between the Lagoon and the rest of the town in the event of an external attack from the coast.

12 See N.A.I C.S.O 5/9 Kosoko's Declaration, 7 February, 1863. This runs contrary to information that many of the traditional institutions of the Ijebu people, including the office of the *Oloja*, (the traditional ruler of Epe in pre-Kosoko era) had been emasculated in the period they deserted the town.

13 So strong was his influence in these areas that his monopoly control of slave trading activities and of the export trade in palm oil and salt on the Lagos and Orimedu rivers rivaled the British in Lagos.

After a while, some of Kosoko's senior military chiefs, such as Akinpelu Iposu and Ajeniya, Agoro and Oshodi Tapa (the fourth, a Nupe-born slave turned chief) naturally assumed responsibility for the defence of the town from the coastal axis. For instance, Kosoko's senior military chiefs were the sole peace negotiators in a series of diplomatic negotiations that took place on the Lagoon between the British administration in Lagos and Epe in the 1850s and 1860s.[14] In the pre-Kosoko era, these roles had been the exclusive preserves of the Ijebu Balogun.

After a sojourn that lasted about ten years, Kosoko returned to Lagos in September 1862. Kosoko's sojourn to Epe can dated to 1854 after a series of diplomatic negotiations with the British colonial government in Lagos. Sequel to the annexation of Lagos in 1861 by the British, it became imperative for the latter to acquire Epe for its strategic economic position, but not without the co-operation of Kosoko. The British feared that the French might outmanoeuvre Britain and acquire a right of Protectorate over the town. Thus, Freeman, the governor of the new Lagos Colony, made fresh overtures to Kosoko to relinquish his claims over his trading ports, especially Palma (Orimedu) and Leke

---

14 The trio of Akinpelu Iposu, Ajeniya and Oshodi Tapa played commendable roles as Kosoko's military chiefs. For details on the career of Akinpelu Iposu, see: I.H. Tijani, "The Career of Akinpelu Iposu in Lagos and Epe *Circa* 1790-1875" in. J.F Kolapo, and K. Akurang-Parry, (eds.), *African Agency and European Colonialism: Latitude of Negotiation and Containment*, (Lanhan-Maryland: University Press of America, 2007), p. 17-24.

(Lekki), which then rivalled Lagos in terms of volume of trade and revenue. In return, he was offered a pardon, re-settlement as *Baale* in Ereko, a section in Lagos, annual stipend and a peaceful reconciliation with Dosunmu, the King of Lagos, among other perquisites. An ageing Kosoko did not hesitate to accept the offers and succumbed because, among other reasons, he did not want to die in exile.[15]

But not all his chiefs and warlords returned with him. With the exception of Oshodi Tapa, who was probably the most intimate of his lieutenants, other senior military chiefs, namely Akinpelu Iposu, Iyanda Oloko, Ajeniya, Agoro, Agbaje and another chief simply described as Balogun, and their family members, soldiers and retainers decided to remain in Epe.[16] The decision of the *Eko –Epe* war-chiefs to remain in the town

---

15 Kosoko could no longer rely on the support of Ibadan chiefs because of their brigandage tendencies if they defeated Ijebu-Ode in the on-going Ijaye War in the interior of Yorubaland, even though they were once his allies. Similarly, he was certain that if the Ijaye-Egba allies on whose side the Awujale fought, were victorious, Ijebu Ode would route him out of Epe for ceding their territories to the British. See excerpts from the following colonial papers: C.O.147/1 Freeman to Newscastle, 1 July, 1862 and C.M.S CA2/021, Annual Letters of James Berber, 31 December, 1857 cited in G.O. Oguntomisin, *The Transformation of a Nigerian Lagoon Town, Epe,* Chapter 5, footnotes 52-55, p. 49.

16 Item 40, Declaration signed by Chief Obafemi Awolowo, plaintiffs' solicitors in suit No ID/26/74 holden at Ikeja between Oba David Ajayi Fesogbade II and others (plaintiffs) and M.D. Kasim and others (defendants) dated 14th March, 1974.

was probably because of the economic privileges that they had been accustomed to as Kosoko's eyes and ears in outlying villages under Epe, which they would have to forfeit if they left. For instance, Balogun Akinpelu Iposu was not pleased with the way Kosoko easily yielded his territorial claims and trading privileges, especially Palma (Orimedu) and Leke (Lekki), to the British, with whom he engaged in diplomatic tussles.[17] The remaining Awori immigrants in Epe were latter dubbed *Eko-Epe* (Lagosians in Epe). Subsequently, the administration of the Eko-Epe section of the town passed on to them.

---

17. His decision to uphold the *status quo ante* and not recognize the British dragged Epe into confrontations with the British colonial administration in Lagos, which decided to use force against him after many entreaties. See: I.H. Tijani, "The Career of Akinpelu Iposu in Lagos and Epe (circa) 1790-1875" in F. Kolapo & K. Akurang-Parry, editors, *African Agency and European Colonialism: Latitude of Negotiations and Containment* (Lanham-Maryland: University Press of America, 2007), 17-24.

Eko-Epe chiefs and the emergence of Balogun title holders

It must be emphasized that the Balogun institution was as popular among the *Ijebu-Epe* as it was among their Eko-Epe counterparts, and that the two are independent of each other. Indeed, the Eko-Epe has a rich and unique Balogun institution that is different from that of the Ijebu-Epe, both in structure and culture. While the Balogun chieftaincy orders among the Ijebu-Epe have a semblance of the Ijebu-Ode structure, the Eko-Epe's seems to take after and reflects adaptations of the Ibadan structure.[18] Unlike the Ijebu-Epe Balogun structure with just two offices, namely the Balogun and the Otun Balogun, the Eko-Epe has multiple Balogun titles. In addition to the Balogun and Otun Balogun, they have additional titles including the *Seriki* and *Sarumi*.

The origin of the Balogun institution among the Eko-Epe dates back to the second half of the 19th century after the exit of Kosoko from Epe. The first set of Eko-Epe chiefs to whom the title of Balogun were arrogated were some of his senior military chiefs, while in Epe, namely Chief Akinpelu Iposu, Chief Iyanda Oloko and Chief Ajeniya, supposedly because they were war chiefs with a sizeable number of soldiers under their command with which they had been able to resist British

---

18 The Ibadan Balogun chieftaincy has a long line of chiefs which is almost over 24 titles altogether. See Ibadan Week Festival Programme, 2012, p.68.

occupation of Epe twice in the 1850s.[19] From 1862, each of them—except Chief Ajeniya—took turns to assume the leadership of the Eko-Epe commu-nity for an unbroken period of thirty five years: Chief Akinpelu Iposu (1862-1865), Chief Iyanda Oloko (1865-1875), and Chief Agbaje (1865- 1866). Meanwhile, the Ijebu-Epe maintained an autonomous traditional council comprised wholly of Ijebu chiefs.

Chief Akinpelu Iposu, assumed headship shortly after Kosoko had returned to Lagos. But his reign was nominal until 1863, when the British finally acknowledged him. Prior to 1863, he displayed a nationalistic opposition against a complete British annexation of Epe. He would not recognize Kosoko's treaty which ceded Orimedu (Palma) and Leke (Lekki) to the British, but continued to lay claims to the territories for their economic and strategic advantages. His refusal to shift ground pitted him against the British. As a result, Epe suffered from two major military attacks from British-led expeditionary forces, but they were repulsed. When his uncompromising posture was going to prove disastrous for the town, he agreed to cease hostility with Lagos, and subsequently gave up his claims over Orimedu and Leke and, in return, the British recognized his authority.

However, the reign of Chief Akinpelu was not favourable to the Ijebu-Epe, whom he attempted to cow

---

19 Ibid, p.6.

into submission. He attempted to integrate the two communities into a central administration but failed and voluntarily left Epe for Lagos in 1865, and was succeeded by Chief Iyanda Oloko.

The reign of Iyanda threw Epe into prolonged chaotic inter-group relations between Eko-Epe and Ijebu-Epe. As soon as he assumed office, he embarked on administrative restructuring that would have excluded the Ijebu-Epe from the governance of the town. He made new attempts at reconstituting a central council whose membership would be restricted to senior Eko-Epe chiefs. He appointed Eko-Epe representatives to sit in the ward meetings of the Ijebu-Epe, with the intent that his appointees would serve as intermediaries between them (the Ijebu) and the central council that he presided over.

In what seemed like a bid to consolidate his power, he took the title of Baale (uncrowned ruler) and appointed his loyal followers as envoys in some of the outlying villages. As expected, Iyanda's policy elicited sharp reactions from the Ijebu Epe, who interpreted his actions as an attempt to undermine the traditional authority of the Ijebu-Epe.

Thus, as a counterpoise to Iyanda's ambitious moves, the Ijebu-Epe revived the defunct title of the Oloja and appointed Sagbafara as the Oloja in 1866. Under Sagbafara, many of the traditional socio-cultural institutions of the Ijebu-Epe, including the Osugbo, the traditional age-grade system, among others, were consolidated. Indeed, for about one decade, from 1866 until the demise of Iyanda in 1875, the resilience of the co-existence of the Ijebu Epe and the Eko-Epe was put to the test.

Chief Agbaje succeeded Iyanda. He was a man of easy temperament who worked hard to restore the lost love between the Ijebu-Epe and Eko-Epe. His political reforms were geared towards overhauling his predecessor's administrative misgivings. On assuming office, he advocated and attempted reconstituting a central council in which both the Ijebu-Epe and Eko-Epe would have equal representation of seven members each. He enjoyed the cooperation of the reigning Oloja Okuboyejo, a man of peaceful disposition, who had succeeded Oloja Sagbafara as the leader of the Ijebu-Epe.

Chief Agbaje restored diplomatic ties between Epe and Ijebu-Ode. He accomplished this, first, by referring all judicial matters affecting the Ijebu to the Osugbo and the Awujale palace. His period in office coincided with the reign of Awujale Fidipote. Agbaje was positively endeared to him. His reverence for the monarch was in contradistinction to the disposition of Balogun Onafowokan (aka Otutunbunibon), the sitting Balogun of Ijebu-Ode, who had a penchant for violating the authority of the Awujale. Later, when Awujale Fidipote was ousted in 1883 by Onafowokan, who had become too powerful for the Oba Fidipote enjoyed good relations with Agbaje during his years of refuge in Epe, until he died in 1885.[20]

The death of Oloja Okuboyejo in 1866 and, subsequently, of Chief Agbaje, changed power relations in Epe. Two events characterised the period. The period coincided with the British annexation of Ijebu-Ode in 1892 and the subsequent declaration of full British sovereignty over Epe n the same year.[21]

While the Ijebu-Epe community was in a state of disharmony and disfavour with the British, while the Eko-Epe community enjoyed their patronage because the British expeditionary forces had relied on the support of the latter during their military campaign against Ijebu-Ode. The other was a series of administrative re-structuring that followed the declaration of British sovereignty over the town on November, 4, 1892.

In November 1901, the British promulgated a Native Council Ordinance which provided for the establishment of Native Authority in the Colony of

---

20. For details see Chapter Two of this publication on the Balogun in Ijebuland. Also see O. Olubomehin, "A Survey of Inter-Group Relations in Ijebuland in the Nineteenth Century", p.14-15; T. Falola and G. Oguntomisin, *Yoruba Warlords of the Nineteenth Century*, (Trenton: Africa World Press,1979), 38-139; E, Ayandele, *Nigerian Historical* Studies, (London: Frank Cass and Company 1979) .

21 The Ijebu-Epe community condemned the Eko-Epe for providing the tactical and logistic support that aided the invading imperial British force to sack Ijebu-Ode.

Lagos and the Protectorates. Presumably in recognition of the role of the Eko-Epe in Ijebu Ode expedition, the colonial administration recognized Eko-Epe chiefs as the Native Authority for the town, whose council was composed of Eko-Epe chiefs only.

As a result, the Ijebu withdrew from the Epe Native Council and demanded a separate Native Council for their section of the town; a request which the District Commissioner granted in 1905. Thus, two separate Native Councils with dual administration and two self-governing sub-ethnic groups emerged from Epe. Cut throat rivalries for political dominance between the two groups made a great impact greatly on traditional institutions in the town.[22] The Balogun institution was not spared in the process.

The Balogun chieftaincy among the Ijebu-Epe: an era of crises and compromises

As has been observed, traditional institutions in Epe in the last decade of the 19th century up to the turn of the new century were marred by cut-throat rivalries among powerful contenders. The office of the Balogun was particularly embroiled with succession crises that made the headlines of major newspapers of the time. For instance, following the demise of Balogun Jegede

---

22 Ref: N.A.I, RG/C5: Report on the Administrative Re-organisation of the Epe District Native Treasury Area of the Colony, by H.Child and E. Gibbons, 1939, p.21 – 23.

Baworen on 14th June, 1932, it became very difficult for the Ijebu to come up with a consensus candidate to succeed him. Two major contenders for the office emerged, namely Saka Aguda from *Etitun* and Abudu Kadiri Oluwo from *Itungbeyin*.

The majority of Ijebu in Aleke Quarter (*Itungbeyin*, *Ajaganobe*, and *Eyindi* wards) and the Osugbo led by Okunade Oluwo, their spokesperson, including the Baale, wished Kadiri Oluwo to be chosen as the next Balogun. Their consideration of Kadiri Oluwo for the coveted post ran afoul of aspirations of the promoters of Saka Aguda in the *Etitun* sub-quarter, led by Fetuga, an Ijebu councilor in the Epe Town Council. The latter group claimed that it was the turn of their sub-quarter to supply a Balogun, based on the argument that before the appointment of Jegede Baworen, who was a candidate of the Apakeji Quarter, Itungbeyin had earlier supplied Dairo for the post, after which Etitun supplied the Alausa. The insistence of the Osugbo and the Baale on the choice of Kadiri Oluwo must have come as a surprise to the supporters of Saka Aguda who took exception to the nomination of the former as an imposition and a violation of an unwritten understanding over the distribution of traditional offices in the quarter.

As earlier indicated, the distribution of traditional offices among the Ijebu in Epe was between the two main Ijebu quarters in Epe, Apakeji and Aleke. At the level of the sub-quarters, the arrangement further provided for a situation whereby each of the sub-quarters that make up a quarter should take it in turn to fill vacancies in traditional offices that were allocated to the larger quarter they belong to. The argument was that:

> It is the custom of the people to select a Balogun from each quarter [and] in turn he [will] eventually succeed to the Baaleship. In other words, [if] the Baale is from one quarter, the Balogun [must be] from the other.[23]

The argument was contained in a petition Etitun sent to the acting district officer in Epe in 1932 in which they demanded that their nominee to the Balogun vacancy be installed.[24] They seemed to have lost confidence in the Osugbo to give them justice on the matter. The question is: Why did the Osugbo and the Baale, who should have been the custodians and protectors of the customs of the Ijebu people, act contrary to the subsisting rotational agreement between the sub-quarters and insist on Kadiri Oluwo as the suitable candidate for the vacant chieftaincy position?

The first explanation was probably due to the personality and popularity of Kadiri Oluwo. According to a newspaper report, Kadiri Oluwo:

> ... was a prosperous trader and a very influential man in the community. A grand old man,

---

23 NAI, F.O/Dispatch No: E.32/1923/27.The District Office in Epe to the Administrator of the Colony of Lagos, 19 October, 1932.

24 Ibid.

cheerful and kindhearted, he was the offspring of an ancient and respectable family of the early settlers ... A devoted Muslim, it was due to his effort that the Jamat Mosque was in its present fine state.[25]

The preference for him among the majority of Ijebu as a most suitable candidate for the highly revered office of the Balogun must have been informed by the popularity he enjoyed among the people.

Second, it was, perhaps, an attempt to compensate him for his acts of generosity, especially towards the construction of the Ijebu Jamat Mosque, which was much appreciated by Ijebu Muslims, who had for decades carried the burden of building a large Mosque for the Ijebu Muslim jamaah in the town, who needed to justify their commitment as devout Muslims.

The Islamic factor in the inter-group relations in Epe cannot be overemphasized. Some of the tussles between the Eko-Epe and Ijebu-Epe for dominance had strong religious overtones, as to which group was more qualified to earn the credit for the esteemed position that is associated with Epe as a prominent centre of Quranic learning—*Epe o ni Qurani* (Epe the custodian of the Holy Quran). As it were, if by 1862, the first Epe Central Mosque had been built at *Oke Balogun* (Balogun's Hill), in an area occupied by the Eko-Epe community. By 1891 *Baado Sale* (Lower Baado)— another section of the town

---

25 See *Daily Times*, May 3, 1939.

largely populated by descendants of Kosoko and their associates — and Oke Balogun, had become the centers of Islamic education in Epe,[26] then the intervention of Kadiri Oluwo in the building of the Ijebu *Jam'at* Mosque would have been too great a favour to be ignored among the Ijebu.

Third, the Ijebu-Epe needed a man like Kadiri Oluwo with immense social popularity, wide political clout and the financial means to represent them and redress some of the perceived imbalances in membership of, as well as in tax and revenue allocation, and other issues relating to judicial matters in Epe Native Council and, subsequently, in Epe Town Council, which had generated a lot of ill-feelings among the Ijebu-Epe since the Eko-Epe Native Authority was created in 1901.[27] Under the Native Authority Ordinance system which came into force in 1901, traditional chiefs were granted civic jurisdiction over their Native Authority Areas. The first head of the Epe Native

---

26 In 1935, a European visitor to Epe captured the mood of Islam in the town graphically: 'I observed with surprise that about 75% of the inhabitants of the town are Muslims, not by name only but by being keen in their religious observance, and can read and understand very well the word of their leader as written in the Holy Quran'. See NAI, A report of a visit to Ikale Community by E.A Kenyo in Akede Eko, 23/02/1935.

27 In 1901, when the Native Authority system was established in the Colony of Lagos, a Native Authority was created for Epe. Ref: N.A.I, RG/C5: Report on the Administrative Re-organisation of the Epe District Native Treasury Area of the Colony, by H.Child and E. Gibbons, 1939, p.21 – 23.

Council, Baale Buraimoh Edu, exercised this power and appointed only the Eko-Epe chiefs as members. The Baale also nominated one of his chiefs to join him as the sole representatives of Epe in the Lagos Central Native Authority.[28]

By the 1920s, the need of the Ijebu to appoint a Balogun figure who could speak up against and redress their long standing alienation in their own town had become more pressing after the Baale of the Eko-Epe had continued to act as the joint president of the now separate Ijebu-Epe and Eko-Epe Native Councils. He also arrogated the responsibility for overseeing developments in the Ijebu-Epe Native Council, including how they should spend their funds, while the British Administration in Lagos continued to recognize him as the Senior Native Authority with political power over Epe and its outlying territories.[29]

Then, there was the less noble reason of the pedigree of Kadiri Oluwo being the son of Okunade Oluwo, the current *Oluwo* or *Apena* and the leader of the Osugbo cult, who were the main kingmakers in Epe. The Oluwo had enormous influence on chieftaincy appointments among the Ijebu. In traditional gover- nance among the Ijebu-Epe, in the absence of the Oloja, the Oluwo has

---

28 See, G.O. Oguntomisin, "*The Transformation of a Nigerian Lagoon Town of Epe: 1852-1942*", (Ibadan: John Archers Publishers,1999), p.62.

29 Ibid.

been described as 'the most influential Ijebu chief'.[30] It stands to reason, therefore, that, even if the entire members of the Oloja council had differed with the candidacy of Kadiri Oluwo, his father could have invoked his influence as the head of the kingmakers and the most influential member of the Ijebu leadership conclave to impose his son on the town.

In spite of all the above reasons, the acting district officer of the Colony stationed in Epe, to whom the tussle between the two sub-quarters and candidates had been referred for mediation, seemed to have other reasons to approve the nomination of Kadiri Oluwo as the next Balogun of the Ijebu. In a letter to the commissioner of the Colony of Lagos dated 19 October, 1932, he stated his reasons for the approval thus:

> The Osugbo, and I should estimate that three-quarters or more of the Ijebu population in Epe, including the Baale, are in favour of Kadiri Oluwo. Kadiri Oluwo is a wealthy trader and, as far as I can ascertain from my files, has always been an influential man in Epe circles.[31]

As shown by the contents of his letter, the British official had no choice but to approve the nomination of Kadiri

---

30 See N.A.I, RG/C5: Report on the Administrative Re-organisation of the Epe District Native Treasury Area of the Colony, by H.Child and E. Gibbons, 1939, p.32.

31 NAI, F.O/Dispatch No: E.32/1923/27. The District Office in Epe to the Administrator of the Colony of Lagos, 19 October, 1932.

Oluwo because, apart from the fact that those who supported him formed a majority among the Ijebu, his sponsors were power brokers in traditional politics in the community.

Subsequently, in a meeting between the acting commissioner of the Colony, Mr. E.M Falk, and Ijebu-Epe chiefs held on 17th November, 1932 in the Court House at Epe, Abudu Kadiri Oluwo was confirmed as the new Ijebu Balogun and was 'installed publicly'. In addition to his duties within the traditional system, his other 'duties of office', which he was advised to 'keep in mind . . . at all times', were spelt out by the commissioner. They included 'loyalty to the government and the district officer' and ensuring 'harmonious co-operation with the Lagos [Eko-Epe] and Ijebu Baales and Balogun.[32] Whether or not some of the contentious issues raised by the other contenders had been satisfactorily resolved was inconsequential. What was incontestable and which the duties of the new Balogun indicated was that the colonial officer needed a balogun figure that was as popular among the Ijebu-Epe as he was among the Eko-Epe, and who could deploy his influence to ensure harmony between the communities.

Even so, there are indications that the installation of Abudu Kadiri Oluwo as the Ijebu Balogun was accomplished amidst great compromises and denials.

---

32 See N.A.I RG/C5: Extracts from the minutes of a meeting between the Acting Administrator of the Colony (E.R Falk) and Epe chiefs held on 17th November, 1932 in the Court House at Epe.

For instance, in the minutes of a meeting that he held on 18th October, 1932 with representatives of Etitun and Itungbeyin, the Osugbo and the two contenders for the vacant Balogun office, the acting district officer attempted to put to rest the controversies surrounding the supposed rotational arrangement between the sub-quarters. He denied knowledge of the existence of a rotational agreement between the wards. He affirmed:

> I could find no trace of there being any arrangement whereby each quarter in turn should fill vacancies.[33]

In the absence of a prior written agreement that 'each quarter in turn should fill vacancies', the excuse of the district officer seemed reasonable. It, however, revealed a weakness that is usually inherent in any tradition that is anchored by oral covenants. Despite the alibi, he assured the Etitun party that he would make a note in the file to the effect that when another vacancy arises, the sub-quarter of Etitun should be favourably considered, if the candidate they put forward was suitable. Whatever those words of commitment meant, resolving the crises that way seemed amicable enough.

However, the seeming peaceful resolution of the Balogun Abudu Kadiri Oluwo versus Saka Aguda saga generated more questions than it actually resolved. The

---

33 See N.A.I RG/C5: Extracts from the minutes of a meeting between the Acting District Officer in Epe and Epe chiefs held on 17th October, 1932.

constitutional issue of rotational allocation of chieftaincy rights and privileges, which was fundamental to peaceful intra-group relations, was swept under the carpet. Also, the fact that he committed the colonial machinery to such a future cause could only mean that he envisaged the practicality of the approach, but why he failed to employ the option in the case at hand leaves so much to the imagination. A probable explanation for the inconsistencies of his decisions and facts of the case was because he was under immense pressure from the Osugbo and the Baale to approve the candidacy of Abudu Kadiri Oluwo, who was their anointed nominee. If this were true, the compromise revealed the latitude and limits of compromise and co-operation between colonial machineries and traditional institutions in Epe.

It could be adduced from the foregoing that the verdict was a most compromising way to resolve a succession crisis. It appeared that the *proviso* that the prospective candidate for the office should be 'a suitable man' pushed considerations for the age-long right of the quarters or sub-quarters to field candidates for chieftaincy vacancies, to the margins in the process and politics of allocation of traditional chieftaincy right and privileges in Epe. Hence, the district officer surely had wittingly or inadvertently set a new precedence for the politics of allocation of traditional chieftaincy rights and privileges among the Ijebu in subsequent years.

Subsequently, upon the death of Kadiri Oluwo on May 31st 1939,[34] Chief Ajakonri from Apakeji Quarter was appointed to succeed him. Subsequent appointments to the office of the Balogun were done in strict compliance to consensus on rotational turn taking among the quarters. Hence, when the Apakeji ran their course after the death of Balogun Ajakonri, the office was reverted to Etitun in Aleke Quarter with the appointment of Mojidi Oluwo. Upon his death, he was succeeded by Balogun Moibi Oluwo of Ebode in Apakeji Quarter. The title returned to Aleke Quarter in 1997 when Lanre Razak from Eyindi became the Balogun.

The changing status of the Balogun institution and new social accords and cooperation in Epe

The latter part of the 1990s marked a turning point for the Balogun institution in Epe. The institution passed on to a new generation of grassroots mobilizers, philanthropists and community men whose influence cut across all ethnic, religious and political constituencies in the town. One individual whose personality embodied the new order of leadership was Balogun Lanre Razak.

Chief Lanre Razak succeeded Chief Moibi Oluwo as Balogun of Ijebu Epe, having been the Otun Balogun during the tenure of the latter.[35] Razak's maternal great

---

34 See *Daily Times*, May 3, 1939

35 See appendix one, for a biographical sketch of Balogun Razak.

grandfather, Fagbayi, was a direct descendant of Ojuro, Chief *Olorogun* Agbaje of Lagos. Thus, Balogun Razak's pedigree suitably positioned him for the title.

The influence of the office of the Balogun in Epe has extended into communities to the south and west of the town. At the 70th birthday of Oba A.K. Hassan, the *Abowa of Agbowa*, a small town of about 10 kilometres on the eastern fringes of Epe, the celebrant made a request to all the other obas and paramount rulers in attendance for the conferment and the recognition of Chief Lanre Razak as the Balogun General of Epe Division. His Royal Highness, Oba Akeem Okunola Adesanya, the *Alara* of *Ilara*, who is also the chairman of the Council of Obas in Epe Division, was in attendance. The request was unanimously granted.[36]

The implication of the recognition for power politics within Epe Division is that henceforth Balogun Lanre Razak would become 'first among equals' as far as the Balogun chieftaincy title holders are concerned in the towns that make up Epe Division. Taken further, it means that whoever emerges as the Balogun of Epe in subsequent years will likely assume the exalted title of the Balogun General.

Even though lines of demarcation between traditional institutions of the Ijebu-Epe and Eko-Epe are clearly visible, however, much of the political and cultural chasm that once separated them has gradually

---

36 An interview with Chief Lanre Razak, current Balogun of Ijebu community in Epe, on May 17, 2015 in Lagos.

constricted and given way to a new era of peaceful co-existence. For instance, even though the Balogun of the Eko-Epe and his Ijebu-Epe counterpart have been separately responsible for the defense and security of their respective areas of influence, they also jointly work and co-operate on matters that affect both communities. One of the platforms on which they jointly operate as security chiefs is the Police Community Relations Council (PCRC). The Balogun of the two communities are members of the PCRC.

More importantly, they are both members of the Epe Club. The club was formed in 1974 to promote harmony and peaceful co-existence of the Eko-Epe and the Ijebu-Epe communities. Through the instrumen-tality of the Epe Club, the Eko-Epe and the Ijebu-Epe groups have lived together harmoniously, though under their separate traditional institutions, and their respective subjects freely intermingle. For instance, the current Olu-Epe of Epe, His Royal Majesty, Oba Adewale Shefiu was a past chairman of the Club, while the sitting Balogun of the Ijebu –Epe, Chief Lanre Razak, has been the president since 2012. The current Balogun of the Eko-Epe, Chief Ikuforiji, is also a member of the club.

Besides, an important influence on the cultural landscape of Epe town is the *Kaykayo* festival, which is believed to have been introduced into the town by the Eko-Epe. The Kayokayo is a pseudo-Islamic commemoration of Prophet Noah's Ark after the Great Flood. The festival has become one of the most significant traditional ceremonies bringing together Ijebu-Epe and the Eko-Epe. The Balogun of the Ijebu and other traditional title holders are usually regular guests at the festival.

Above all, generations of men and women on both sides have developed strong social and political connections, marital affiliations, economic interdependence, as well as the co-membership of various social and grassroots associations that have enriched the multi-cultural complexion of the town.

Conclusion

This chapter has shown the changing fortunes of the Balogun in Epe from the 1850s. We have traced the origins of the institution as a warrior class chieftaincy title usually reserved for military aristocrats within the traditional system of government. The evolution of the Balogun institution followed the same pattern, as two parallel lines of the chieftaincy emerged in the town before the end of the 19th century.

The constant conflicts for political dominance between the Ijebu-Epe and the Eko-Epe in the post-Kosoko era, warranted administrative reorganisation under colonial rule, which climaxed with the emergence of a composite political structure in the town. The new composite structure, though intended as a solution to the tension and acrimony between the two cultural factions, further diminished the tendency to reconcile their differences. Part of the fallout includes inter and intra-group rivalries over the allocation of chieftaincy rights and privileges between and within the two groups. The Balogun institution has mediated conflicts between intra and inter-group cultural politics from the second half of the 19th century. Among the Ijebu-Epe, for instance, the struggle over the allocation of rights and privileges for occupying the position compelled some eminent indigenes—competing claimants—to get embroiled in controversies. The question of 'who gets what and how?' was addressed through civil negotiations, mediation and delicate compromises.

Despite the challenging scenarios of the past, the Balogun chieftaincy has grown in popularity and significance, not just within the town, but also in neighbouring communities. The chieftaincy has become one of the means of diffusing the perennial conflicts between various subgroups in a community Holders of the Balogun title are in the forefront of community mobilisation, as well as community spokespersons.

6
The Balogun Institution in Egbaland
Lanre Davies

Introduction

The Egba are a sub-group of the Yoruba who inhabited an area between Remo and the present Oyo town many years ago before the disturbance that destroyed their abode at their *orile* (homestead), consequent upon the Owu war. According to Samuel Johnson (1921), the Egba originally occupied an area bounded by certain imaginary lines drawn from Ijaiye to meet the Ogun River at Olokemeji and another from the same point via Ibadan to the west of Ijebu Remo down to the coast.[1]

In the aftermath of the Owu War, the nearby Egba kingdom which had in no way been overtly involved in the original problems that led to the Owu War got punished for their neutrality. The victors accused the Egba of secretly helping the Owu during the war, while some surviving Owu laid siege against some Egba towns, accusing them of not coming to their aid. In the process, the Egba towns became divided, some joining the aggrieved Owu to fight other Egba towns, while between 1825 and 1827, the victorious army of Ijebu, Ife,

---

[1] S. Johnson, *The History of the Yorubas*, (Lagos: CMS, 1921), p. 17.

and Oyo continued to destroy one Egba town after the other.² The Egba subsequently dispersed and finally migrated to Abeokuta after making some stop-gap measures at Ibadan, and the Odo-Ona transit camp, from where Sodeke of Iporo led them to Abeokuta, around 1830.

Origin of the Balogun Institution

Any meaningful analysis of the evolution of the institution of the Balogun chieftaincy title in Egbaland must take cognisance of the situation in the Egba forest before the Egba migrated to Abeokuta in 1830. In retrospect, the experience of the Egba under the yoke of the Oyo Empire was instrumental to the institution of the Balogun chieftaincy title in the Egba forest. During the time that Gaha was the Bashorun of Oyo, the Alaafin's direct authority over the Egba forest diminished. The Ilari/Ajele managed to convert Oyo's problems to their advantage. They became despots without any religious or political sanctions which had previously made their presence acceptable.³ The Ilari/Ajele were no longer contented with the collection of annual tributes. They virtually usurped power from the Egba rulers. They tyrannized the Egba by making

---

2 I.A. Akinjogbin, "Wars in Yorubaland, 1793-1893: An Analytical Categorisation", in A. Akinjogbin, editor, *War and Peace in Yorubaland*, 1793-1893,(Ibadan: Heinemann,1998), p. 33-51.

3 H.A. Gailey, *Lugard and the Abeokuta Uprising, The demise of Egba Independence*. (London: Frank Cass, 1982), p. 1.

excessive demands from them and also harassing their women.[4]

The activities of the Oyo Ajele in the administration of the Egba at their Orile made Lisabi Agbongbolo Akala, an Itoku man, who grew up at Igbein, to organise the Egba men into a mutual assistance society called *aaro*[5] in every Egba town. The Egba leader (Lisabi), later converted the society into the olorogun society (war society) which he used to rid the Egba of the excesses of the Ilari/Ajele stationed at the Egba forest in the various Egba towns in the three provinces, Egba Alake, Oke-Ona, and Gbagura.[6] His principal lieutenants were Amosu of Ikija in Oke-Ona; Arinkotu of Ojo; and Akila of Iddo in Gbagura.

Lisabi and his associates armed their followers secretly with bows and arrows, slings, spears, daggers, swords, hatchets, and clubs. The violent uprising began in Lisabi's Igbein and soon spread to every other Egba town at their Orile. It is estimated that over six hundred Ilari/Ajele were murdered by the Egba.[7] Thus the Egba olorogun uprising under Lisabi brought an end to the political domination of Egbaland by Oyo.

---

4 T. Falola, and G. Oguntomisin. *Yoruba Warlords of the Nineteenth Century*. (Asmara, World Press, 2001), p. 114.

5 See A.K. Ajisafe, *History of Abeokuta*, (Abeokuta: Fola Bookshop, 1964), p. 15; Falola and Oguntomisin, Ibid, p. 2.

6 Ibid.

7 Ibid.

The attempt by the Alaafin to re-conquer Egbaland proved abortive. An Oyo army made up of troops from Oyo, Ibarapa, and Egbado, crossed the River Ogun at Mokoloki and advanced towards Igbein, Lisabi's town. Lisabi had, however, hid the women and children of the town in a ravine called Melegu. When the Oyo army entered Igbein, they found it deserted. As the invading army was busy ransacking the town, Lisabi's militia suddenly and swiftly descended on them and put them to rout and the Egba regained their independence.[8] It has been argued that, apart from the military tactics employed by Lisabi, the Egba victory could also be attributed to the weakness of the Oyo army under Alaafin Abiodun's prosperous reign (1774-1789). During his time, the Oyo army became inefficient; as a result, it was defeated by Borgu in 1783, Ife in 1791, and Lisabi's militia in 1796.[9]

The transformation of Aaro into the olorogun society was very significant in the initiation of the Balogun chieftaincy title among the Egba who had hitherto relied on the Ode society (hunters) for defence. The hunters of each town performed police duties and engaged in reconnoitring activities which were not effective in defending the Egba against external aggression. Therefore, the Egba placed themselves under the protection of the Alafin of Oyo. With the

---

8 Gailey, op cit.

9 Falola and Oguntomisin.

creation of the olorogun society, Lisabi now led a standing militia that could be used to defend the Egba forest whenever occasion demanded.

The victory of the Egba over the Oyo army made the Oke-Ogun people to enter into a treaty of peace with the Egba under Lisabi. This treaty was kept till the end of the Agbaje War, when it was broken by the Oke-Ogun people as a result of their frequent attack on Egba territories, consequent upon the internal feud among the Egba after the demise of Lisabi.[10] According to Falola and Oguntomisin:

> With Lisabi at the head of this new force the Egba could now raise their own national force under a commander like their Oyo, Owu and Ijebu neighbors. With the existence of the olorogun, the Egba would no longer need the protection of the Alafin of Oyo against external aggressors as the military society could be mobilized for defense.[11]

The alliance with the Oke–Ogun people made the Egba to pursue an active common frontier policy against Dahomey who raided Oke-Ogun periodically. Lisabi built a fortress on a hill in order to watch the activities of the enemies more easily. He remained in this fortress at

---

10 Ajisafe, op cit.

11 Falola, and Oguntomisin, op cit.

the head of a garrison.[12] Therefore, it can be submitted that Lisabi was the first commander of a united Egba army, even though he was not officially addressed as Balogun of the Egba. He, however, functioned as the Jagunna, which was the Egba equivalent of the Balogun title at that time. Ajisafe has shown how the Jagunna had been the commander-in-chief of the Egba army. According to him:

> The title "Jagunna" ranks higher than the title "Balogun"; it is a royal appointment and is equivalent to "Minister of War." The Jagunna rules all the Baloguns either of his province or of all the other provinces. He is responsible to the king (Alake) alone, and is to wear his cap before the king when all other warriors would or must uncover their heads [sic].[13]

As a military leader, he organised an army that was capable of defending the sovereignty of the Egba. His army was divided into three columns—the centre, the right, and the left—each under a commander. The centre was commanded by the Jagunna, the right by the Lukotun, and the left, the Lukosi.[14] Lisabi also taught the Egba how to protect their towns by erecting

---

12 S.O. Biobaku, *The Egba and Their Neighbours, 1842-1872*, (Oxford: Clarendon Press, 1957), p. 10.

13 Ajisafe, op cit.

14 B.O. Sonuga, "A Comparative Study of Lisabi and Sodeke as Egba Statesmen". *Historia* no. 3, (1966): 23.

fortifications around them. He is also remembered today by traditional historians as a man who strictly enforced laws and taught the Egba how to protect their civic institutions.

But his achievement went beyond commanding the Egba forces. He became a military and a political leader under whom the Egba were not only united, but also prosperous.[15] The Egba people took advantage of their newly won independence and security to engage in trade beyond their immediate neighbourhood. They traded in kolanut with the Hausa of northern Nigeria, and also engaged in coastal trade at Badagry. These commercial activities brought prosperity to the Egba people. Losi recorded how Lisabi was used to saying that "I fought for them (the Egba people) to wrap alari cloth and I warred for them to wear sekini cloth."[16]

Despite the achievements of Lisabi in the areas of peace, unity, prosperity, and security of the Egba nation, he later became unpopular among his chiefs. Ajisafe, Losi, Biobaku, and Falola and Oguntomisin have given various reasons for his unpopularity ranging from: jealousy of his fame by his chiefs, war weariness, resentment of conscription of young people who could be used on the farms into the army, to his old age among others. As a result of all these, Ajisafe noted how Lisabi was tricked to a hill in the Egba forest by some of his

---

15 Ajisafe, op cit.

16 J.B.O. Losi, *History of Abeokuta*, (Lagos, 1924), p. 9.

chiefs who were critical of his government, and pushed into the ditch below where he was seen no more.[17] Biobaku however, argued that Lisabi either perished in a Dahomian raid on the Egba frontiers or mysteriously took his own life in the forest.[18]

The importance of the military arrangement under Lisabi in the Egba forest cannot be over-emphasized. Local differences had been submerged under the spell of his personality and the need to combine to meet an external foe. His demise however, brought about a return to *status quo ante* which meant a return to town rivalries and jealousies, and the ineffectiveness of the old federal authorities which according to Biobaku "was neither clearly defined nor able to assert itself."[19]

With local differences and rivalries re-emerging among the various Egba towns, it was not long before civil wars occurred in the Egba forest. Although Biobaku has argued that many of these might have occurred in the Egba forest before the Owu war,[20] the first to be recorded in Egba history was the Ogedepagbo War between Igbein and Itoku which was the result of an attempt to run a salt monopoly which Igbein "had either imposed or violated."[21] When the parties to the dispute

---

17 Ibid.

18 Biobaku, p. 11.

19 Ibid.

20 Ibid.

21 Ibid.

threatened to involve all the other Egba Alake towns, the blockade runner or smuggler (Ogedepagbo of Itoku) was condemned to death and executed by the *Oro*.

The second civil war was as a result of a chieftaincy dispute between Asalu and Depolu in Ilugun under Oke-Ona province. Some of the Egba Alake townships tried to intervene to stop the war but their overtures were rejected. They thereafter aided one of the parties to the dispute (Depolu) to expel his arrogant rival (Asalu).[22] The third, was the Agbaje civil war. The war broke out because seven Egba Alake towns (Itoko, Erunwon, Ijeun, Itoku, Oba, Itesi, and Itori) formed their own court at a central place called Kosofe, where their combined Parakoyi gave such impartial justice that they completely ignored the Alake's court (Ile Ogboni Ake).

When this rival court began to withhold a portion of its fees which it formerly sent to Alake Okikilu, he decided to move against it by enlisting the assistance of Agbaje, a notable warrior from Ijanna in the Egbado country who brought a large army into the Egba forest. The Egba raised a large force and besieged the Alake at Ake. Alake Okikilu fled to Kemta after Agbaje forces had been defeated at Itori. It has been argued that Alake Okikilu died either by accident or design.[23] Okikilu was the last Alake in the Egba forest and another Alake was

---

22 Ajisafe, p. 46-47.

23 Ibid, p. 48-49.

not appointed until 1854 after the Egba migrated to Abeokuta.

The fourth outbreak of war in the Egba forest was between Itoku and Oba. The cause of the outbreak is not given in recorded history but Ajisafe has noted that it was the fiercest and the most horrible war ever fought in the Egba forest.[24] According to him, one Lakoso a powerful war chief in Ijeun, helped the Itoku people and this enabled the Itoku people to subdue Oba people even though Lakoso himself received a mortal blow in the course of the war.[25]

The civil wars resulting from the collapse of the first military arrangement initiated by Lisabi emphasized the weakness of the federal civil authorities in the Egba forest. Even though the Alake was *primus inter pares*, and was universally acknowledged as the supreme judicial authority, there was no binding obligation to resort to his court as a powerful individual could ignore it altogether. There was the will to act collectively in settling inter-town disputes (as in the Ilugun civil war) but it did not bear fruit in the absence of recognisable military machinery as experienced under Lisabi. When the Egba Alake towns established a central Parakoyi court, their success tempted them towards separatism. Again when Alake Okikilu failed in his attempt to deal

---

24 Ibid, p. 49.

25 Ibid.

with seceding towns, his office fell into abeyance simply because there was no central coercive machinery.

Their lack of cohesion and mutual jealousies proved fatal to the existence of the Egba towns at the time of the upheaval which engulfed Yorubaland in the second decade of the nineteenth century, when the allied forces of Ife, Ijebu, and Oyo refugees invaded the Owu kingdom, whose territory was adjacent to the Egba forest. After the destruction of Owu, the victorious forces attacked one Egba town after the other. The Egba lacked the leadership and internal cohesion to contain or even repel the attack of the enemies. Instead of evolving an all Egba military machinery as practiced under Lisabi, the Egba townships aided the enemies against their fellow Egba towns and even rejoiced at the fate of such towns until the same fate befell them. As a result, the whole Egba forest was completely devastated by the allied forces.[26]

Institutionalisation of Balogun chieftaincy among the Egba

As noted earlier the inability of the Egba to unite against the invading forces of Ife, Ijebu, and Oyo spelt doom for the Egba towns which were destroyed by the enemies. In the demoralizing atmosphere of the period, the Egba failed to perceive the advantage of a united defensive action. The calamity that befell the Egba rendered many

---

26 Falola and Oguntomisin, op cit.

Egba towns desolate. Apart from Awe, Fiditi, Iloba, Abena, Akinmorin, Agerige, Aran, Kojoku, and Oroko, which had submitted themselves to Oloyo,[27]

Dispersed and chastened, the Egba wandered for some time before they finally resorted to Ibadan, now under Okunade, the Maye of Ife, and the commander-in-chief of the allied forces, which proved to be the rallying point of the Yoruba and later the bulwark of the Yoruba defence against the Fulani.[28] It was at this time that all the foreign war titles with the exception of Bashorun and Aare Ona Kakanfo were introduced to the Egba.[29] According to Biobaku:

> At Ibadan, the Egba regrouped themselves and evolved the first truly federal organization, an all-Egba military command. They adopted Oyo-Yoruba ideas and titles for their forces. Yisa of Itoko... became the Balogun... of the Egba, Debaoku of Ijemo, the Seriki. Each had his right- and left-wing commanders. There was also the cavalry, led by the Sarumi and his lieutenants. The old militia, the *olorogun*, had given way to an organization approaching a national army except that its units were still organized according to the old towns.[30]

---

27 Ajisafe, op cit.

28 Biobaku, op cit.

29 Ajisafe, op cit.

30 Biobaku, op cit.

Thus, Yisa of Itoko became the first Egba man to assume the title of Balogun in Egba history. He was said to have become conspicuous for his bravery and military tact. Subsequently, he was made the first Balogun of the Egba army in Ibadan under Maye, while Deboku of Ijemo became the Seriki of the Egba army.[31] However, when they began to age, the two military men retired from active service.

Lamodi succeeded Yisa as the Balogun of the Egba army, while Denlu succeeded Deboku as the Seriki. Denlu was later succeeded by Sodeke of Iporo as Seriki of the Egba army. It is important to note that at the time Lamodi emerged as the Balogun of the Egba army, Lakanle was the Balogun of the Oyo army; Kale was the Balogun of the Ijebu army, while Ege was the Balogun of Ife army, all of whom were under the command of Maye, the commander-in-chief at Ibadan.[32]

The situation in Ibadan at the time that Lamodi emerged as the Balogun of the Egba did not encourage the continued co-existence of the Egba with the other Yoruba groups in the town. At this time, the motley assemblage of people in Ibadan lacked food and other means of livelihood. As a result, the Oyo, Ijebu, and the Ife allies were in the habit of kidnapping the Egba and selling them into slavery.[33] The Egba people tried to

---

31 Ajisafe, op cit.

32 Ibid, p. 58.

33 Ibid.

prevent this to no avail as they were outnumbered by the hostile forces in Ibadan. When the situation became unbearable, the Egba people decided to vacate Ibadan and encamp far away from the hostile forces on the western side of the Ona River. This decision was communicated to Maye who initially refused and charged the Egba leaders with rebellion. He later ruled that unless the sincerity of the Egba to vacate Ibadan was proved by the casting of Kola in their favour, the Egba people would be destroyed. The Egba however, managed to extricate themselves of Maye's charge and finally encamped at the Ona transit camp under Sodeke.[34]

Before the Egba departed from Ibadan, the Egba leaders under Balogun Lamodi had arranged that some Egba should remain in Ibadan to forestall any surprise attack by the hostile army. Therefore, Balogun Lamodi, Agburin of Ilugun, Soge of Ibadan[35], and Lasilo, the Osiele, with all their followers remained in Ibadan, while Sodeke the Seriki of the Egba army led the remaining Egba people to the western side of the Ona River. The military strategy employed by Balogun Lamodi and other Egba leaders to leave some Egba behind in Ibadan paid off as it actually prevented Maye, the commander-in-chief of the allied forces, who

---

34 Ibid.

35 This is the original Ibadan belonging to the Egba Gbagura now occupied by the allied forces.

regarded the Egba as his bondsmen from attacking them.

However, when the allied forces realised that the presence of Balogun Lamodi in Ibadan would frustrate their plan of attacking the Egba, they conspired against him. They invited him to a friendly meeting presided over by Maye, where he was to be assassinated. Balogun Lamodi attended the meeting with some of his followers. According to Ajisafe, the sight of Balogun Lamodi overawed the conspirators who *ab initio* could not do anything but for the intervention of the bard of Balogun Ege of Ife, who sang his praise thus:

> O mighty Ege ! how strange it seems to me - Brave and powerful as thou art --- Yet a coward should be ! What ! The hind legs of the dreadful wolf have been caught and held fast ; And yet there's none to confront him ! [sic][36]

Chief Ege, the Balogun of Ife, was said to have been so moved that he took his loaded gun and fired at Balogun Lamodi but he missed. In self defence, Balogun Lamodi shot and killed his assailant. He was said to have fired another shot at Chief Maye, but missed his target.[37] Consequently, the conspirators and their followers attacked Balogun Lamodi and his followers who were pursued towards the Egba encampment at Oke Ona.

---

36 Ajisafe, op cit.

37 Ibid.

In an attempt to rescue his son, Osota, from the conspirators, Balogun Lamodi was fatally wounded but still managed to get to the Egba camp on the western side of River Ona. He died the following day. Before his death, he urged Sodeke the Seriki, and other Egba leaders to save the Egba from annihilation by the hostile forces by securing a better place of abode for them.[38]

Not satisfied with the new development, the allied forces under Chief Maye regrouped and decided on a final onslaught on the Egba at their Oke-Ona Camp. Maye's forces arrived at Oke-Ona to discover that the Egba although outnumbered were prepared for the attack under their new Balogun, Sodeke. With daring courage, the Egba defended themselves against the firepower of the combined Ibadan forces under Maye. They fought with the desperation of a people whose very existence was threatened. After a fierce battle with the allied forces, the Egba soldiers under Balogun Sodeke put the allied forces to rout. The allied forces fled in all directions and were mercilessly pursued by the Egba soldiers who captured Chief Oluyole and his horse in the process.[39] He was later released by Balogun Sodeke through an entreaty by Chief Maye. His horse was released to him much later.

Thereafter, the Egba decided to vacate their Oke-Ona camp for a safer place. It was clear to them that the

---

38 Ibid.

39 Ibid, p. 61.

trans-Ona camp was too close to Ibadan for their safety. Balogun Sodeke had heard of a site far away from Ibadan, where three hunters had escaped in the course of the disturbance that swept away the Egba towns. Tradition claims that the site was the farm of a man from Itoko who was also a member of the Ogboni. It was this man that introduced the Olubara into the Ogboni statecraft. Other traditions maintain that the site belonged to an Egbado man called Adagba.[40]

Whatever it was, Balogun Sodeke quickly dispatched some hunters to make the necessary investigation preparatory to settlement in the area. Having also made the necessary enquiry from Ifa, through soil sample taken from the site, Balogun Sodeke led the Egba to the new settlement "under the stone." It was this site which grew to become a formidable city called Abeokuta.

A notable chief of Ikija, Ogunbona, who later became prominent in Abeokuta, joined the Egba shortly before they left their trans-Ona settlement. Hotly pursued by the allied forces under Maye, Chief Ogunbona escaped by denying that he was an Egba man; he claimed to be an Ijebu because of the *ebe* marks on his back.[41]

The evacuation was carefully planned. Chief Sodeke detailed an advance party to cut a wide track through the forest to the chosen site. Sodeke the Balogun himself,

---

40 Biobaku, op cit.

41 The *ebe* marks are incisions made by the Ikija people and some Ijebu on their backs.

and the Egba Alake people constituted the vanguard; they were followed by the Egba Gbagura people led by Agbo; the Oke-Ona people brought up the rear and were led by Lumloye, the Balogun of Ilugun. A skeletal force under Agburin of Ilugun, Soge, and Lasilo the Osiele of Ilugun, protected the rear and used delay tactics against Maye's forces.[42] Both Agburin of Ilugun and Soge of Ibadan, later joined the others at Abeokuta while Lasilo, the Osiele of Ilugun settled at an outpost named after him to forestall any surprise attack on Abeokuta.[43]

The Balogun institution in nineteenth century Abeokuta

The Balogun institution in nineteenth century Abeokuta was instrumental to the effective defence and administration of Abeokuta right from the time the Egba settled in Abeokuta till the end of the century. An all Egba olorogun was established for the whole of Abeokuta. Even though there was an attempt to re-create the old Egba townships, a federal Egba olorogun was preferred to the civil government of the Egba forest, as the Egba found themselves in a chaotic situation Abeokuta. From 1830, when the main body of the Egba entered Abeokuta, they settled on the western side of the Olumo rock from where the remnants of the old towns formed townships or quarters to which they gave

---

42 Biobaku, op cit.

43 Ibid.

the names of their former towns. Some pre-fixed *Ago* (camp) to the names in order to keep alive the desire to return to the old location in less troubled times in the future.[44]

At Abeokuta, Chief Sodeke allowed all Egba refugees to settle in Abeokuta, and very soon, there congregated in Abeokuta the three main Egba groups of Egba Alake, Egba Gbagura, and Egba Oke-Ona, who were later joined in 1831, by the Owu. The Egba surrounded the new settlement with a wall which was constantly adjusted as new refugees arrived and formed their own quarters. Balogun Sodeke allotted land to the new-comers and the settlement quickly spread over parcels of land formerly farmed by the people of Itoko and Ijemo.[45]

However, the Egba were confronted in Abeokuta by two immediate problems—food shortages, and insecurity. Food, clothing, and money were very scarce when they got to Abeokuta. The food supplied by the Itoko, Ijemo, and their Ibara, Isaga, and Ilewo neighbours was not enough to feed the teeming population. So great was the famine that occurred that some of the settlers pawned their children and wives to the Ijemo and Itoko people for food.[46] Balogun Sodeke solved this problem by asking the people to take to

---

44 Ibid.

45 Ibid.

46 Ajisafe, op cit.

farming and within one year of settlement in Abeokuta, the Egba were able to produce food in abundance for all and sundry.[47]

In the area of defence, Balogun Sodeke, like Lisabi before him had a clear vision that unless the Egba could consolidate their strength in the defence of a single town, they were doomed as a people. This explains why he threw open the gate of Abeokuta to all Egba refugees, the Owu, and much later the Saro returnees, in order to render the town by sheer number an impregnable fortress. No doubt, this put severe strain on the nascent town as the Egba were hard pressed for food and other supplies but as said earlier the people soon got over the problem.

The nascent settlement was soon threatened by the old enemies of the Egba—the Ibadan and Ijebu marauders— who overran the newly established farms of the Egba and kidnapped in broad daylight anyone who ventured beyond the town wall. Balogun Sodeke and the olorogun drove the marauders off and pursued them far into the Ijebu country and within sight of the coast.[48]

In order to keep their Ijebu attackers at bay, Sodeke and the Egba soldiers attacked Ijebu Remo towns, capturing Offin, Makun, Ogere, Ilishan, Ode, and Isamoro. They also attacked Ota, which they suspected

---

47 Falola and Oguntomisin, op cit.

48 Biobaku, op cit.

was aiding the Ijebu.[49] A combined Ibadan and Ijebu force drove the Egba from Ota and they returned to Abeokuta via Agbamaiya on the Ogun River. The Egba attack on Ota revealed that the Egba desired to control the trade route to the coast at their new location which Ibadan and Ijebu were trying to forestall. Hence they were desirous of crushing the Egba before they became too powerful.

After the Egba's attack and capture of Ijebu Remo towns, Ijebu and Ibadan planned a joint attack on Abeokuta. However, because of Ibadan's involvement in war with Ipetumodu, Ibadan could only sent a small detachment under Oluguna. Thus the Owiwi War of 1832 was fought mainly between the Ijebu and the Egba. Balogun Kalejaiye and six other Ijebu generals led the Ijebu soldiers, while Sodeke personally led the Egba soldiers. In the first encounter, the Ijebu defeated the Egba with heavy casualties. The Egba retreated to Ibara and drew reinforcements from Abeokuta. When the news of the defeat reached Abeokuta, some of the Egba panicked and drowned themselves in the Ogun River rather than fall victim to the Ijebu invaders or resume another period of wandering and suffering in the forest.[50]

Balogun Sodeke gathered the remaining Egba soldiers and also sought the assistance of Oba Adele of

---

49 Falola and Oguntomisin, op cit.

50 Biobaku, op cit.

Lagos who not only procured arms and ammunition for the Egba, but also led his own force personally to assist them.[51] Moreover, the Egba were said to have accidentally forestalled a major attack on their position at Ibara and pursued the disconcerted Ijebu into Egbado territory.

Again, acting on information provided by Ishaga spies, the Egba intercepted an Ijebu convoy which was taking gunpowder to the Ijebu army. Equally important was the fact that the Egba were protected on their southern flank by a neutral Ota, which was then under the leadership of Ajano. In addition, before Sodeke finally attacked the Ijebu, a plague broke out in the Ijebu camp to compound their problems.[52] Therefore when the final battle was fought, the Ijebu were at a great disadvantage. Although, the Ijebu fought brilliantly, the result was a complete rout for them. Balogun Kalejaiye and the remaining six Ijebu war generals were captured, executed, and their heads taken as trophies to Abeokuta where they were buried in front of Sodeke's compound at Iporo.[53]

Strengthened by their victory over Ijebu, the Egba accused the Egbado towns of collaborating with Ijebu, and so sent a detachment under Apati the Bada of Kemta to punish the Egbado. Apati destroyed several

---

51 Falola and Oguntomisin, op cit.

52 Biobaku, op cit.

53 Ajisafe, op cit.

Egbado towns, notably Ijanna, Imala, Kesan, and they also attacked Ilaro, their capital. The Olu of Ilaro was driven to Itoro, where he was captured and slain.[54] The people of Ilaro fled to Idogo, and elected another Olu, whose reign was short. The Egba later forced the people of Ilaro to re-settle at Ilaro and made them install a pro-Egba Olu, and also to accept an Ajele from Abeokuta to supervise the administration and to collect annual tribute for the Egba.[55]

Having conquered Egbado towns and their principal town subjugated, the Egba attained supremacy in the Egbado country and also succeeded in keeping the trade routes to the coast open. The major routes in their foreign policy were Lagos, Badagry, and Ota. The Egba watched events in these areas with keen interest.

The Baloguns also protected the Egba against armed bandits in Abeokuta when the nascent town was infested by armed robbers led by one Dado a chief of Igan, in the Egbado country, and Ibadan marauders. Between them, they raided and laid waste the north-western farms of the Egba in 1834. Initially, Balogun Sodeke established a system of day and night watch but this proved inadequate. Then a sufficient force under Agana, an Igbein chief, was sent to either capture or kill Dado. The first force sent by Balogun Sodeke was driven back. But a second one under Apati the Seriki of the

---

54 Biobaku, op cit.

55 Ibid.

Egba drove back the marauders at Samore, and captured a lot of booty.[56]

Not long after this, the Egba were confronted by the great might of Ibadan. In 1835, Bashorun Oluyole led a very large force to invade Abeokuta. The Ibadan people were supported by Kurunmi of Ijaiye, the Aare Ona Kakanfo of Yorubaland, and Ayo of Abemo,[57] two notable war generals, who joined Oluyole at Olokemeji. The grand forces hoped to sack Abeokuta by surprise. The Egba sentries however, spotted the invading forces and alerted the Egba soldiers. Balogun Sodeke quickly mobilized an Egba force to engage the enemy on a hill close to the town. In the first encounter, both sides were forced to retreat and encamped. The invaders camped on the other side of the Arakanga stream and began a regular siege on Abeokuta for over three months. The Egba regrouped and launched a vigorous attack on Ibadan and their allies and put them to flight. The Egba pursued them as far as Olokemeji killing many of them and also capturing many as slaves. Balogun Sodeke returned to Abeokuta triumphantly with his forces and booty.[58]

The defeat of Ibadan at the Arakanga War of 1835, elicited various reactions at the time. The Ibadan gave excuses for their resounding defeat—the campaign was

---

56 Ibid, p. 22-23.

57 Falola and Oguntomisin, op cit.

58 Biobaku, op cit.

badly planned and ill executed; junior chiefs followed their leaders half-heartedly and carried fake kegs of gunpowder which were in fact filled with yam flour.[59] Johnson also argued that the Ibadan merely attacked Abeokuta to avenge the death of Oshun, the chief of the Oyo cavalry, who was killed at Oniyefun in the aftermath of the Owiwi War, and not to destroy Abeokuta.[60] Whatever was the reason for Ibadan's defeat, the Egba had defeated not only the strongest military power in Yorubaland, but also some of the best war generals in Yorubaland, and had succeeded in driving back Ibadan permanently.

The victory of the Egba over the Ibadan also marked a turning point in Egba history. Refugees poured into Abeokuta between 1836 and 1842. Balogun Sodeke's fame spread far and wide. All the Egba who had hidden in the forest during Egba's dispersal from the Egba forest now found their ways back to Abeokuta. Inhabitants of friendly towns especially from Oke-Ogun, who fled before invaders found refuge in Abeokuta. Captives of war, especially of Oyo, Ife, and Ijebu, brought back by the olorogun, when not sold into slavery were absorbed into Egba households as domestic slaves.[61] Thus Abeokuta was fortified with immigrants and hence became more impregnable than

---

59 Johnson, op cit

60 Ibid.

61 Biobaku, op cit.

ever to withstand any attack. More importantly, the Egba were now confident enough to embark on the offensive.

The Egba attacked the people of Iperu whom they believed supplied Ibadan with gunpowder during the Arakanga War. The Balogun of Odo, Aiyejorun, led the Egba force by the quickest route to Iperu, but failed to surprise Iperu, which had appealed to Ibadan for help. The Egba were said to have feigned a retreat, drew the besieged out, and then fell upon them with deadly results. The arrival of an Ibadan force led by Lakanle saved Iperu. The Egba then withdrew having lost Aiyejorun. They returned to Abeokuta with some Ibadan captives.[62]

Politically, the Balogun institution was effectively used to administer Abeokuta under Balogun Sodeke. It should be noted that during the brief stay of the Egba in Ibadan, they had resuscitated the olorogun not only as a unifying force, but also as their militia. Under Lisabi, the olorogun transformed from a socioeconomic organisation into an essentially military society. Under Sodeke in Abeokuta, the society was restructured along the model of the Oyo army with its hierarchy of officers. Balogun Sodeke organised the olorogun society at federal and local levels. Sodeke himself was the Balogun and commander in chief of the Egba army. Chief Apati of Kemta succeeded Degeshi as Seriki after his death,

---

62 Ibid, p. 24.

Lumloye of Ilugun in Oke-Ona, was appointed Otun (commader of the right wing), while chief Agbo of Gbagura, was made the Osi (commander of the left wing) of the all Egba forces.[63] The new high command was now made the representative of all the Egba sections.

Nonetheless, the old township Ologun remained. Many war chiefs did not have federal titles. They merely took township titles until there were vacancies in the federal high command. The olorogun of each township was responsible for its administration while the central olorogun concerned itself with matters affecting Egbaland as a whole. A central olorogun house was built behind Sodeke's house where the central olorogun chiefs discussed matters ranging from the appointment of military officers, defence, and military expeditions, to foreign policy. The central olorogun council also decided on matters referred to it from the township or local olorogun councils. Decisions reached at the central olorogun council were taken to the various Egba townships for implementation. Sodeke led the olorogun and presided over its central council meetings until his death in 1845.[64] Thus under Balogun Sodeke, as in the days of Lisabi, the olorogun became an instrument of political cohesion in Egbaland.

---

63 Ibid, p. 21.

64 Falola and Oguntomisin, 122.

The olorogun under Balogun Sodeke led the Egba when there was no civil authority in Abeokuta before any Egba section appointed civil heads. The government presided over by Balogun Sodeke in the exigency of the period was essentially military which made the commander-in-chief to be very powerful. In spite of the awesome power possessed by Sodeke, he was unlike Kurunmi of Ijaiye, far from being autocratic. It has been argued that the federal nature of the Egba military government, especially the representative structure of the central olorogun council meant that decisions reached at the council represented the wishes of all sections of the Egba in Abeokuta. In addition, the presence of such powerful men as Deliyi, the Balogun of Ijemo, Apati of Kemta, Ogunbona, and Ogundipe Alatishe, provided adequate checks on Sodeke.[65]

Just as in Ibadan, rivalry was very common among these chiefs. Ajisafe noted how Chief Deliyi once challenged the supremacy of Sodeke as the overall head of the Egba in Abeokuta, an incident that would have resulted into serious breakdown of law and order but for the tact of Tejuoso, an Ifa priest, who awarded the honour to Sodeke, but fined him because he risked the safety of the new town under him in civil strife.[66] After this incident, his supremacy was no longer challenged by any of his colleagues.

---

65 Ibid.

66 Ajisafe, op cit.

The olorogun institution under Sodeke also influenced the development of civil authority in Abeokuta. Balogun Sodeke realised that a civil constitution must be established as soon as the emergency which gave rise to the olorogun was over. A new civil authority, under Losi, a descendant of an Alake in the Egba forest was put in place as an attempt to organise an all Egba Ogboni. A grand lodge (Ile Ogboni Egba) was built at Itoko and its officers were drawn from various townships of the Egba Alake section.[67] The idea of a federal civil authority in the 1830s was new and also short-lived, as Losi, the Oluwo of the all Egba Ogboni, built an Ogboni lodge at Ake his own quarters. Other all Egba Ogboni leaders followed suit in their various quarters but these civil authorities were all overshadowed by the olorogun.

The liberated Egba who had been set free at Sierra Leone by the British Naval Squadron were encouraged to return to Abeokuta as a result of the peace provided by the olorogun under Sodeke. By 1842, their population had risen to more than five hundred. Balogun Sodeke allowed them to practice their own religion, appoint their own headmen, and administer their own community. It was on their advice that Sodeke favourably received Christian missionaries, such as Thomas Birch Freeman (1842), and Henry Townsend

---

67 Biobaku, op cit.

(1843).[68] The favourable disposition of Sodeke to the Christian missionaries created a very conducive atmosphere for the work of the missionaries in Abeokuta, when they finally decided to settle down even after the death of Sodeke in 1845.

Shortly before the death of Balogun Sodeke, the cordial relationship between the Egba and the Ota broke down. It has been argued that the Ajano of Ota "demanded from the Egba an exorbitant price for his friendship that safeguarded their trade route to Lagos."[69] The Egba took up the challenge and sent a force under Lumloye, the Otun Egba, to reduce Ota. Ibadan, Kosoko of Lagos, and Ado, had offered to help Ota, but the Egba quickly surrounded Ota in such a way that prevented Ota from receiving the desired help from its allies. After a long siege that weakened Ota's resistance, the Egba stormed the town and took it in 1842. The Ota people were allowed to remain in the town for as long as they did not rebuild the town walls, and the Egba also placed an Ajele there to collect tribute for the Egba.[70]

After the fall of Ota, Lumloye wanted to proceed to Ado but Sodeke disagreed. He realised that unlimited expansion in the Egbado region might bring the Egba into an unnecessary clash with Dahomey. The conquest

---

68 Falola and Oguntomisin, op cit.

69 Biobaku, op cit.

70 Ibid.

of Ota was necessary as it had kept the trade route to Lagos as far as Ebute-Meta open. Balogun Sodeke was always mindful of the danger from Ibadan and did not want the Egba forces to be tied down elsewhere in case the Ibadan re-appear from the north. Hence he overruled Lumloye who died shortly after his return to Abeokuta. A small force sufficient to continue a siege but not to conquer Ado was therefore left outside the town.[71]

Moreover, renewed hostility between Abeokuta and Ado-Odo resulted in the Egba declaring war on Ado-Odo. The Egba accused Ado-Odo of interfering with Egba trading activities along the Badagry route. Dahomey being on good relations with Ado-Odo saw the Egba siege as an opportunity to attack Abeokuta on the grounds that Ado-Odo was tributary to Porto Novo. Gezo (the Leopard) led the invasion himself, but he underestimated the Egba. The Egba forces led by Ayikondu met Dahomey at Imojulu and drove Dahomey back. Gezo (their king) narrowly escaped capture, while his war charms, stool, and royal umbrella made from the skins of different animals were seized by the Egba.[72] The Egba took these trophies to Abeokuta and Dahomey vowed to regain them at all cost.

Reverend Samuel Johnson has argued that Dahomey negotiated the return of the items to Dahomey all to no

---

71 Ibid.

72 T.I. Tunde *A Victim of the Egba Dahomey Military Confrontations (1862-1951)* (Ibadan: International Publishers Limited, 1998): 23.

avail as they had been destroyed. King Gezo was said to have vowed that he would not live without the destruction of Abeokuta.[73]

After the defeat of Dahomey, the Egba continued their siege of Ado-Odo more actively such that when Henry Townsend returned from England, he could not proceed immediately to Abeokuta, because the Egba had blocked the route. So, Townsend had to negotiate with the authorities in Abeokuta for safe conduct. While negotiating for this, Sodeke died.

The death of Sodeke raised serious constitutional issues and this protracted Townsend's negotiations with the Egba. Sodeke had welcomed the advent of Christianity and European influence. He had applied the necessary restraint on the Ologun, without which they would have endangered the new settlement by dissipating their energies on slave raiding. Although Balogun Sodeke's leadership lacked traditional sanction, he proved to be a leader of the highest calibre.

The demise of Balogun Sodeke brought about a decline in the fortune of the Balogun institution in Egbaland. His demise resulted in the factionalisation of the olorogun institution in Abeokuta. Apati the Seriki, expected to succeed to the vacant office of the Balogun of the Egba because he had been next in rank to Sodeke. However, Ayikondu the Balogun of Igbein was chosen instead in conformity with the traditional practice

---

73 Ibid.

whereby Igbein supplied the supreme commander of the Egba armies, which dated back to Lisabi's time.[74]

Since the the Egba's dispersal from their forest, township affiliations had been ignored in the choice of federal Ologun. Yisa of Itoko and Sodeke of Iporo had held the office at different times. Only once was the holder of the office (Sodeke) challenged by Deliyi of Ijemo. In the more settled state of affairs in 1845, the Igbein people asserted their traditional privilege to the title of Balogun of Egbaland which they refused to surrender to Apati, a Kemta chief. Moreover, Apati was believed to be from a slave lineage. Apati's real name was believed to be Humpati. His father was an Egun slave while his mother was of Oyo descent.[75]

Although Ayikondu offered to step down when Apati vigorously asserted his right to succeed Sodeke, the people of Igbein eventually kept their traditional title, while Apati imported a higher rank which satisfied his pride. He purchased the Oyo imperial title of Bashorun from Oluyole its holder in Ibadan. At about the same time, Anoba of Ago-Ika in Gbagura, purchased the title of Aare Ona Kakanfo from Kurunmi of Ijaiye.[76] Biobaku has argued that the titles were personal to their holders and that their introduction to Egbaland was a concession to "over-mightiness, and the innovation

---

74 Biobaku, ibid.

75 Ibid.

76 Ibid.

encouraged extra-constitutional actions on the part of the Ologun whose pretensions were not recognized within the framework of the Egba traditional constitution."[77]

However, neither Apati nor Ayikondu was able to succeed to Sodeke's prestige and leading position among the Egba. The civil authorities regained some influence. Thus Henry Townsend had to negotiate his safe conduct with both the leaders of the Ologun and the Ogboni. Apart from writing a letter to Apati the Bashorun, and Okukenu, the Sagbua of Ake, Townsend also did a letter to Ogunbonna, the Balogun of Ikija, another influential chief.

Moreover, events in Lagos, after the demise of Sodeke, revealed the decline in the power of the Ologun further. When Akitoye ascended the throne in 1841, he recalled all exiles including his ambitious nephew, Kosoko, who lived in Porto Novo and Whydah, where he became acquainted with Portuguese slave dealers. So when in 1845, Akitoye decided to admit the English to Lagos, abolish the slave trade, and promote legitimate commerce, Kosoko placed himself at the head of the supporters of slave trade on the island and rebelled against his mild uncle.

After a twelve day civil war, Akitoye was defeated by Kosoko, and many of Akitoye's followers were captured and slain. Akitoye therefore took refuge in

---

[77] Ibid.

Abeokuta with friends and relations.[78] A pro-Kosoko's party in Abeokuta opposed Akitoye's stay and demanded his head to be sent to Kosoko in Lagos. Okukenu the Sagbua of Ake, and the head of the Ogboni provided refuge for Akitoye, in his own township of Ake. The Ogboni supported Akitoye not only because his mother was an Egba, but also because he opposed slave trade while the leading Ologun supported Kosoko because of his support for slave trade.[79]

Hence, the question of asylum for Akitoye created a rift in Abeokuta after the demise of Sodeke, as a result of which the pro-Kosoko party led by Basorun Apati attacked the Ake people by burning their houses. The people of Ake in consequence moved and Ake quarter was established on its present site which was then on the outskirts of the town.

The support of the leading Ologun for slave trade resulted in the Abaka raid of 1846. According to Biobaku, the raid on Abaka in Oke-Ogun "might be explained as the action of a slave-trade party who wanted to carry on business with Domingo Martinez at Badagry"[80] The Abaka raid illustrated further the

---

78 A.B. Aderibigbe, "Early History of Lagos" in A. B. Aderibigbe, editor, *Lagos: The Development of An African City*, (Lagos, Longman, 1975), p. 1-26.

78 H.B. Harunah, "Lagos – Abeokuta Relations in 19th Century Yorubaland" in A. Adefuye, editor, et al, *History of the Peoples of Lagos State*, (Lagos: Lantern Books, 1987), p, 199.

80 Biobaku, op cit.

division and weakness of the Egba state. The leading Ologun and their forces were now a law unto themselves. The slave trade party was in the ascendancy among the Ologun at this time. It completely disregarded the official policy of the Egba, which until the death of Sodeke, had been against the slave trade. After the Abaka raid, fresh agitation against Akitoye broke out, and Okukenu, the Sagbua of Ake, judged it best to allow Akitoye to leave Abeokuta. Akitoye was therefore, escorted to the frontier of the town of Imowo and handed over to the people of Badagry, who were charged to protect him from Kosoko or risk the wrath of the Egba.[81]

By the middle of the nineteenth century, the Ologun institution in Abeokuta was no longer as powerful as it was under Balogun Sodeke. In 1848, when Henry Townsend returned to England, it was clear that the civil authorities under Okukenu, were in the ascendancy as Townsend took a letter from Okukenu, the Sagbua of Ake, and chiefs of Abeokuta, to Queen Victoria. The Egba used the letter to profess hatred for the slave trade and identified Lagos as its stronghold. The Egba wanted to navigate the Lagos lagoon and link Abeokuta to the coast through the Ogun River.[82] The land route from Badagry via Ado-Odo to Abeokuta was becoming more and more unsatisfactory and must be replaced by an

---

82 Ibid.

83 Ibid, p. 35.

inland water-way which would be within Egba jurisdiction. In this way, the missions and traders would receive their stores and supplies in safety, and the Egba a more secure trade route. Only the British preventive squadron could guarantee this.

After Henry Townsend's return to Abeokuta from England in 1850, the immediate problem confronting the Egba was the survival of Abeokuta against Dahomean attack. Aside from the persecution of the Christians especially at Itoku, in 1848-49, in 1850, (at Igbore), the slave trade and its proponents were still active. This was as a result of the absence of a central authority, which Ologun adequately provided under Sodeke. Despite the disagreement between the leading Ologun and the civil authorities in Abeokuta, at a meeting with Consul Beecroft where Sokenu the Seriki, was the spokesperson, the Egba jointly requested for the fortification of their town, and also suggested that Akitoye be reinstated at Lagos.[83]

While the British were still thinking about the reinstatement of Akitoye, Dahomey attacked Abeokuta, on March 3, 1851, just two days after the installation of Somoye as the Basorun.[84] Before Dahomey attacked Abeokuta, its soldiers had encamped at Isaga, in the Egbado country where the people under their king, Asade Okogan, had feigned submission and at the same

---

84 Ibid, p. 43.

85 Apati, the Basorun, died in 1849. This cleared the way for Somoye, a princely Ologun to assume the mantle of leadership.

time warned the Egba of the approaching army. The Isaga people also advised the Dahomey soldiers to attack Abeokuta in the daylight instead of under the cover of darkness and led them to wade through the Ogun River at a deep point where their powder was lost or became wet.[85]

The actual attack was launched upon the Aro gate where the Isaga had directed them. The wall around the Aro gate had just been repaired by Okukenu, the Sagbua of Ake, and other pro-missionary chiefs. Although the Dahomean soldiers approached Abeokuta in a stolid and discipline manner, firing on their enemies with grim determination, the Egba soon discovered to their chagrin that foremost among their assailants were the Amazons and were revolted at the thought of yielding to women. Sokenu, the Seriki, led an out-flanking move which soon demoralized the besiegers. The attempt of Akati, the commander of the Dahomean forces, to rally round his demoralized troops proved abortive. He perished in this attempt and his leaderless forces broke into a retreat. The retreating forces were pursued by the Egba who arrived Isaga just in time to save the people of Isaga from punishment for their deceit. The retreating forces never lost their cohesion as they recrossed the Yewa River, and laid waste to Egba farms on their way and took some prisoners home.[86]

---

86 Tella, p. 24-26.

87 Biobaku, p. 44.

The perennial difficulty at Abeokuta since the death of Balogun Sodeke had been the absence of a strong central authority. In its place there was a plethora of chiefs and authorities. Henry Townsend succeeded in persuading the Egba authorities to resuscitate the defunct title of the Alake. The missionaries favoured a strong king who could control the activities of the Ologun and lend executive support to the missionary programme of agricultural regeneration of the area. Their candidate was Ogunbonna. After he had however, planted the traditional shade trees at the Afin at Ake, the Egba people recalled the incident in which he had denied his Egba nationality and rejected him. Biobaku has, however, argued that the Ologun actually preferred a weak candidate and so defeated Henry Townsend's real aim of ensuring their subordination.[87] The Losi of Ake was chosen but he died before a general agreement could be reached. Okukenu, the Sagbua of Ake, was therefore, elected in 1854, as the first Alake in Abeokuta.[88] In real terms, Okukenu transformed into the Alake without any appreciable increase in his authority. No doubt the diminishing power of the Ologun was clearly aided by the Ologun's selfishness. The leaderdership of the Ologun abhorred a strong centre that would prevent the Ologun to wield and use power as it suited their whims and caprices. Under Sodeke, members of the military were prevented from being

---

88 Ibid. p. 52.

89 Ajisafe, op cit.

over-bearing subjects. From time to time, they were checkmated from engaging in any military recklessness by Sodeke.

The death of Okukenu on September 4, 1862, resulted in the appointment of Basorun Somoye as regent and was accorded the royal greeting of Kabiyesi without any serious change in the fortunes of the Ologun. In view of the Makun War, Somoye could not exercise any control over the Ologun. Robbery was rife, and trade was disrupted. In addition, after the destruction of Ijaiye on March 18, 1862, the Ijaiye refugees had congregated at a separate quarter in Abeokuta, thus swelling the rank and file of Ologun in Abeokuta at the detriment of adequate central authority.

The disagreement among the Ologun did not help matters at all. This affected so many things in Abeokuta at this time. It reflected in the *Ifole* of 1867, where there was no Ologun of any means to restrain the activities of the mob in Abeokuta. It was only at Ikija that the Christians were saved by Ogundipe Alatushe. In other sections of Abeokuta, the mob had a field day and the missionaries and the converts suffered a great loss. The death of Bashorun Somoye in 1868, worsened matters as the Ologun supported two rival candidates, thus fuelling the embers of discontent in Abeokuta. One of the candidates (Ademola) eventually got installed by the

Ogboni in 1869.[89] This however did not deter the other group from installing their own candidate (Oyekan). The result was serious factionalisation of the Ologun and the lack of unity in Abeokuta.

The rift in Abeokuta politics resulting from the conflict over the choice of Alake among the Ologun lingered for about three decades. Again, there was the emergence of herculean subjects, as some powerful Ologun dominated Abeokuta politics even when there were sitting Obas. First, it was Ogundipe Alatishe who dominated the politics of Abeokuta until his death in 1887; second, there was the rule of the triumvate – Chief Osundare, addressed as Oba Nlado of Kemta, who had at times rivalled Ogundipe, Ogundeyi Magaji of Iporo, who later assumed the title of Basorun, and Sorunke the Jagunna of Igbein, who was the Balogun of Abeokuta. Third, there was the dominance of Aboaba, the Balogun of Abeokuta.[90] During this time, the Ologun split internally. Even when Chief Aboaba of Igbein became the dominant power in Abeokuta, the Ologun was still factionalised and so, the Ologun institution could not play the desired role as played by Sodeke, who was the last Balogun that wielded effective power over the whole of Abeokuta.

Balogun institution in twentieth century Abeokuta

---

90 A. Pallinder-Law, "Government in Abeokuta with Special Reference to the Period of the E.U.G.", PhD thesis, Goteburg, (1972), p. 52.

91 Ibid, p. 59.

No doubt, the Balogun institution in twentieth century Abeokuta, was not as effective as it was in the preceding era, especially from the third decade of the nineteenth century up till the death of Balogun Sodeke. The assumption of the office of Balogun by Chief Aboaba did not bring any significant change to the institution in spite of the power and wealth of Aboaba. The internal division among the Ologun still remained. Besides, the Igbein people under Balogun Sorunke and Aboaba had claimed the Ogun River as belonging to the Igbein township and as such claimed the duties from the Isheri customs. This created a lot of confusion in the latter part of the nineteenth century in Abeokuta, to the extent that Balogun Aboaba was deported to Ibadan in 1898.

However, the ascension of Gbadebo as Alake, in 1898, coupled with the re-organisation of the Egba Government (E.U.G.), brought a serious setback to the Balogun institution in Abeokuta. Alake Gbadebo was a very powerful king who was wise, bold, and very strict. His character and conduct were said to have incurred the displeasure of the people of Egbaland.[91] The activities of the Lagos government at this time aided the power and prestige of Alake Gbadebo at the expense of the Balogun institution. The government of Lagos supported Gbadebo against any internal division. The re-organisation of the Egba government supported by the Lagos government was based on the authority of the Alake, while Aboaba and the Seriki of Abeokuta, including the sectional Oba were recognised as advisers

---

92 Ajisafe, op cit.

to the Alake in Council.⁹² So, it became more and more difficult if not impossible for the Ologun to play a prominent role in Abeokuta politics, especially after the Ijebu expedition of 1892, and the signing of the Treaty of Friendship and Commerce with Lagos by Abeokuta.

In addition, the issue of external war had become a thing of the past by the twentieth century. The Dahomean menace which was a serious threat to Abeokuta had ceased in 1875, when the Egba fought the forces of Dahomey for the months of March, April and May, before Dahomey could be defeated successfully and finally.⁹³

Thus, the continuous menace of Dahomey which started in 1844, finally came to an end in 1875. Hence, the opportunity used by the Ologun to gain ascendancy among the Egba was removed completely. By the end of the nineteenth century, all external aggression against the Egba people had ceased. Nonetheless, internal problems such as the Itori crisis of 1901, the Kemta trouble of 1903, the Ijemo massacre of 1914, the Adubi rising of 1918, and the disturbance of 1947-48, still occurred in Abeokuta.⁹⁴

The re-organisation of the Egba government in the name of the Egba United Government (E. U. G.), the 1898 agreement with Sir MaCallum, and the annexation of Abeokuta by Lord Lugard after the Ijemo massacre of 1914, brought about a stop in the overbearing authority

---

93 Pallinder- Law, p. 59.

94 Ajisafe, p. 133-134.

95 G.O. Davies, "The politics of interregnum in Egbaland 1947-48."

of the Ologun in Abeokuta. Their prominence as war chiefs directing affairs in Abeokuta, effectively ceased in the more settled situation of the twentieth century where the Egba government now functioned as part and parcel of the colonial administration in Nigeria. The Ologun's traditional role as the military cadre now underwent a transformation to being ceremonial institution. The Balogun institution was not discontinued, but its military prowess was no longer a criterion for the office. Prominent indigenes of Abeokuta were honoured from time to time with military offices, without necessarily being military officers.

It should be noted that declarations relating to the appointment of suitable candidates for the six Ologun chieftaincy titles in Abeokuta, were approved by the colonial government on November 12, 1958. These Ologun chieftaincy titles were: Balogun Egba (zoned to Egba Alake section); Otun Egba (zoned to Oke-Ona section); Osi Egba (zoned to Gbagura section); Ekerin Egba (zoned to Owu section); Seriki Egba (zoned to Egba-Alake section); and Ashipa Egba (zoned to Egba-Alake section).[95]

The holders of these offices must have become the Balogun in their various towns before they could be appointed to the central Ologun offices. Oral investigation revealed that since performance in warfare or military prowess is no longer a criterion, the contribution of the recipients to their various townships

---

96 Lisabi Day Celebration, Souvenir Programme, p. 31.

in particular and Abeokuta in general was the raison d'être for such conferment.[96]

Conclusion

This chapter has examined the institution of the Balogun chieftaincy among the Egba from its inception up till the twentieth century. It has been demonstrated that the Balogun institution among the Egba underwent various stages before it was finally demilitarized and institutionalised. It has been argued that Lisabi initiated the process through which the Balogun chieftaincy later became institutionalised among the Egba. It has also been shown that Yisa, an Itoko man was the first person to assume the title of Balogun in recorded Egba history. Traditionally, the Egba war chief was known as Jagunna, a title the Egba war chief assumed until the Egba's sojourn at Ibadan, where they picked the title of Balogun.

However, the Balogun institution underwent changing fortunes in the period under study. From the time of Lisabi, through Yisa of Itoko, Lamodi, and sodeke, the institution provided effective military and dynamic political leadership for the Egba at various crucial periods when they were in need of liberation from political servitude first under the yoke of Oyo; and then under the tyranny of the allied forces at Ibadan; and later for defence against the allied forces of Ijebu and Ibadan, at the Owiwi War; and the allied forces of

---

97 In discussion with the author by several informants.

Ibadan, Ijaiye, and Abemo, at the Arakanga War; and the Dahomean menace in the 1840s.

Under Sodeke, the Egba in Abeokuta were able to build a new home that repelled the attacks of all their neighbours and emerged as one of the successor states to the Old Oyo Empire. Indeed, Lisabi, Yisa, Lamodi, and Sodeke, were not only able to defend the Egba against their enemies, but also succeeded in infusing a sense of unity into the Egba through their leadership qualities, and through their military acumen, they led the Egba to achieve an imperial offensive and resounding success.

The post-Sodeke period, however, brought about a decline in the fortunes in the Balogun institution. The unity of purpose that characterised the earlier era was dumped for selfish reasons. The Ologun became divided among themselves at the expense of the Balogun institution. Thus none of the Baloguns that succeeded Sodeke could not control the Ologun as a group. Again those who emerged as Balogun after Sodeke were not necessarily the most powerful or important Ologun.

The importation of the title of Basorun into the military hierarchy of the Egba in Abeokuta did not help matters. Those who eventually emerged as Balogun were not as powerful as the Basorun under Apati, Somoye, or Ogundeyi Magaji. This development created serious cleavage in the Balogun institution. The type of leadership provided by the Balogun institution under the status quo ante was non-existent in the post-Sodeke period.

Consequently, the civil authorities started sharing power with the military in Abeokuta from the 1840s until the end of the nineteenth century, when political expediency finally sealed the fate of the Ologun in any meaningful power sharing with the civil authorities as the Ologun now functioned as advisers in the Alake council. Thus, the military institution moved from a position of prominence and reverence to one of insignificance towards the end of the nineteenth century.

186   The Balogun in Yorubaland...

7
The Changing Status of Military Chiefs in Ijeshaland
Monsuru Muritala

Introduction

In Yorubaland during the pre-colonial and colonial periods, important personalities in society were recognized and honoured with chieftaincy titles. These titles can be classified into hereditary, traditional and open titles, which are similar in some societies and settlements, but different in designation and responsibilities from one community to another. While it is impossible to define 'chief' in pre-colonial terms, it is possible to define it in colonial terms.[1] This is because the title chief under the British colonial rule was used to designate African in positions of authority.

The power, influence and designation of these chiefs began to change under colonial rule and continues to change right to the present time. It is within this purview that this paper examines the changing status of

---

1 M. Crowder, and O.Ikime, editors, *West African Chiefs: Their Changing Status under Colonial Rule and Independence*, (Ile Ife: University of Ife press, 970), p. x.

the military chiefs in Yorubaland, with special focus on Ijeshaland.

Political structure of Ijeshaland in historical perspective

Ijeshaland lies in the Yoruba-speaking region of southwestern Nigeria, around the upper reaches of the Oshun, Shasha, and Oni rivers which flow south and southwest to the Lagos Lagoon, some hundred miles away.[2] Its location in the forest, adjacent to the savannah, has been the most important geographical parameter of Ijesha history. Ijeshaland lies in the rainforest of northeastern Yorubaland, a very beautiful landscape, with hills ranging from 900 feet in the forest of Oni valley to around 300 feet above sea level as in Imo hill and 1800 feet in the hills around Okemesi, towards the north, and about 1,900 feet in Olumiririn Waterfalls and others around Erinmo, forming the boundary with Efon Alaaye and other allies in Ekiti and Igbominaland.[3] Though there is evidence that human settlements in some parts of the deep rain forest to the south is ancient,[4] the general movement of the Ijesha

---

2 J.D.Y.Peel, *Ijeshas and Nigerians: The Incorporation of a Yoruba Kingdom, 1890s-1970s*, (Cambridge: University Press, 1983), p.19.

3 A. Agunlejika, *Ijesha Chronicles: A historiographic Tribute*, (Lagos: Itunuade Publishing, 2011), p.13.

4 See T. Shaw. *Nigeria: its Archaeology and Early History*, London (1978), p. 45-51.

settlement seems to have been from the drier and more open northern parts of the forest southwards.

Ilesha, situated more or less in the centre of the two Ijesha divisions (now called Obokun and Atakumosa local government areas) was probably founded about the early sixteenth century; but it was apparently not the earliest center of the kingdom.[5]

It has been established that the traditions of the foundation of the Ilesha, as with the other major kingdoms of the region, take the form of a dynastic migration from Ile-Ife, the sacred origins of the Yoruba people.[6] Five or six of the early rulers in the dynasty are associated with places other than Ilesha, particularly, in and around Ibokun, some fourteen miles to the north.[7] The foundation of Owa Obokun Adimula monarchical dynasty, both ancient and modern, can be traced to Ajibogun Orun Aganiyeye Ekun, the great progenitor of the Ijesha people whose memorial statue can be seen at the Ilesha city centre. The historical account has it that after his heroic fetching of the ocean waters to heal his father, Odua Olofin-Aye of old age blindness, he became

---

5 J.D.Y. Peel, "Kings, titles and quarters: a conjectural history of Ilesha: the traditions review", *History in Africa*, vol.6, (1979), p. 53-109.

6 Peel, 1983, p. 19.

7 P.A. Francis, "Power and Order: a study of litigation in a Yoruba Community", Unpublished Ph.D thesis, Liverpool, (1981), cited in Peel, *Ijeshas and Nigerians....* p.19.

the lord of a very vast territory today known as Ijeshaland.[8]

In like manner, the successors to the throne of the Ijesha kingdom after the demise of Owa Obokun Adimula, followed in his footsteps and engaged in military exploits that incorporated many towns and villages into the Ijesha kingdom. Prominent among these are Owa Obokun Obarabara Olokun-Eshin, Owa Obokun Adimula Owaluse, Owa Obokun Adimula Owari and Owa Obokun Adimula Atakumosa.

It was Adimula Atakumosa who captured and took possession of Osi—an ancient kingdom located within Ondo territory. In fact, it has been argued that Owa Obokun Adimula Owari and Owaluse transformed and reshaped the Ijesha traditional government, to include military supervisors, under Ajaka Ajibogun, the commander- in-chief of the Ijesha armed forces.[9] In its earlier days, before Ilesha outstripped all other Ijesha settlements in size and power, the kingdom might have been more of a federation, with the *owa* as a kind of primus inter pares.[10]

The political structure of Ijesahaland comprised six *Agbanla*, four members of the Aare council of royal

---

8 A. Agunlejika, *Ijesha Chronicles: A historiographic tribute*, (Lagos: Itunuade Publishing, 2011), p.15.

9 Ibid. p.17.

10 Ibid. p.20.

counsellors and administrators; and three Elegbe military war commanders.

The Agbanla included Obaala of Ilesha, Ogboni of Ibokun, Ogboni of Ijebu-jesa, Ogboni of Ipole, Ogboni of Ilesha and Obaodo of Ilesha. The Agbanla cadreorder is also referred to as the Agba-Ijesa — the Ijesha parliament of the first realm established by Owa Obokun Adimula Owaluse. In fact, they are also known as *iwarefa*. Also important in the political administration of the kingdom are the four members of the Aare council of royal counsellors and administrators. They are Odole of Ilesha, Risawe of Ilesha, Saloro of Ilesha and Arapate of Ilesha.

The last tier in the political structure are the Elegbe military war commanders: the Lejoka of Ilesha, the Loro of Ilesha and the Lejofi of Ilesha.[11] It is important to mention that these thirteen wise men represent a vast variety of opinions from every nook and cranny of the Ijesa Obokun kingdom. The Ijesa Obokun council of kingmakers is part of this political structure and to date the traditional composition has remained the same.

The inference from the pattern of the foundation of the kingdom is that the geopolitical expansion of the kingdom was predicated on conquest and military exploits of the founding fathers, who were warriors. Thus, the following posers may be raised, at what point did the role of the commander-in chief of the armed

---

11 Agunlejika, p.37.

forces shift from the king to the military chiefs? What role did the Yoruba internecine wars of the nineteenth century play in the changing fortunes of the military class in Ijeshaland? Did the Oyo Empire influence the military prowess and changing fortunes of the military class? What has become of the titles of the warlords in modern times? This chapter will therefore examine the roles of the military class and the changing fortunes of military chiefs in Ijeshaland, from the pre-colonial to post- colonial period.

Warlords and chieftaincy titles in Ijeshaland

In most Yoruba kingdom, the Balogun in the pre-colonial and colonial period was synonymous with the head or leader of the military group. In other words, the Balogun refers to the person who possessed the courage, charms and military prowess to guarantee the security of life and property in his society. This nomenclature actually became popularised as a result of the military exploits of the Ibadan people, where a large number of the people in the society, especially slaves and *iwofa*, worked for warriors.[12] The military chiefs in Ibadan were always looking for excuses to wage war so as to acquire wealth and increase their followers. It was an established custom for a new Balogun to attack a town and be successful if he wanted to retain the people's confidence, demonstrate his ability to protect them,

---

12 T. Falola, *The Political Economy of a Pre-colonial African State: Ibadan, 1830-1900*,(Ile-Ife: University of Ife Press, 1984), p.194.

acquire wealth and gain more followers.[13] Others, not directly in their service had to contribute to support them. It was compulsory for everybody to have a *babaogun*, "father-protector" who must be obeyed. The people had to give part of their produce to the babaogun, and follow him to war when called upon to do so.[14] They also constituted his force when he wanted to build or repair his compound, clear or construct roads or carry out any other important task. The inference here is that, the title of Babaogun as popularized by the Ibadan people, later transformed to Balogun, which was embraced by some Yoruba speaking societies to honour their warlords.

In the case of Ijeshaland however, the warlords were referred to as Elegbe—war commanders, whose titles as mentioned earlier, are Lejoka, Lejofi and Loro. This of course, is a departure from the chieftaincy titles synonymous with warriors in Yoruba societies; especially the title of Balogun. However, in spite of these differences in nomenclature, the title holders of Lejoka, Lejofi and Loro in Ijeshaland shared similar characteristics with the Balogun of Ibadan. The chiefs in pre-colonial and colonial Ilesha wielded enormous power. For instance, in the mid-nineteenth century, the chiefs (probably the Elegbe) are said to have levied tolls of two cowries per traveller at each of Ilesha's seven

---

13 Ibid, p.128.

14 Ibid

gates.[15] Suffice to say that the military leaders performed the function of revenue collectors, aside from fighting. Also, in the late nineteenth century, traders throughout Yorubaland lodged with chiefs and gave them presents in return for lodging and protection.

In the late 1890s, Lejofi Esan, an Ilesha chief, for example, acted as host to Ilorin traders, who stayed in his house for several weeks at a time and from whom he received cloth, tobacco, ostrich feathers and other gifts; if he received two cloths, he would send one as a present to the *Owa*.[16]

The military chiefs devised a way in which the power of their people was mobilised to maintain the title system. The rewards of military success—booty and slaves (*eru*)—won by a citizen army organized under quarter chiefs, was divided in such a way as to support the established hierarchy. Though the exact details for Ilesha before the nineteenth-century upheavals are not available, it is likely that something like the Oyo-Yoruba convention prevailed: one-third of captives to the Owa, one third to the chiefs, one third to the ordinary citizen-

---

15 NAI, CMS paper1/17, P.J. Meffre, account of 'a Brasilian' Ijesha trader, in the valuable documents.'Towns destroyed by the Ibadans in Ijesha Country', (1882), p.5.

16 Oral interview, Reverend D.B. Esan, son of Lejofi, 23 Feb.1974, cited in J.D.Y. Peel, (1983), p.45.

soldiers.[17] In fact, so large a body of slaves belonged to the Owa that in the 1890s, any individual around the town who was not known to the citizens would be considered an eru Owa.[18]

Ijesha traditions suggest that the periods of successful war had a destabilizing effect on the relations between the Owa and his subjects, producing tyranny on the one hand and rebellious reaction on the other; for the sudden accession of slaves through the centre would have encouraged those in political authority to ignore the claims of their ordinary constituents.[19]

If the period of boom and successful military campaigns attracted more slaves, who were incorporated into the society, then what happened to the military class or war lords during the Yoruba internecine wars? The examination of the changing fortunes of the war lords in Ijeshaland during the nineteenth century Yoruba civil wars will illuminate the temporary changes in the political structure of Ijeshaland and the subsequent change in status of the war lords in the colonial and post-colonial periods.

---

17 See A.G. Hopkins, editor, (1910), A report on the Yoruba (a document prepared for the British authorities by six educated Yoruba , of whom one, C.A.Sapara Williams was of Ijesha origin)

18 Peel, 1983, p.45.

19 Ibid.

Yoruba Internecine wars and the changing status of Ijesha war chiefs

By 1831, the great Oyo Empire had collapsed. Consequently, Ibadan—one of the towns which emerged from the ruins of Oyo, saw it as an opportunity to take control of the whole Yoruba nation. It is on record that after a short period of rest, Ibadan started their military exploits which began with the recruitment of young and energetic men from all over Yorubaland; these included Ijesa's Ogedengbe Agbogungboro who hailed from Atorin and Fabunmi Oraralada of Okemesi.[20] The recruitment of these men by Ibadan marked the beginning of Ibadan influence in the political structure of the Ijeshas, especially the military aspect. As it will be recalled, by the 1840s, Ibadan started her expansionist campaign and incursion into the north of the Ijesha Obokun Kingdom and also into Ekiti territories but Ilesha remained untouched. In fact, the first European visitors in 1858 found Ilesha itself in good order, its defenses well-maintained, but its authorities intensely wary.[21]

In spite of this state of fortification, Ilesha was still capable of military initiatives in pursuit of traditional objectives. In 1860-62, when Ibadan was occupied far away in the Ijaiye war, Ijesha forces subjugated Efon and

---

20 Agunlejika, p, 6.

21 W.H. Clarke. *Travels and Explorations in Yorubaland*, (Ibadan: Ibadan University press, 1972), p.125.

Ogotun in Western Ekiti.[22] Emboldened by its success, the Ijesha then decided to try to recover Igbajo, the largest of their former subordinate towns in the north. Igbajo called to Ibadan for aid and the Ijesha, weakened by dissension among her chiefs, suffered a severe defeat in 1867.[23] Consequently, Ilesha became a town to be conquered by Ibadan.

By 1870, the continued attacks of Ibadan on Ilesha finally paid off when the city was abandoned by its defenders.[24] A further humiliation followed. The Owa who was captured was accidentally drowned in the river Oshun on his way to Ibadan. Thus, the capture of Ilesha, 'being a town of great strength, both in its fortifications and its able-bodied citizens', as Johnson put it, marked the high point of Ibadan's strength in Yoruba country.[25]

This was followed by a period of internal political turbulence which witnessed the rebellion of a body of young warriors called Ipaiye led by Ogedengbe.[26] Ogedengbe and the Ipaiye drove a wedge between

---

22 S.A. Akintoye, *Revolution and Power Politics in Yorubaland, 1840-1893: Ibadan Expansion and the Rise of Ekiti Parapo,* (London, University of London Press, 1971).

23 Peel, 1983, p.77.

24 Ibid, p.79.

25 S. Johnson, *History of the Yorubas from the Earliest Times to the Beginning of the British Protectorate,* (Lagos: CMS Bookshops, 1921), p.368-71.

26 Peel, 1983, p.79.

Odole Ariyansule and his allies by burning the houses of his allies and blaming him for it; they suborned women who drowned out the Odole's protests at a public meeting by shouts of *ole* (thief!). Ariyansunle left the meeting in anger. When his people began to desert him, he killed himself, and the Ipaiye sacked his house.[27] After the exit of the Odole Ariyansunle, the youthful Ipaiye militant movement had an overriding influence in the Ijesha Obokun polity.[28] It will be recalled that the leader of the Ipaiye movement, Seriki Ogedengbe Agbogungboro had earlier undergone some military training in Ibadan.

The successful involvement of the Ipaiye militant youths in the mainstream of Ijesha Obokun polity climaxed in 1870. By then, the full blown Kiriji intra tribal war had ensued between the Ibadan (under the control of Aare Latosa of Ibadan), Ijeshas and allies: Ekitis and Igbominas.

Thus, there was a remarkable change in the political scheme of things in the Ijesha Obokun Kingdom. The Ijesha power polity gradually shifted from the Aafin Adimula to the Kiriji war camp where Ogedengbe Agbogungboro, Fabunmi Oraralada Obe, Okunade Arimoro, Ogunmodede, Fapohunda, Jowojori Onigbogi, Ogunlae Dagunduro and a host of other Ijesha warlords assumed leadership roles and took custody of Ijesha

---

27 Ibid.

28 Agunlejika, Ibid, p.220.

Obokun Kingdom and prosecuted the war in a most gallant way.[29] Although this singular act by Ogedengbe and his allies partially represented a reflection of Ibadan's influence in the Ijesha political style, Ilesha was not Ibadan because Ilesha's political structure, with its non-lineage military titles, was fairly flexible, and the consequences of successful war and the incorporation of slaves had occurred several times in her civic history.[30]

In fact, the greatest chief of all, Odole Ariyansunle, did not go to war, but was the head of the *Aafin* organization. Ilesha's politics still depended, in good measure, on a highly structured system of titles and not just on the shifting fortunes and alliances of the leading warriors, until some years after 1870 when the center of Ilesha's politics moved to the war camp at Kiriji.

Changing status of war leaders: the Kiriji war camp connection

The alliance against Ibadan brought together the allies of Ijesha, Ekiti and Igbomina to form the Ekiti Parapo. This alliance saw a change in the status of Ogedengbe, who had joined the Ekiti Parapo group as early as 1880. His experience and prestige earned him by common consent of the other *Ologun*, the post of commander-in-chief.[31] The Kiriji camp of the Ekiti Parapo became a

---

29 Ibid, p. 222.

30 Peel, (1983), p.81.

31 Ibid, p.83.

substantial town, with a population that fluctuated seasonally but was estimated at 40,000 strong in 1886.[32] Its structure derived from the relations between the leading Ologun, each with his following. This 'public' force, which certainly carried the aspirations of peace and freedom of the peoples represented there, was in fact, an aggregation of private armies.

The Ijesha, for example, were not a unified contingent but went as the followers of Ogedengbe himself, Arimoro, Ogunmodede, Obe or whoever else they had some connection with.[33] During this period, the status of Ijesha war leaders would have been transformed and fashioned after the Ibadan type polity but the larger followings had something of a stratified command structure, such that Ogedengbe's status was 'under-balogun', who would be with surbodinate captains within his following, rather than lesser Ologun with followings of their own.[34] It is important to state that many of the leaders at Kiriji assumed Oyo-type titles—Fabunmi Okemesi was Balogun, Ogedengbe was *Seri*ki (in theory a lower title than Balogun, denoting the leader of young warriors), Obe was *Bada*, Arimoro was *Asaaju-ija*-but they were purely personal, not indications

---

32 See Akintoye, p. 5.

33 Peel, (1983), p. 83.

34 Haastrup. J.P. (member of the Lagos Ekiti-Parapo Society and sometime Owa Bepo's messenger) to Lt Governor Griffiths, 16 Feb. 1882, in CO 147/149, no.48.

of positions in some fairly stable division of authority.[35] Evolution towards a permanent Ibadan-type order was limited, not just by the break-up of the Kiriji camp, but by the fact that the Oba of the allied communities of the Ekiti Parapo, including the Owa, continued as a kind of parallel authority and implicitly served as reminders of the former order.

In spite of the enormous influence and power of Ogedengbe in Ijeshaland, Ogedengbe's inability to occupy the position of Balogun like Fabunmi of Okemesi at the Kiriji war camp hindered the adoption of the Ibadan title (Balogun) for war leaders in Ilesha.

The implication of the military structure at the Kiriji War camp on the Ijesha polity is that, the Ijesha did not adopt the title of Balogun for their war leaders. Instead, the traditional chieftaincy structure has been maintained even up till the present time. This consists of members of the Agbanla order, Aare and Elegbe military commanders, today known as Agba Ijesha, the Ijesha council of elders, otherwise known as the Ijesha Obokun Parliament.[36] In the Ijesha Obokun tradition, the Aare chieftaincy groups are those of high military command known as Elegbe warlords. The membership includes: Lejoka (head of Elegbe Oke), Loro and Lejofi. Also, Lokiran, Rinsinkin, Sorundi, Salosi, Sawe Ijamo, Lodifi, Losare and Lokoyi belong to Elegbe Odo.

---

35 Peel, (1983), p. 84.

36 Agunlejika, p. .151.

Apart from the above, it is also important to emphasize that in the post-independence period, the feature of Ijesha chieftaincy structures reveals two categories. First are lineage chieftaincy titles which are hereditary. Second are chieftaincy titles which are open to all Ijeshas. The hereditary lineage chieftaincy titles are the exclusive right of the descendants of the first holders of such chieftaincy titles which are as follows: Ogboni Ibokun, Ogboni Ijebu-jesa, Ogboni Ipole and Ogboni Ilesa (lineage hereditary chieftaincy titles in the Agbanla group); Loro, Sorundi, Salosi and Sawe Ijamo (lineage chieftaincy titles in the Elegbe military/war group).

The second group, the open-ended chieftaincy titles which are free and open to all Ijeshas who have distinguished themselves immensely and had contributed to the growth and development of Ijesaland in general. The open chieftaincy titles in the Elegbe military/ war chieftaincy group are: Lejoka, Lejofi, Lokiran, Lodifi, Rinsinkin, Losare and Lokoyi. The inference from this list of chieftaincy titles is that, rather than the title of 'Balogun' which is synonymous with courage and power possession in other Yoruba societies, the deserving Ijesha indigenes are honoured with any of the above titles in the open ended category.

However, the title which was similar to that of Balogun in Ijesaland was the Obanla title bestowed on Ogedengbe for his bravery and military exploits during his lifetime. In fact, Ogedengbe so much cherished this title that he was said to have appealed to his kinsmen at the point of death not to interfere in other chieftaincies in Ijesaland and beyond, except the Obanla of Ijeshaland.[37]

Conclusion

The title of Balogun has gone through metamorphosis in virtually all the Yoruba societies including Ilesha where the warlords were not honoured with Balogun but with other names of the similar status. However, the dynamics in the transformation of this Balogun title, which *abi nitio* emanated from bravery, courage and ability to protect self and members of the community from external attack is that in the modern times, the title of Balogun is a common title in the mosques and in some churches with a few modifications. For instance, deserving members of mosques are awarded the title of Balogun Adini just the same way their counterparts in the church are awarded Balogun Ijo Onigbagbo. Although this practice in the mosque is common in Ibadan, Abeokuta, Ijebu-Ode, Ilorin, Osogbo and some other Yoruba towns, it is rarely practised in Ilesha because the town has a predominantly Christian population and the few mosques in Ijeshaland seem not to be fascinated with the title because there is no traditional basis for it, unlike in other Yoruba towns.

---

37 S.B. Amusa, "Ogedengbe Agbogungboro of Ilesa: A 19th century Yoruba warlord", In S. Oyeweso, editor, *Ijesa Icons and the Making of Modern Nigeria,* (Osun State University:
College of Humanities and Culture, 2011), p.12.

Thus, the Elegbe military titles of Lejoka, Lejofi, Lokiran, Lodifi, Rinsinkin, Losare and Lonsikin are traditional titles awarded to deserving citizens in Ilesha in both ancient and contemporary times, which are similar in honour and responsibility to the title of Balogun in other Yoruba societies.

8

The Balogun Institution in the Akoko Area of Northeastern Yorubaland

Olusanya Faboyede

Introduction

Akokoland is a sub-group in the northeastern part of Yorubaland. Akoko comprises forty-five towns and villages.[1] Most towns and villages, groups and sub-groups consist of settlers whose origins are diverse. Like their neighbouring kith and kin in Ekiti, Edo (Benin), Owo and Owe, agriculture has been their main occupation, with a majority of the population having small to medium holdings. Their progenitors laid claim to Ife ascendancy,[2] and unlike their counterparts in other parts of Yorubaland, the towns and villages in Akoko are different in some respects, especially in the areas of

---

1 Culled from the attendance list of Akoko obas in a Traditional Rulers' meeting held in Ikare Akoko on 5th December, 2007.

2 The traditional history of the origin and migration of the Akoko people evolves around Ife myths, which claim that 16 sons and princes of Oduduwa, the progenitor of the Yoruba conquered their hosts, absorbed them and established their own kingdoms. See C.O. Akomolafe, "Akoko under British Rule, 1900-1935" Master's thesis of Philosophy (History), University of Ife, Ile-Ife, 1976, p. 4-12.

language dialect. Also, in Akoko there is no single paramount ruler, like the *Alake* of Egbaland, the *Awujale* of Ijebuland and the *Alaafin* of Oyo.³ As such, many communities in Akokoland have been embroiled in incessant chieftaincy disputes and protracted conflicts which have challenged their peace and progress.⁴

The origins of the *Balogun* institution in Akokoland

Every sub-group in the Akoko confederacy has evolved its own Balogun institution under different circumstances, especially in the course of migration and dispersal from Ife during the processes of state formation. However, two events were significant in the evolution of the Balogun institution. It has been acknowledged that territorial warfare and expansion was the basis for the emergence of war chiefs in Akokoland.⁵

---

3 A. Oyedele, "Alaafin Carpets Soun over Beaded Crown", *Sunday Punch*, News, January 11, 2009, p. 9.

4 "Secret: Ondo State of Nigeria, Report of the Ondo State Judicial Commission of Inquiry on Chieftaincy Matters, Comprising Chieftaincy Declaration, Paramountcy, Prescrib-ed and Consenting Authorities Part II", January 1999, p. 1-25, 110, 124-149. Also, see The Asin Oka Chieftaincy: A Case for Its Recognition.

5 Interview held with Malam Adebayo Balogun, c. 60 years, farming. He was interviewed at his residence 68, Owanikun Street, Ikun-Akoko on 14-04-2013.

In the nineteenth century inter-group warfare among the Yoruba in pre-colonial times precipitated the emergence of the Balogun institution in almost all Akoko towns and villages.[6] The Ekiti and Ijesha warlords and Ibadan war adventurers launched attacks on the people of Akokoland, especially when Ayorinde found a settlement at Irun in Akokoland in 1856. Akintoye referred to Ayorinde as the lord of Akoko and Ido-Ani.[7] The Nupe military forces also raided towns and villages in Akokoland during the reigns of the various Etsu Nupe rulers, such as Masaba, Maliki and Usman Zaki.[8] The only exception was Oka town which proved impregnable to the Nupe soldiers.[9] The recklessness of the external warlords was checkmated, when the various Akoko towns and villages came together and rose against external attacks.[10] The proliferation of war chiefs, of which the Balogun

---

6 Ibid.

7 Akintoye, "Revolution and Power Politics in Yorubaland, 1840–1893" in Obaro Ikime, editor, *Groundwork in Nigerian History*, (Ibadan: Heinemann Books,1980) p. 68-69; and M. Mason, "The Jihad in the South: An Outline of the Nineteenth Century Nupe Hegemony in Northeastern Yorubaland and Afenmai", *Journal of the Historical Society of Nigeria* (JHSN), 5 (2) 1970: 197.

8 Mason, p. 193-197 & 199-200.

9 A.O. Olukoju, "Oka", in G.O. Oguntomisin, editor, *Yoruba Towns and Cities*, volume one, (Ibadan: Bookshelf Resources, 2003), p. 85.

10 Akintoye, p. 76.

institution was an important component, was part of traditional military tactics developed not just to prosecute intra-group warfare, but also to ward off incessant external attacks. The emergence of such personalities like Balogun Ogedengbe, Aduloju in places such as, Ikare, Oka, Ajowa, Okeagbe, Oyin, Arigidi, Ipesi, Ifira, among others, was linked to their ability to perform excellently on the battle field.[11] Hence, the assertion that the Balogun institution in its entirety was a product of power and gallantry of individuals in war.[12]

In addition, the period of the Balogun evolution towards the end of the eighteenth century also coincided with the period of the slave trade, when European slave traders demanded slaves to be obtained through local slave raiding networks in the interior.

The role and status of the Balogun in pre-19th century Akoko

Maintaining security was a major issue at the level of power relations in Akoko society, because every town and village maintained its independence from the

---

11 G.I. Olomola, "The War Generals in Eastern Yorubaland", in Adeagbo Akinjogbin, editor, *War and Peace in Yorubaland 1793-1893* (Ibadan: Heinemann Educational Books, 1998), p. 181.

12 S. Johnson, *History of the Yorubas from the Earliest Times to the Beginning of the British Protectorate*, (Lagos: CMS Bookshops, 1921), p. 132

others.[13] The traditional military institutions had power to cause and control conflicts. Sometimes, they played overt and covert roles and engaged varying forms of state patronage as emergent informal security groups until the evolution of a formal security agent. Hence, they could instigate or forestall communal clashes for the essence of slave raiding and for either state or personal wealth or both.[14] The Balogun often stage-managed and controlled rivalries among towns and villages in Akoko. This was evident in the conflicts between Ikanmu and Oka, Ifira and Ipesi, Iboropa and Oka, Omuo and Ogbagi. The Baloguns in these towns and villages rivalled one another during the period under study.[15]

The Baloguns often dual roles in the internal and the external security of Akoko communities they were supposed to protect. The Balogun was the traditional institution who had to maintain peace by preventing crises, especially over land disputes, border or boundary problems for both economic and supremacy reasons. Here, the Balogun was the primal local military agent

---

13 Interview held with Chief A. Ajanaku cited.

14 Ibid.

15 A. Olukoju, "The Siege of Oka, ca.1878-1884: A study in the Resistance to Nupe in Northeastern Yorubaland" in T. Falola & R. Law, editors, *Warfare and Diplomacy in pre-Colonial Nigeria: Essays in Honour of Robert Smith*. (Madison: African Studies Program, University of Wisconsin-Madison 2003) p. 104 & 107.

around whom the entire traditional military institution in Akoko revolved.

Adopting the nomenclature of indigenous traditional title holders, the war troops were headed by the Balogun and organised in line with the administrative divisions of communities in Akoko. The title holder of Balogun was the head of the warriors or guilds such as *ode* (hunters) and *ologun* (the association of warriors). Internally, the Balogun in Akoko commanded the veteran soldiers. In other words, he was the *de jure* leader of all the military warlords in the land.

The title also had political significance. He was a member of the community council and participated in deliberations on the socio-political activities in the town. In this second role, the Balogun controlled the vassal towns and villages. Many of these towns and villages paid tribute through the Balogun, who presided over the imposition and collection of levies by selected officials (*Ajele*).

During the revolutionary years in Yorubaland, the Balogun was the *de facto* leader in major towns such as, Ikare, Arigidi, Oka, Ifira, Ipesi, Iboropa, Ogbagi, Okeagbe, Oyin, among others, where he played the role of *Baale* (mayor or vassal chief).[16]

Two categories of Balogun emerged in Akoko, namely the hereditary Balogun and the non-hereditary

---

16 Johnson, p.90.

or honourary Balogun. In the first instance, the hereditary line of the Baloguns was mainly in charge of the traditional military services or armed forces, whose responsibility was to take action on territorial defence and expansion in the pre-19th century.[17] Due to his status within the elite military class, a Balogun with hereditary status had considerable influence in socio-political affairs of his domain, particularly prior to colonial period. The Balogun customarily exercised fierce control over enemies, virtually for political dominance and to secure economic power over vassal states.[18]

In appointing a Balogun, character was a major attribute for consideration, apart from dexterity in warfare as previously noted. As for the honorary Balogun holders, the title only confers civic responsibilities.

The position of the Balogun in the 19th century

Prior to British incursion into Akoko, the Balogun was prominent and famous as the leader of the traditional military elite in the land. He had both political and military power to safeguard his people. The Balogun

---

[17] Interview held with Chief A. Ajanaku, the Balogun of Owake-Oka, c. 56 years. He was interviewed on at No. 68, College Road, Opposite Magistrate Court, Iwaro-Oka on 16-02-2013.

[18] Ibid.

was physically present at battlefields, and maintenance of security was vested in him although with the consent of the *Oba*. The stability of Akoko society depended on the patriotic role of the Balogun and his lieutenants in the 19th century, which was to preserve and protect his people within their domain. Principally, as a result of the inevitable role of the Balogun, the Akoko region became prominent in the socio-political affairs in the comity of towns and villages in the north-eastern part of Yorubaland.

In Akoko region, the Balogun had a large slave estate that produced food for the military armies and oil palm for Nupe merchants and traders in the interior. The Balogun was entitled to half of the *iko-gun* (war booty) assigned to his lieutenants and the other half was equally divided among the subordinate war chiefs.[19]

The Balogun had effective power and jurisdiction over all military subordinates in his territory. The Balogun also had control over the tributary areas; mainly their slaves and followers became vested in the various groups of his descendants.[20] In wider terms, the Balogun regulated security activities around his environment. In discharging his duties, he had to

---

19 Ibid, p. 133; Also, see J.S. Eades, "The Yoruba Today", online version; and B. Awe, "Militarism and Economic Development in Nineteenth Century Yoruba Country", *Journal of Africa History (JAH)*, 14 (1) 1964: 654.

20 Interview held with Chief A. Ajanaku, cited.

engage in military training. As a reflection of his duty, the Balogun and his subordinates had to consult the Oba, to discuss and take decisions on social and security problems. This way, the Balogun institution provided easy access to useful information on security issues and other matters of concern to its members.[21]

It will be recalled as observed by Akintoye that the emergence of the Balogun as the *de facto* Baale was revolutionary in the history of northeastern Yorubaland.[22] The oba had no profound control over the Balogun in the course of embarking on war expedition, a product of power relations, which potentially threatened the position of the oba. In this respect, the oba was no longer *kabiyesi* (he that could not be questioned or challenged by his subjects). The emergence of the new military elite, their power, fame, style and wealth from tributes that were extracted from conquered towns and villages and gifts of slaves enlarged the influence of the Balogun institution particularly in terms of power relations with the monarch.[23]

However, the Balogun was under the authority of the oba, although he might, sometimes have influenced the decision of the oba and the chiefs in council. The

---

21 Ibid.

22 Akintoye, p. 77.

23 Ibid.

outstanding example was in Oka community, where the Balogun, during the reign of *Olusin* Ajamaye Ologunogeh (1895-1910), the head of Olusi kingdom, Chief Koku Ologunagba, turned down the royal order of the chief to wage war against Oba Akoko in 1890, for the reason that Koku's mother was from Oba Akoko.[24] The Balogun became prominent after the reorganisation of the security structure to withstand Ibadan imperial-ism. The Ibadan army was defeated at the battle of Ogidi between 1896 and 1897.[25]

The changing position of the Balogun institution under colonial rule

The introduction of colonial police officials to oversee the collection of taxes under the Native Authority during colonial rule opened a new phase in the role and place of the Balogun institution which had been the military custodian up to the 19th century. A divisional council was eventually created and the Balogun institution was no longer recognised and had no authority to carry out the exercise of prosecuting warfare in the society. And with the changed nomenclature of the native administration to local government, there was a provision for the local

---

24 J.J. Olusin Ologunagba II, "The Brief History of the Balogun Chieftaincy in Owalusin Oka", n.p. n.d., p. 4-5.

25 Ibid., p. 37.

government police, supervised by the regional commissioner of police.[26]

The Balogun was particularly forbidden to declare war on real or imagined enemies, as was the case in the past and again, could not impose punishments on offenders in his suzerainty. Other than this, and subject to approval of the colonial administration, the oba and his Balogun continued to administer and deliberate upon sensitive issues affecting the security of the towns and villages in line with tradition, and making sure that peace, harmony and tranquillity was sustained.[27]

It was the district officer (DO) that had the power, under the new dispensation, to ensure peace and order with British troops stationed at strategic places. To perfect a gradual loss of traditional authority on the coordination of defence, the Oba was elected by the district officer based in Owo (from 1919) to do the bidding of the colonial government.[28]

Subsequently, the exalted positions among both hereditary and non-hereditary elite groups in north-eastern Akokoland became obsolete. The appointment

---

26 Olukoju, p. 203.

27 Interview held with M.O. Osantuyi, *Elejemo* of Irun-Akoko on 25-04-2013.

28 Interview held with Chief (Hon.) I.A. Olukoju, c. 80 years, former honourable member of the defunct Western Regional House of Assembly, Ibadan. He was interviewed at his residence, No. 1, Sabo street, Iwaro-Oka on 16-02-2013.

of the Balogun was overtaken by modernism and western democracy. The Balogun institution lost its independence and relevance in the political affair of the community beginning from the 1940s, when the native authority police came on board.[29] The colonial arrangement affected the role and status of the Balogun. It replaced the Balogun and the traditional military institutions that were once the symbol of loyalty. It was advanced by an oath of allegiance among members of chieftaincy holders. Thus, the management of security was modernised. In other words, the Balogun was only fit for physical extortions and later functioned as an adviser.

Following the 1910 native authority proclamation, the native authority order prevented crimes, arrested and deported any known felons and enforced law and order.[30] The result of this proclamation was community policing with vigilante groups.[31] As a matter of fact, the Balogun institution and the traditional military institution were no longer in charge of diplomatic

---

29 Ibid.

30 S.T. Okajare, "Akoko-Owo Relations from the Earliest Times to 1935: A study of Inter-group relations in northeastern Yorubaland". Ph.D Thesis, Department of History and International Studies, Ekiti State University, Ado Ekiti, 2012, p. 140.

31 Interview held with Chief Matthew Shaba Oluwole, c. 90 years, the Shaba Olukanmu of Simerin Ikanmu-Oka. He was interviewed at No. 1, Agbadotun Street, Ayepe, Iwaro-Oka on 16-02-2013.

relations, despite the absence of internecine warfare, except in resolving conflicts over fertile portions of land and various economic considerations.

218 The Balogun in Yorubaland ...

9

The Balogun Institution in the Ilorin Emirate since 1823

Saad' Yusuf Omoiya

Introduction

The pivoting role of the military class in the emergence, sustenance and changes in any given polity, at the micro or macro level, cannot be underestimated. It explains why the military has been the major institution from which most African polities have originated. This embraces the social, political and economic aspects of the people's lives. Despite their central role in nation building, different societies at different times, have identified the military class as a distinct unit, insulated from direct governance. This was perhaps to ensure necessary checks and balances.

In the African political system, most of the leaders combined their political leadership with military control. For instance, the Shaka of Zulu led his people in war.[1] For some parts of Benin Empire's history, the Oba led

---

1 S.Y. Omoiya,"The Impact of Colonial Administration on Political Institutions in Ilorin 1897 – 1960",M.A. Ibadan.1988, p. 32 - 33.

his people in war until the revolution of Oba Ewuare.[2] However, in most parts of Yorubaland, specifically in the Oyo Empire, a separate place was carved out for the warriors, for they were not allowed to live in the same town with the Alaafin. The military commanders only responded to the directives or command of the political head, the Alaafin, who is the head of all the institutions in his domain.

An example of the sophisticated Yoruba political structure as it affected the military can be located within the Old Oyo Empire's political system, where the head of the military was called the *Aare Ona Kakanfo* (the generalismo of the imperial army). Even with the tradition of checks and balances to guarantee the stability of the empire, the personal relationship between an Alaafin and his Aare Ona Kakanfo was central to the actual realization of stability.

The founding of Balogun Institution in Ilorin

The personal animosity between Alaafin Aole and his Aare Ona Kakanfo, Afonja, started when Aole, after his installation as the Alaafin named Aare Afonja as one of his enemies, who by Oyo tradition, had to be executed to make the reign of the new Alaafin a peaceful one. Aare Afonja camped at Ilorin, because by another Oyo tradition, he was not allowed to live in the same

---

2 Ibid.

environment with the Aalafin. He remained calm and waited to see who would carry out the tradition of killing the declared enemy of a newly installed Alaafin.

The refusal by the army to execute Aare Afonja propelled the Alaafin to embark on another scheme to get rid of him. This, the Alaafin did by conniving with the palace guards. The guards were directed to carry a message from the Alaafin to the Aare to undertake a military expedition against a place that was not to be disclosed to him.[3]

Word of the second scheme of the Alaafin to get rid of him had reached the Aare before the arrival of the *Eso*, but he followed them without asking any questions as the order could not be disobeyed.[4]

Iwere, was the maternal home of Alaafin Abiodun, which by Oyo tradition, could never be attacked by the Empire's army due to the blood relation.[5] Any such misadventure would be bound to fail. And if any military expedition failed, the Aare Ona Kakanfo would have to commit suicide.[6] Apart from the consequence to the Aare for defying a tradition by using the Empire's army to wage war against a town that had blood relations with the Alaafin, the town of Iwere was also

---

3 Samuel Johnson, *The History of the Yorubas*, (Lagos: CMS Bookshop, 1921), p. 188 - 192.

4 Ibid, p. 5.

5 Ibid.

6 Ibid.

protected because it had the geographical advantage of being surrounded by rocks. It was at Iwere that the Aare ordered the massacre of the Eso, sparing only one of them. The Aare ordered the sole survivor to carry an empty calabash to the Alaafin, as a sign of being rejected by the people, and thus obliged to commit suicide.[7] The Aare subsequently declared independence for Ilorin. He was supported by Onikoyi and Opele of Gbogun who also declared independence for their respective areas.[8]

Aare Afonja adopted two military strategies to fortify his position as the political head of an independent Ilorin. One of these was to source for independent spiritual powers that would defy the powers and influence of an Alaafin as the head of all traditional institutions.[9] The second strategy of the Aare, was to inject new blood into his army.[10] Preferably strangers, on whom he could build his confidence. Through his age long friend, Sholagberu, the Afonja got in contact with a Muslim cleric of Fulani origin, to prepare Islamic oriented charms to fortify his spiritual powers.

To further fortify his position, Aare Afonja recruited the slaves that had run away from their masters at Old

---

7 Ibid.

8 J. Atanda, *The New Oyo Empire*. (London: Longman Group Ltd. 1973).

9 Ibid, p. 15.

10 Ibid, p. 15 - 35.

Oyo township to Ilorin. These slaves had fled to Ilorin looking for sanctuary, to save themselves from being recaptured. Certainly, the Aare took advantage of this to secure and to build absolute confidence in the new recruits, since they were strangers in the environment.

The rapacious activities of the slave soldiers led Fagboun, the left wing commander of Aare's army, to send a report to the Aare. In reaction to this report, the Aare embarked on an internal reorganization of his army.[11] This led to a mutiny by the slave soldiers who took the life of Aare Afonja in about 1817.[12] The death of Aare Afonja created a vacuum in the political leadership of Ilorin.

The Aare Afonja's Muslim cleric, and later friend, Shehu Alimi, was said to have remained in Ilorin until his death in about 1823. He committed himself to his clerical work after the Aare was killed by his slave soldiers. However, the death of Shehu Alimi in about 1823 opened Ilorin to another era of change which eventually filled the political vacuum left by Afonja's death.

The succession to Shehu Alimi's position as an imam of a mosque, which was contested for by Abdulsalami,

---

11 Abdullahi Smith, "The Early States of the Central Sudan" in J.F. Ade Ajayi and Michael Crowder, editors, *History of West Africa*.(London: Longman, 1971) p. 55-85.

12 Ibid.

Shehu Alimi's first son and a man simply referred to as Bako, from Serikin Gambari's family, illustrates that the position held by Shehu Alimi in Ilorin was purely religious and not necessarily hereditary.[13] The support given by Sholagberu, Shehu Alimi's friend and some other Yoruba friends of Shehu Alimi, gave Abdulsalami victory over Bako. Thus, he succeeded his father as an imam of a mosque, out of many mosques that were in Ilorin at the time.[14]

It was by coincidence that the slave soldiers who had killed the Aare observed their daily prayers in the mosque where Shehu Alimi was the imam. The succession by his son, Abdulsalami, initially meant little or nothing to the people because the new imam was seen as a complete gentleman. Shitta, the younger brother of Abdulsalami, developed a close relationship with the slave soldiers. Shitta was said to have raised a false alarm that some people were trying to kill his elder brother, the imam.[15] He pointed to the settlement of Islamic clerics at Okesuna among others, and incited the slave soldiers against the clerics at Okesuna. These clerics were massacred. This strange incident enraged Sholagberu, Shehu Alimi's friend, who had been

---

13 S.A. Balogun, "The Gwandu Emirates" Ph.D Ibadan, 1970. p 69 - 72.

14 Ibid, p. 35 - 38.

15 S.Y. Omoiya, *The Origin and British Colonial Impact on the Cosmopolitan Community of Ilorin in the 20th Century*, (LINCOM GmbH 2009) p. 72 - 104.

Oyo township to Ilorin. These slaves had fled to Ilorin looking for sanctuary, to save themselves from being recaptured. Certainly, the Aare took advantage of this to secure and to build absolute confidence in the new recruits, since they were strangers in the environment.

The rapacious activities of the slave soldiers led Fagboun, the left wing commander of Aare's army, to send a report to the Aare. In reaction to this report, the Aare embarked on an internal reorganization of his army.[11] This led to a mutiny by the slave soldiers who took the life of Aare Afonja in about 1817.[12] The death of Aare Afonja created a vacuum in the political leadership of Ilorin.

The Aare Afonja's Muslim cleric, and later friend, Shehu Alimi, was said to have remained in Ilorin until his death in about 1823. He committed himself to his clerical work after the Aare was killed by his slave soldiers. However, the death of Shehu Alimi in about 1823 opened Ilorin to another era of change which eventually filled the political vacuum left by Afonja's death.

The succession to Shehu Alimi's position as an imam of a mosque, which was contested for by Abdulsalami,

---

11 Abdullahi Smith, "The Early States of the Central Sudan" in J.F. Ade Ajayi and Michael Crowder, editors, *History of West Africa.*(London: Longman, 1971) p. 55-85.

12 Ibid.

Shehu Alimi's first son and a man simply referred to as Bako, from Serikin Gambari's family, illustrates that the position held by Shehu Alimi in Ilorin was purely religious and not necessarily hereditary.[13] The support given by Sholagberu, Shehu Alimi's friend and some other Yoruba friends of Shehu Alimi, gave Abdulsalami victory over Bako. Thus, he succeeded his father as an imam of a mosque, out of many mosques that were in Ilorin at the time.[14]

It was by coincidence that the slave soldiers who had killed the Aare observed their daily prayers in the mosque where Shehu Alimi was the imam. The succession by his son, Abdulsalami, initially meant little or nothing to the people because the new imam was seen as a complete gentleman. Shitta, the younger brother of Abdulsalami, developed a close relationship with the slave soldiers. Shitta was said to have raised a false alarm that some people were trying to kill his elder brother, the imam.[15] He pointed to the settlement of Islamic clerics at Okesuna among others, and incited the slave soldiers against the clerics at Okesuna. These clerics were massacred. This strange incident enraged Sholagberu, Shehu Alimi's friend, who had been

---

13 S.A. Balogun, "The Gwandu Emirates" Ph.D Ibadan, 1970. p 69 - 72.

14 Ibid, p. 35 - 38.

15 S.Y. Omoiya, *The Origin and British Colonial Impact on the Cosmopolitan Community of Ilorin in the 20th Century*, (LINCOM GmbH 2009) p. 72 - 104.

instrumental to his relationship with Aare Afonja which had eventually led to his settlement in Ilorin. He contacted Onikoyi for assistance which made the rampaging slave soldiers to go after him and eventually kill him.

After the killing of the prominent groups and personalities in Ilorin by Shitta and the slave soldiers, Shitta encouraged his brother, the imam, to declare himself an Emir in Ilorin. In this, the children of Shehu Alimi, Abdulsalami and Shitta, with the support of the slave soldiers, were conscious of their restraints in consolidating the new political status proclaimed by Abdulsalami. Therefore, they schemed together to embark on internal and external strategies to secure the proclamation of Emirship on Ilorin.

At the internal level, Abdulsalami sought the co-operation of the existing leaders of the major linguistic groups including the Yoruba, Hausa and Fulani in Ilorin. This he did by co-opting them into the Emirate Council, with the title of Balogun. Apart from the fact that these co-opted leaders would represent their respective linguistic groups in the Emirate council, they were technically mobilized to be prepared to secure the new Emirate administration.

At the external level, the new Emir sent a letter to the Caliph at Sokoto, pledging his allegiance and seeking to be accommodated as part of the caliphate. In response to the letter written by Emir Abdulsalami, (translated by Professor Abdullahi Smith, captioned as "Emir of the

Yaraba"), the caliph accepted Abdulsalami's request to be accommodated into the caliphate because he had pledged to operate on the tenets of the Holy Quran and the Hadith. The letter went further to respond to some of the questions raised on the issue of Sharia (Islamic legal code). It was concluded with the promise to continue to assist the administration.[16]

The questions deserving answers at this point are: why was Yoruba title, Balogun chosen for the different leaders in the Emirate council of Ilorin? What were to be the responsibilities of these Baloguns? Being a Yoruba title for war commanders, it clearly illustrates that the widely spoken language in Ilorin was and still is Yoruba and it gives credence to the dominance of the Yoruba in the area. The fact that the Baloguns were chosen from the existing leaders of the major linguistic groups, suggests that they were to continue to exercise their leadership control over their respective peoples and to secure their loyalty to the new Emirate structure.

The status, responsibilities and contributions of the Balogun in Ilorin

A holistic discussion or evaluation of the Balogun institution in Ilorin, would require us to appraise it both from the Emirate structure in which it exists and from the Yoruba political organogram to which the title could be directly linked. According to S.A Balogun, in his Ph.D

---

16 Ibid.

thesis which examined the Gwandu Emirates, the Balogun institution in Ilorin is unparalleled in its structure and responsibilities compared to other Emirates under Gwandu. Apart from the fact that it is only in the Ilorin Emirate that the title of Balogun exists, its responsibilities are so central to the administration of the Emirate that it can be said to form the pillars on which the Ilorin Emirate itself was built.

The function of the Balogun institution in the Emirate council as representatives of the diverse linguistic groups that make up the population and its service as the military arm of the administration accounted for the Balogun's dominance in the affairs of Ilorin. At operational level, it was the main institution that engaged in the wars that allowed the Emirate to survive the protracted wars with the authority of the Old Oyo Empire, that brought about the consolidation of Ilorin as a political entity and that led to the expansionist project of the Emirate which made Ilorin prominent in 19th century Yoruba warfare.[17]

In relation to the Yoruba political structure, the Baloguns in Ilorin existed as a unit of administration, rather than just a unit of commanders in the military.[18] In addition to their responsibilities as members of the Emirate council which determined the administrative

---

17 Ibid.

18 R. A. Adeleye, *Power and Diplomacy in Northern Nigeria 1804 – 1906*. (London: Group Ltd London 1971), p, 187 - 192.

policy for the Emirate, the Baloguns of Ilorin also had control over given areas in the fiefs under the Emirate as well as adjudicating in their own domains. This distinguished the Balogun institution in Ilorin from other Baloguns all over Yorubaland.

It also explains why the Balogun institution became dominant after the Emirate's wars of survival, specifically after the reign of the Emir Shitta (1835-1861). This was when the Ilorin Emirate army engaged in the wars of consolidation and wars of expansion. The process by which leadership evolved amongst the Baloguns in Ilorin, after the first set of Baloguns, which began with three and later increased to four began to die, prevented any form of rancour amongst the four Baloguns. The oldest surviving Balogun on the council automatically assumed the position of the Balogun Agba.[19] The respect from the other Baloguns and the authority enjoyed by the Balogun Agba, over the entire population of Ilorin were so enormous that the recognition and power of the Emir gradually faded.[20]

From the time that the first and second Emirs, Abdulsalami (1823-1835) and Shitta (1835 – 1861) proclaimed themselves as Emirs, it became the responsibility of the Emirate council, led by the Balogun Agba together with religious leaders from the three linguistic groups, to consider and select from among the

---

19 Ibid.

20 Ibid.

contesting princes the new heir to the throne of Emir. It is interesting to note that although the Emirate council selects a new Emir, with the Balogun Agba as the head of the council, and the other Baloguns playing prominent roles, the succession to the position of Balogun is entirely left to the family of the respective Baloguns. The family only presents the chosen candidate to the Emir for turbanning, which is equivalent to taking an oath of office.

The impact of colonial rule on the Balogun institution in the Ilorin Emirate

The engagement of the Ilorin Emirate in protracted wars of survival, consolidation and expansion which spanned its existence, naturally placed the Balogun institution at an advantage by choosing leadership for the Emirate. The role of the Emir therefore became advisory.[21] The superior authority of the Balogun was clearly demonstrated when the Balogun Agba, Karara of Gambari, decided to avenge the role said to have been played by Offa in the Ilorin-Oshogbo war, which was popularly referred to as the Jalumi war. As part of the expansionist war of Ilorin, she chose to bring Oshogbo under her control by crossing the bridge on Otin River to engage the Oshogbo army.[22] Oshogbo being aware of

---

21 Ibid.

22 Ibid.

its limitations, decided to bring in the generals from Ibadan to save her from the Ilorin incursion.[23]

As part of the war tactics, the allied forces of Oshogbo and Ibadan decided to attack the Ilorin army camp at night to forestall the advantage of Ilorin Calvary.[24] The allied forces of Oshogbo and Ibadan were also said to have instructed Offa to damage the bridge on the Otin river to cut off the supplies from Ilorin. Offa's faithfulness in carrying out the assignment and the night attack on the Ilorin camp, forced the Emirate army to retreat. This hasty retreat of the Ilorin army resulted in heavy casualties of men and horses in the Otin river. Those who survived, crossed the river on the dead bodies of men and horses.[25]

The Balogun Agba decided to punish Offa for its alleged act of treachery against Ilorin. Since the Offa people knew the consequences of an attack from Ilorin, the elders of Offa decided to send an emissary to Emir Aliyu (1868-1891) to plead with the Balogun. The Emir's attempt to dissuade the Balogun Agba on his planned revenge on Offa met with a threat of dethronement for the Emir by the Balogun Agba. The Balogun eventually sacked Offa.

---

23 NAK/SNP/15/11 Carnegie to H. C. July, 1900 (Situation report on Ilorin).

24 NAK/SNP/15/11 P. Dwyer to H. C. August, 1900.

25 NAK/SNP/15/11 H. C. to P. Dwyer, September, 1900.

Another significant display of the power of the Balogun Agba over the Emir occurred when the successor to Emir Aliyu, Emir Mama (1891-1895) attempted to undermine the authority of the Balogun. This the Emir did by linking with the colonial governor in Lagos through secret correspondences. The Balogun perceived this as an act of treachery. He is said to have mobilised the Emir's younger brother, Alege to mount a military siege on the Emir who was consequently forced to commit suicide.[26]

The role played by the Balogun Agba, then Balogun Alanamu Inakoju Ali, in the appointment of Emir Sulyman, (1895-1915) further illustrates the power of the Balogun Agba over the Emir. It explains why the first set of colonial residents in Ilorin, David Carneige and P. Dwyer confirmed to Lord Lugard in their respective reports on Ilorin, that the actual ruler in Ilorin at the time, between June and July 1900, was Balogun Inakoju Ali of Alanamu.[27]

The consequences of the Baloguns' resistance of the British colonial rule

The appointment and posting of the first British colonial resident, David Carnegie to Ilorin in June, 1900 opened a new phase in the power play between the indigenous

---

26 The Holy Quran, Chapter 8, verse 65, Reviewed and Edited by Ismail International Organization, 1997.

27 Ibid.

chieftaincy institutions and the British colonial authority. For instance, the Balogun Agba, fully supported by the other Baloguns, jointly expressed their resentment against the arrival of David Carnegie as the British resident in the area because the Balogun saw it purely as foreign domination and an erosion of their power and influence. On the other hand, the Emir was warm towards him (the resident),[28] since he neither had any political power nor influence to lose.

The position taken by the Emir directly opposed the stance of the Baloguns and the people of Ilorin on the one hand, and the tenets of Islamic faith on the other. It provided a good opportunity for the colonial residents to exploit the discord between the indigenous ruling classes and facilitate the establishment of colonial rule in the area. David Carnegie observed that the Emir was powerless and that the actual rulers in Ilorin Emirate were the Baloguns and the other chiefs, who were said to enjoy the good following of the people.[29]

The colonial resident quickly took advantage of this discord and suggest to the Colonial High Commissioner, Lord Lugard, to forcefully back the weak, that is, to support the Emir against the powerful chiefs in Ilorin represented by the Baloguns. It was not long after this that David Carnegie took ill and died.

---

28 S. J. Hogben, *The Muhammedan Emirates of Nigeria*, (Oxford University Press, 1930), p. 161–163.

29 Ibid.

He was replaced by P. Dwyer.[30] In the situation report of the new colonial resident in July 1900, he confirmed the enormous power of the Balogun in the administration of the Ilorin Emirate. He went further to say that Balogun Inakoju Ali of Alanamu had been the actual ruler of Ilorin for the previous six years.[31] He then suggested that the only way by which the colonial administration could be established in the Ilorin Emirate without much cost, was by deposing and deporting Balogun Alanamu, who was identified as leading the other Baloguns and the people of Ilorin against the establishment of British rule in the area.[32] Dwyer also confirmed the empty status of the Emir in the administration of the Emirate. According to Dwyer, the deposition and deportation of Balogun Inakoju Ali of Alanamu would serve as a warning to the other Baloguns to stop their resistance against the establishment of colonial rule.

In reply to P. Dwyer, the High Commissioner agreed with all the suggestions made by the resident but advised that he should wait until the arrival of the forces from Asante, before swinging into action against Balogun Alanamu. Lugard also advised Dwyer to

---

30 S.Y. Omoiya, "The Life and Times of Balogun Inakoju Ali 1827 – 1910" B.A. Long Essay. Submitted to University of Ilorin. 1986, p. 33 – 35.

31 Ibid.

32 NAK/ILO/PROF/1/1 Report No 6 January 1903.

constantly monitor the movements of Balogun Alanamu, to be able to charge him for an offence, thus providing rational grounds for his deposition and deportation.

The Emir, perceiving the British intention to weaken the power of the Balogun, continued to demonstrate his loyalty to the British. This support was demonstrated in the Bida incident of 1900. In August of that year when Bida was under pressure from the imperial forces, she approached Ilorin for military assistance. As the Balogun and the people of Ilorin were ready to offer their assistance, the Emir reported the incident to the colonial resident. The Emir feared that if the resistance of the people of Bida was successful, they could easily support the Balogun and the people of Ilorin to drive the British away. Consequently, his treachery would be made into a case against him.

Another incident that proved the pro-British stance of the Emir involved the Caliph in Sokoto. This time, the Emir received a letter from the Caliph in Sokoto, Attahiru the First, asking him to create a disturbance in Ilorin so as to divert the attention of the British army away from their planned attack on Sokoto. It is likely that the caliph was trying to buy time to prepare and defend the caliphate from an attack from the British. As custom demanded, the Emir read the Caliph's letter aloud to the people. As he did in the case of Bida, the Emir sent the Caliph's messenger with the letter to the British resident in Ilorin. By so doing, Emir Sulyman handed over the Caliph to the British. The Balogun Agba, the other Baloguns and the people of Ilorin maintained a watchful eye on the Emir's relations with the colonial resident and they were hopeful that time would soon catch up with him.

From a religious point of view, the behaviour of Emir Sulyman negated the principles and practice of the Islamic religion. Going by the tenets of the Holy Quran and the Hadith, it is an obligation for a Muslim to resist leadership by non-Muslims, who are commonly referred to as infidels. For a leader of a Muslim community, such as Ilorin, to submit to the rulership of the British was totally un-Islamic.

The friendship of Emir Sulyman with the colonial resident was an indication of his preference for political power and influence as opposed to Islamic reformist interest often ascribed to him by the jihadists. It exposed the motive of taking over political power by the children of Sheu Alimi in Ilorin. The decision of the Emir to forge a relationship with the British agent rather than his traditional administrative team, clearly illustrates the strong desire of the Emirs in Ilorin to rule rather than to serve as mere religious leadership symbols.

On the part of the Baloguns, the experience of their encounter with the British-led West Africa Frontier Force, which brought about the conquest of Ilorin in February, 1897 was still very fresh in their memory. This explained why they tried to avoid any form of open confrontation with the British when they formally established colonial rule in Ilorin.

The relegation of the Baloguns' powers to the Emir

The full demonstration of Emir Sulyman's support for British colonial interest was manifested by his non-support of the Baloguns in Ilorin against British rule. The betrayal of sister emirates such as Bida and even the caliphate in Sokoto, must have encouraged the colonial administration to create more authority for the Emir in Ilorin. By 1902, the stage was set, and Balogun Inakoju Ali, the Balogun Agba (Alanamu) became the first victims of the colonial government's schemes to subjugate and subordinate the Baloguns who were the actual rulers of the Ilorin Emirate. As S. Hogben put it:

> The Emir, finding himself backed up by the resident, broke away from the constraining hands of Alanamu and other chiefs and commenced to act up to his position in a way which showed that he realised how the tide had changed. No longer was he a figure head shaking in his shoes with dread of a sudden death, but an Emir, supported by the government, who insisted on the payment of tributes.[33]

---

33 S.J. Hogben *The Muhammedan Emirates of Nigeria*, (Oxford University Press, 1966), p. 161 – 163.

Hogben goes further to narrate how the Balogun Agba, Balogun Inakoju Ali of Alanamu was caught in the trap set by the colonial government. The Balogun Agba was immediately arrested and deported to Jebba, where a contingent of the colonial army was already waiting in preparation for any eventuality that might follow the deposition order.[34]

The large group of people who went from Ilorin to Jebba to support the Balogun and demonstrate their allegiance to his cause made the colonial government appreciate the fact that it was not an issue they could control by the mere presence of the army, without resorting to violence. Thus, to avoid unnecessary bloodshed, Balogun Inakoju Ali was moved from Jebba to Lokoja,[35] a place further away from Ilorin. It must be appreciated that the Emir represented the minority group, while the Balogun, especially Alanamu and the others represented the majority. The large number of people from different ethnic groups in Ilorin who went to Jebba despite the heavy presence of the colonial army, to forestall any form of violence that could accompany the deposition of Balogun Alanamu, confirmed the popularity of the Balogun.

Apart from the people's demonstration of support for Balogun Inakoju Ali, the actions of the other Balogun and the people totally went against the postulations of

---

34 Ibid.

35 Ibid.

both the colonial resident in Ilorin, P. Dwyer and Lord Lugard that the removal of Balogun Inakoju Ali of Alanamu, would prevent others from fomenting further trouble. The other Baloguns instructed their people to ignore both the colonial resident and the Emir, by not abiding by the colonial instructions passed through the Emir.[36]

The failure of the colonial administration to realize the peace they had hoped for by the exile Balogun Inakoju Ali, the Balogun Agba in Ilorin made them to look inward for another solution to the problem. The colonial administration had to moderate its intention to forcefully subjugate the Balogun to the control of the Emir. The British realized that the Balogun had to be carried along too if they wanted to succeed in gaining control of Ilorin. It was for this purpose that the government decided to award second class chieftaincy status to some of the Baloguns while the Emir was awarded first class status.[37]

Even with the recognition accorded the Baloguns by the British, in contrast to their original plan to forcefully impose the Emir on them as sole administrator, friction between the Baloguns and the Emir over the operation or implementation of colonial policies in Ilorin continued to generate crises between them and their

---

36 Omoiya, The Life and Times of *Balogun* Inakoju Ali 1827 – 1910" p 33 – 35. See fn 30.

37 Ibid.

followers. The reaction of the other Baloguns and the majority of the people of Ilorin was premised on the fact that the colonial administration had decided to confer on the Emir the status of sole authority in Ilorin, whereby all the other political institutions in the Emirate would be accountable to him. This was done by referring all matters relating to the Emirate only to the Emir and the position taken by the Emir on them was always supported by the colonial administration.[38] Added to this was the fact that all instructions from the colonial administration were passed through the Emir. This policy of the colonial administration negated the traditional structure in the Ilorin Emirate whereby collective leadership rather than sole authority had been the system that had sustained the Ilorin Emirate as an entity. Through the natural process of political development and changes in the Ilorin Emirate, the Emir only reigned, while the Balogun ruled.[39]

The attempt by the colonial administration to forcefully impose the Emir as sole authority, naturally generated protracted reactions such as the uncooperative attitude of the Balogun and the people of Ilorin towards the British. This situation explains why the colonial administration continued to change its policy of administration in Ilorin until the other traditional

---

38 NAK/ILO/PROF/1/1 Report No 6 January 1903.

39 Omoiya, 'The Life and Times of Balogun Inakoju Ali," op. cit.

political institutions in the Emirate were effectively integrated into its colonial system.

The accommodation of more interest groups in the Emirate Council

The limited achievement recorded by the colonial administration in ensuring a peaceful acceptance of their presence forced the colonial administration to continuously change its policies, until it recognized the indigenous ethnic balancing in the administrative structure of the Emirate. The implementation of the recommendations of the Palmer Commission of Enquiry of 1913, wherein, more Yoruba were brought into the Emirate council, with the inclusion of the Aare and the Baba Isale, both of whom were from Aare Afonja's family, eventually provided the balance needed for the colonial administration to establish peace in Ilorin.

The establishment of British colonial rule in Ilorin can therefore be said to have generated two contradictory historical issues. The first was the disunity between the indigenous political ruling classes, which the British exploited to their advantage and the second was the recognition by the British of the need for ethnic balancing in administering Ilorin.

The Balogun in Ilorin after 1960

Since the elevation to the status of Balogun Agba was by natural circumstances and any of the four Baloguns could become the Balogun Agba, after the demise of the incumbent, the ethnic representation and balancing was secured. Hence, there had never been acrimony amongst the four Balogun over leadership succession. However, the failure of the British colonial administration to achieve the status of sole administratorship for the Emir, by forcefully backing him, even after the dethronement of two Balogun Agbas in succession, and the continued crisis in the polity gave the colonial administration a reason to review its policies.

By 1913, the colonial administration had to initiate an enquiry into the situation in Ilorin, to adjust its policies and bring about the desired peace for the administration to be successful. The recommendation of the 1913 Palmer Enquiry included the full involvement of the Baloguns, among other chiefs, in the administration of the Emirate. It also recommended the inclusion of more Yoruba in the Emirate council, that is, the inclusion of the Magaji Aare and the Baba Isale, who were direct family members of Aare Afonja. The recommendations of the Palmer Enquiry must have stemmed from the need for more ethnic representation in the Emirate council, because of the multiethnic composition of the population of Ilorin and the ratio of representation.

At this point, it needs to be stressed that of the four Baloguns in Ilorin, two of them were of Yoruba origin, while the Hausa and Fulani were represented by one each. Therefore, the recommendation for more Yoruba in the Emirate council, clearly illustrates the percentage of the Yoruba in Ilorin which can be put at about 80 percent, while the other Hausa speaking minority groups—the Fulani, Nupe, Bornu and Kamberi fell into the remaining 20 percent.

From 1935, when the recommendations of the Palmer Enquiry were implemented, the relationship between the Emir, the Baloguns and the other chiefs has been based on mutual respect. The amiable personality of Emir Abdulkadiri (1919-1959) was said to have cemented relations between the Emir and Baloguns on one hand, and the Emir and the other chiefs on the other. Indeed, the cordiality and the collective action of the Emir and the Baloguns to prevent the erosion of their power and influence made them once again to work together closely.

The revolutionary group, "the Ilorin Talaka Parapo" led the people to rise up against oppression from the implementation of the colonial policies and the imposition of members of the family of the traditional ruling oligarchy to represent the Emirate in both the Council of Ilorin Native Authority and in the Northern House of Representatives.

The alliance between members of Ilorin Talaka Parapo and the Action Group of the Western Region accorded victory to the Talaka Parapo over members of the traditional ruling oligarchy, both at the elections to the council of the Native Authority and representatives into the Northern Regional House of Assembly in the

1956/57 elections. It was the unity of the traditional ruling oligarchy, supported by the Northern Regional Government and the Northern People Congress, (NPC) that overturned the ITP/AG alliance's electoral victory. The litigation process that followed, where Chief Richard Akinjide, represented the Workers Union against the N.A. Council led by the Ilorin Talaka Parapo and Chief Rotimi Williams represented the Council of the Ilorin Native Authority, illustrates the sophistication of the struggle.

The death of Emir Abdulkadir in 1959 gave all the stakeholders concerned with sustaining the power and influence of the Emirate system in Ilorin, the opportunity to ensure the enthronement of a literate Emir, Emir Sulu Karnani Gambari in 1959. Given the challenging political climate in Ilorin and the threat to the power and influence of the traditional ruling oligarchy, from the experience of the short Ilorin Talaka Parapo led administration, Emir Sulu Karnani Gambari wielded enormous power. He was able to suppress the possible continuation of the activities of the Talaka Parapo and the reconsolidation of the power of the traditional ruling authorities. The fact that the Emir operated a special court that even sat at night to adjudicate on matters, ended up committing all leaders of the Talaka Parapo to various terms of imprisonment.

The exercise of seemingly absolute power of Emir Gambari in Ilorin history, soon brought him into conflict with the powerful traditional elite who mobilized for the Emir's removal by 1963. It necessitated the intervention of the Northern Region's premier, Sir Ahmadu Bello, who had to come to Ilorin to settle the matter. The power of the Emir was reduced by the abrogation of the Emir's court and insulation from his influence in party matters. The need for the Emir to embark on fence mending remained the only viable option.

The fortunes of the Baloguns in Ilorin since 1967

The aftermath of the January 1966 military coup and the counter coup of July of the same year, brought about the restructuring of Nigeria from a regional structure to the creation of twelve states. Amongst these new states was Kwara State, with Ilorin as capital. The military governor, Major David Lasisi Bamigboye, commenced his administration by dividing the new state into smaller administrative units. Among the new divisions were Ilorin Division, Igbomina Ekiti Division, Oyun Division and Lafiagi Pategi Division.[40] The creation of these administrative units provided opportunities for the traditional ruling institutions, by attracting recognition from government to the exclusion of the Baloguns in Ilorin. The feeling was that what remained of the Ilorin Emirate after division was an entity which should have the Emir as the only recognised chief.

---

40 Information obtained from publication series, by the Kwara State Ministry of Information, Ilorin, 1968 – 1990.

It is important to acknowledge the fact that the whole of Igbomina, Ekiti and Ibolo carved into divisions were part of the Emirate structure. They were actually administered by different Baloguns that had conquered them. Therefore, to exclude the Baloguns from government's recognition which would have given them new responsibilities and remunerations, in order to respect of the Emir did not go down well with them. This explains the undercurrent misgivings between the Emir and the Baloguns on the grading of the Baloguns in Ilorin. At any given opportunity, the Baloguns operate together to press home their requests. Both historical evidence and moral justifications were often advanced to support their claims.

By 1982, when the civilian administration of Alhaji Adamu Atta, of the NPN, tried to create more local government areas in the then Kwara State, the Baloguns among other institutions within and outside the Ilorin metropolis gave their tacit support to the pressure groups that were pressing for the consideration.

Within the Ilorin metropolis was the Joint Wards Association, made up of elite from all segments of the society, which fronted for the creation of local government areas within Ilorin township. The reigning Emir, Sulu Karnani Gambari, (1959 – 1992) was not disposed to creating additional local government areas and the government backed the position of the Emir. The masses mobilised by the elite, saw the behaviour of the Emir and the government as being against the people of Ilorin. This eventually led to public revolt and protest. It took the state's house of assembly to pass a vote of 2/3 majority of members to create Oloje, Pake and Agbeyangi local government areas out of the then Ilorin local government area. The creation of the local government areas was seen as the first step needed to represent the grading of the Baloguns among other chiefs. The process was still ongoing when the military coup of 1983 was launched and the major actions of the preceding government were annulled.

The opportunity did not come up again until Colonel Oga became the military governor in Kwara State. The pressure from the Baloguns, supported by the elite, forced the government to institute a Chieftaincy Review Panel, to look into the plea of the Baloguns to be graded, among other requests.[41] The government white paper on the findings and recommendations was not released until a new civilian government under Late Admiral Mohammed Lawal came on board. The implementation of the government white paper on the grading of the Balogun Agba and the Aare to first class status and the other three Baloguns to second class status, created open hostility between the Emir and the late governor, which extended to the electoral campaigns. The coming to

---

41 Information obtained from Department of Chieftaincy Affairs, Governor's Office, Ilorin, January, 2013.

office of Dr. Bukola Saraki as the state governor in 2003 led to a reversion of the Baloguns' grading.

Conclusion

An overview of Ilorin history starting from when Aare Afonja declared Ilorin independent of the Old Oyo Empire's authority, through to the implementation of the Aare's scheme to consolidate his authority in the area and the eventual mobilisation of his slave soldiers against him indicates the militarisation of Ilorin. The killing of Aare Afonja by his slave soldiers created a political leadership vacuum that provided an opportunity for the children of Shehu Alimi, Aare Afonja's Islamic spiritual associate, to proclaim Ilorin an Emirate. They successfully deployed the slave soldiers to massacre groups of Islamic clerics and kill individuals who they felt could resist their political ambition. This trend of military engagements led to the emergence of the Balogun institution which sustained the Emirate as an entity. The leading role of the Baloguns in the affairs of the Ilorin Emirate administration before the advent of colonial rule is the true traditional administrative system that evolved in Ilorin. The efforts of the colonial authority to erode the Balogun's powers and influence to the advantage of the Emir were dictated by exigency. The struggle for government recognition and grading of the Baloguns remains a potent issue for government attention.

248 The Balogun in Yorubaland ...

APPENDICES

Appendix One

APPENDIX ONE

A Biographical Sketch of Balogun Lanre Razak

Balogun Lanre Razak began his career in public service in 1979 when he emerged as a councillor and chairman of the Committee on Works in the old Epe Local Government until 1983. Shortly thereafter, he was summoned to duty again during the administration of Group Captain Gbolahan Mudasiru's military administration of Lagos State (January 1984-August 1986), to mediate between the state government and Epe community at the height of a tax and tenement rate crisis, which had degenerated into a protracted face-off between the government and the people. Through his timely intervention, the prolonged crisis was resolved within two days.

These accomplishments earned Balogun Razak the honour of being elected the executive chairman of the Epe Local Government from 1994 to 1995. Shortly after leaving office, arguably in recognition of his meritorious services, he was appointed as the commissioner for public transport in Lagos State from 1996 to 1997. He had barely relinquished this assignment when tradition beckoned to him to assume the vacancy created by the demise of the sitting

* Balogun Razak's photograph appears on the front cover of this volume.

Appendix One

Balogun of Epe. Chief Razak had spent barely two years as the Balogun of Epe in 1999, when he was appointed the state chairman, and later the national vice chairman Southwest and, subsequently, deputy national chairman of the All Nigerian Peoples Party (ANPP).[1]

A distinguishing feature of the office of the Balogun is the prestige that surrounds it. During festivals and ceremonies for instance, especially during *Eid El Fitri* and *Eid El Kabir* ceremonies when the Muslim faithful march in procession to the Eid for prayer, the Balogun rides with pomp and pageantry on a lavishly decorated stallion, accompanied by a large entourage of gun-firing and horse-trotting admirers. The glamour of the entourage of the Balogun on these festive occasions has always attracted many spectators.

Since 1997, however, more than it had in recent history, Balogun Razak's entourage has had a distinctly youthful composition, which seems to imply that the Balogun institution is growing stronger in popularity, especially among the younger generations of indigenes and non-indigenes alike.[2] But, more importantly is Razak's proclivity as a grassroots mobilizer, philanthro-

---

[1] Interview with Chief Lanre Razak, current Balogun of Ijebu community in Epe, on May 17, 2015 in Lagos.

[2] This claim is based on eye witness accounts by the author.

pist and politician, as well as the leadership role he continues to play in community-based organizations

The popularity of Balogun Lanre Razak among the younger generation was put to the test in 2005 when a bloody confrontation erupted between the Ijebu-Epe and the Eko-Epe, which the police quickly quelled. However, some Ijebu-Epe youths alleged that the police did not play the role of a neutral arbiter of peace in the crisis between them and their Eko-Epe counterparts. Dissatisfied with the way the police handled the crisis, more than ten thousand youths of Ijebu-Epe took to the street brandishing various types of lethal weapons. They marched on the police station in *Oke Oyinbo* chanting war songs and demanding that justice be done, while a meeting between the divisional officer (DPO) and over twelve obas from towns surrounding the Epe area was holding. All efforts to placate the rampaging youths were to no avail. Meanwhile, Balogun Razak was out of town and had to be summoned to intervene in the matter. He met the irate youths on the night of his arrival and was able to accomplish a cessation of hostilities before dawn.

Balogun Razak stands on a social platform that has earned him undeniable acknowledgment as a traditional and political colossus rolled into one.

APPENDIX TWO

A commentary on the institution of the Balogun in Yorubaland, with special reference to Owu

The endemic wars of the 19th century in Yorubaland presented an opportunity for warlords to acquire power and influence in their various states and kingdoms. Properly understood and correctly interpreted, the Balogun in Yorubaland in the pre-colonial era was a fearless soldier of fortune who garnered wealth and power from his conquests.

This multi-authored book examines the origins of the Balogun in eight Yoruba city-states/kingdoms. The adaptation of the case study approach allows the authors to detail the intricate and fluid history of the institution in specific Yoruba societies. This is, as posited by the editors, an attempt to generate context-based data and avoid drawing generalizations of historical realities and to reduce biases.

The book examines the Balogun institution from the circumstances of its emergence as a purely military figure to a political heavyweight within the social, cultural and political developments from pre-colonial to the post-nineteenth century. Given the context within which the Balogun institution emerged, the different writers did justice to the subject matter by examining the traits and experiences of various holders of the title within specific historical contexts, drawing attention to the exploits of heroes and villains and how they brought about change and continuity.

Politically, the office of the Balogun in pre-colonial Yorubaland was one of the major power centres in the palace; the Balogun enjoyed a pre-eminent position particularly among the chiefs. These warlords wielded both military and political authority by virtue of their ascriptions, other than by right of succession.

In essence, this is book highly readable and adds clarity to a difficult subject. Similar projects ought to be initiated to highlight crucial institutions of our cultural, social and political development even though they experience the vagaries of external subjugation and oppression.

Perceived Roles of the Balogun in Modern Day Nigeria

With reference to the views expressed in the book, a Balogun is that citizen who possesses towering courage, charisma and leadership qualities to guarantee the security of life and property in his society. Indeed, the countless titled Baloguns in Yorubaland particularly among the Owu (from Alugbua to Olufakun), were not only able to defend their people against the oppression of tyrants or tyrannical machinations but, also succeeded in infusing a sense of unity into their lives to achieve an imperial offensive and resounding success.

The evolution of the position of the Balogun among the Owu people rested on circumstances of the times. The inference here stems from the fact that, after the Owu War ended the Owu people dispersed to every corner within Yorubaland, becoming like the proverbial wandering Jew. Thus in every place or community in which they relocated, the Owu managed to preserve their identities and cultural distinctiveness (like their facial marks and annual festivals). To this distinctiveness was the evolution of the Balogun title traced from Alugbua to Olufakun in pre-colonial times.

Adubi and Sogade were valiant leaders in the post-nineteenth century struggle. Their undaunted valour and courage guaranteed the safety and prosperity of the Owu over space and time under the Balogunship of Adelekan.

What duties and responsibilities were the Baloguns shouldered with, within the traditional administration of their towns?

The duties and responsibilities of the Balogun in the traditional administration of towns can be traced to the creation of the *olorogun* (war-chiefs) titles, within which the Balogun functions. Though initially an essentially military figure rather than political, the responsibilities of the Balogun included adequate checks on the excesses of internal and external individuals or groups.

Commentary on the Institution of the Balogun

In terms of ranking, the position of the Balogun was not critically different from other chieftaincy titles. This is because a number of titled chiefs were created to oversee different activities in the three townships in the Owu quarters in Abeokuta. Amongst the top ranking and most important positions compared to the Balogun were the Ogboni titles of Akogun, Obamaja, Orunto, Osupori Oyega, Omolasin and Olosi; the ologun titles as well as those of the parakoyi or trade chiefs. The installation of these titleholders as well as the Olowu's was executed in the traditional manner of the time.

The status of the Balogun, in terms of power relations in traditional politics of the town, can be culled from the actions of Baloguns in Yoruba societies where their courage and leadership prowess saw them as the primus causa to almost every policy formulation and execution that affected their towns.

Is the position of Balogun hereditary, by appointment, or compensatory?

From Alugbua to Adelekan, it is obvious the position was not hereditary, but rather a position by royal appointment and recognition of service to the community.

The special qualities considered before being appointed Balogun are basically courage, leadership skills and general or particular services to the community. In certain instances, philanthropic works and personal achievements are considered. These qualities however transcend space and time not only among the Yorubas but every human society.

Definitely there are differences between the traditional responsibilities of the Balogun in pre-colonial, colonial and post-colonial times. This is as a result of circumstances of the times within which a particular Balogun alternates functions and responsibilities.

The Balogun title is now being awarded by religious organizations–is this welcome?

The honorary and compensatory Balogun titles now conferred on distinguished individuals, especially in churches and mosques, are modern day adaptations to suit new socio-political realities in Yorubaland. Whether these distinguished individuals uphold the tenets of the progenitors of Balogunship is left to be seen.

What characteristics of the Balogun title should be preserved in terms of the socio-cultural and political environment of today?

First, with renewed human demands that may lead to developmental growth, I expect the continuous but gradual mutation of the Balogun chieftaincy from its purely traditional duties and responsibilities to a situation where the Balogun title no longer wields military power as a sine qua non. Second, the preservation of the institution should be promoted because as part of a culture, it is a mirror to look through a society's historical development. Third, the Balogun should be in the forefront of the struggle of the community against oppression in any form and the struggle for political, economic, social, educational, cultural and general progress of the community. The Balogun must be a leader in community development and primus inter-pares among the leading chiefs of the community.

History is a continuous discourse between man and his environment. This unending dialogue and diachronic exchange are centred on the past and the present. Any enquiry into the historical development of society is an attempt to stimulate new ideas and research that will extend the frontiers of knowledge beyond the present scope of the subject matter. This book surely will stimulate more discourse on this historically relevant institution.

OLUSEGUN OBASANJO

Abeokuta, February 2016

INDEX

Abeokuta

first *Alake* installed (1855), 9; reverted to civil rule, 11; Balogun Sodeke led the Egba to the new settlement "under the stone", 154; Sodeke's demise (1845), 166, 168; post-Sodeke period, 181, 182; decline in the power of the Olorogun, 170

Aburumaku, Bale of Ogbomoso (1865-69), 66-67; first Balogun in Ogbomoso, 67; died 1869, 67;

Son, Otunla seized power 1869, 67

Ade Kola title, general, 24, 6, 53

Adechegou (Adesegun) title, divisional general, 24, 26, 53

Adesoye, Chief Fasasi (Ijebu-Ode) 1951-1961; paramount Balogun under the British, 33, 40-41; appointed by the Awujale, 44; transport magnate, 41, 42, 45, 46

Ado-Ekiti

Balogun Aduloju, 12; *Osoko Ekiti Soko Akoko*, 12; arrested by British (1898), 12

Ajobo, Balogun (Ibadan), 88-89

Akintola, Balogun (Ibadan), 93

Akintuyi, Balogun (Ibadan), 86

Akoko region

northeastern Yorubaland, 205; no overall paramount ruler 206; balogun institution, 206-217; every Akoko town had its own balogun, 206; in defense against Ibadan, Ilesha and Nupe 207; and the slave trade, 208; each town had its own defence system, 209; rivallry among balo-guns, 209; played both a military and political role, 210-211, 212; both hereditary and appointed, 211-212; under colonial rule,

261

215; stripped of power and authority, 215; 1910 Native Authority Proclamation, 216-217

Alaafins

Obalokun (1689), 3; Ajagbo, 56; and Ogbo-Oro War, 56; warriors and Alaafin's abode, 220; Abiodun (1774-1789), 142

Alake(Abeokuta)

Okikilu, 147-148; Gbadebo, crowned as Alake in 1898, 178;

Alatishe, Chief Juniad (Ijebu-Ode); appointed Otun Balogun by the Awujale, 44; appointed paramount Balogun, 45; the 10-year litigation, 45

Alesinloye, Balogun Ban-kole (Ibadan) 86

Alimi, Malam (Ilorin)

warned against trying to take Ogbomoso, 63

Awujales in Ijebuland

Fidipote, 19, 27; removed from office by Balogun Otutunibon, 28

Fusigboye, 19

Tunwashe, 35 Gbelegbuwa II, 43

and appointment of baloguns, 45-50

Adetona, 501

Baloguns

origins of the institution, 1, 192; in Ijebuland 15-16, 18-19; in Ogbomoso, 57-61; In Ibadan, 89-90; in Epe, 103; in Ijeshaland, 192

its prominence by 1882, 27; other names for, 2, 3; responsibilities, 2; and 19th century Yoruba internecine wars, 4; [see wars]

and the rise of warlords, 5; in Ekiti and Ijesa, 7; in Ilorin, 6-7; and Ibadan,81-102;decline in power, 8-9; British colonial domination, 10-11;

post-war positions in Yoruba towns, 13-14; as a religious title, 14; received a facelift, early 1900s, 37; subordinate offices, Otun and Osi, 40, 48; institution of in Ijebu-Ode, 27-

Balogun chieftancy titles, 140, 142, 144, 150, 151

INDEX 263

Balogun (other) titles

Fulani, 7; *Gambari*, 7; *Ananamu*, 7; *Ajikobi*, 7; *Olorogun*, 9; *Otun*, 48; *Osi*, 48

Balogun Kalejaiye, 158, 159

Balogun Lakanle of the Oyo army, 150, 163

Balogun Kale of the Ijebu army, 150

Balogun Ege, of Ife army, 150, 152, 153

Balogun Aiyejorun of Ondo, 162,163

Balogun Ayikondu of Igbein, 167, 169, 170

Balogun Lamodi, 150-153

Balogun Sodeke [See Abeokuta]

Balogun Aboaba of Abeokuta, 177

Bashorun Oluyole invaded Abeokuta in 1835, 161

British intercession in Nigeria

Colony of Lagos, 10; bombardment of Lagos, 9-10; and their domination in Yorubaland, 10; annexed Ijebu-Ode, 123-124; Promulgated Native Council Ordi-nance (1901), 124; Governor Carter's peace treaty of 1893, 81-82, 97; and Balogun Ajayi Ogboriefon, 94; slaves captured by Ibadan, 95; Governor Campbell of Lagos, 95; and improv-ed access to trade routes to Lagos, 95-96; Gov-ernor Glover, *Afari Ogun*, 96; affect on the office of the Balogun, 97-99

Christian missionaries, (Abeokuta), favourably received by Sodeke, 168; Freeman, Thomas Birch (1842), 168; Townsend, Henry (1843), 166, 168, 170-175

Church Missionary Society (CMS), 10

Dahomey, 143, 167, 168, 173, 178; King Gezo 167, 168; defeated by the Egba forces, 168

Egba groups/provinces (also see Abeokuta) 141, 159; conquered the Ijebu, 159;Egba United Gov-ernment (E.U.G.), 179; Ekiti Parapo wars, 9-10; ended by British, 9

264 INDEX

egiri, age grade of warriors, 3

Eleduware War (1830s) led by Olisa Adebote, 26

elegbe, war-chiefs, 3

Epe town, the evolution of the Balogun; location, 103; origin traditions, 103-104; Huraka vs. Alara, 103; two main Ijebu quarters; Apakeji and Aleke, 106, 109, 125, 126, 134; current Olu-Epe: Oba Adewale Shefiu, 136

Ijebu-Epe and Eko Epe, 106-107, 125; conflicts between the two, 123 fnt 21, 124; Islamic factor, 128; Ijebu-Epe, 136-137; appointment of Balogun Oluwo, 129-132; traditional governing systems, 106-108; judicial authority, 106;

Awujale recognized as paramount ruler, 108 Balogun's role in government, 108 selecting a Balogun, 109-110, 125, 129-131

duties of, 111; and cut-throat rivalries in late 19th century, 125-127;

Eko-Epe

chiefs, 119; origins of the Balogun title, [Epe] 120; early holders of title Chief Akinpelu Iposu (1863-1865), 120; Chief Iyanda Oloko (1865-1875), 120; Chief Agbaje (1865-1866), 120; Chief Iposu, anti-British, 120-121; Chief Iyanda, took title Bale, 121-122; Chief Agbaje, 122-123

British promulgated Epe Native Council Ordinance (1901), 124 first head, 128; set up IJebu-Epe Native Council Ordinance (1905), 129

Baloguns in Epe under colonial rule

Oluwo, Abudu Kadiri (Ijebu Balogun) 1932-1939), 129-131; son of the Oluwo, leader of the Osugbo, 130-131; British supported appointment , 131, 132; disgruntled elements in the Etitun quarter, 133 ;duties as defined by the Colony, 132; suc-ceeded by Chief Aja-konri from Apakeji quarter, 134;

eso, royal guards. Oyo, 2

Fidipote, Awujale
    exiled to Epe, 123

Foko (war title), 89

Gbebi, Taiwo (Ogbomoso)
    Balogun under Ajibola Eleepo, 72

Gbonka, (war title), 89

Hassan, A.K., the *Abowa of Agbowa*, 135

Ibadan
    and military warlords, 81; recognition of the Balogun, 81; role in governance, 82

    Balogun Oluyole defeated the Fulani, 82

    Bower, Captain Robert in Ibadan, 98

    warlords offered protection to farmers, 85; and the trans-Atlantic trade, 85, 93;

    Balogun Ola, trouble maker, 101-102

    Baloguns in Ibadan (1860s to early 1900s)
        Akintola, Balogun, 93
        Akintuyi, Balogun, 86
        Alesinloye, Balogun Bankole, 86
    Oluyole, Balogun
        defeated the Fulani, 82, 85, 88; named Basorun Oyomes, 85; ruled Ibadan as an autocrat, 85, 86
    Ibikunle, Balogun, 86-88 made concessions to the British (1860s), 94 opening of trade routes to Egba and Ijebu, 96
    Irefin, Balogun, 101
    Kongi, Balogun, 1914, 99
    Latoosa, Aare, 92-93, 97
    Lajubu, Balogun, 86
    Ajobo, Balogun, 88-89
    Ogunmola, Basorun, 1866, 89
    Orowusi, Balogun, 89

Ijebu-Ode
    British invasion of, 11; annexed in 1892 29; and Balogun Kuku, 11, 36-40; and Balogun Ogunsi-gun, 11; led an insur-rection against British, 35

    and the origins of the Balogun, 15-16

and warlords, 16-17; in pre-colonial times, 21; in its satellite towns, 30;

first Balogun, 18-19

and the introduction of Christianity, 31; the decline in promin-ence of the awujale nd balogun, 31

Imagbon war, 31; end of baloguns as military leaders commanders, 31

creation of two subordinate offices of Balogun (Abeokuta); Otun and Osi, 40, 48; paramount Balogun between Odutola and Fasisi, 40-41

Ijemo massacre of 1914, 179

Ikuforiji, Balogun, member of Epe Club, 137

Ilesa

Balogun Ogedenge, 11-12

Oba Hastrup, 12

Ilesha/Ijesha

location, 187-188

founding dynasty, Ajibogun Orun Aganiyeye Ekun, 189-190

political structure of, 190-191; Agbanla, 191; Elegbe, 191, 193; Lejoka, Lejofi, Loro, 193

Babaogun, 193; and booty from war, 194-195

Agbogungboro, Seriki Ogedengbe, 198

leader of Ipaiye movement, 198; recruited by Ibadan as a war lord, 202

Ilorin

baloguns kept in check by British, 12; Royal Niger Company invades, 12-13

Baloguns in, 220

treachery and betrayal in Ilorin 1823- 220; Aare Afonja, enemy of newly installed Aaafin, 220-221; Alaafin plots to execute Are Afonja, 221; Are Afonja declares independence for Ilorin, 222; Afonja recruits slaves for his army, 222-223; Afonja killed by slave army, 223

Imam Shehu Alimi friend to Afonja, 223;

INDEX 267

Abdulsalami declares himself emir of Ilorin, 225

Balogun title remains in use in Ilorin, 226; Baloguns in Ilorin, 226-227; unique in Gwandu Emirates, 227; Balogun Agba head of emirate council, 229, 231-232

arrival of the British resident, 232; considered baloguns a threat to colonial rule, 232-233; Balogun Alanamu, 233, 236; arrested and deported, 237; props up emirs, 234, 235, 239; and Bida, 234, 235-236; and the cali-phate in Sokoto, 234-235; and the West Africa Frontier Force, 235; and the Palmer Enquiry, 241; and Emir Abdulkadiri (1919-1959), 242

Ilorin Talaka Parapo, 242, 243

Emir Sulu Karnani Gambari , 243; removed by Sir Ahmadu Bello, 243

Baloguns in Ilorin from 1967, 244; under military governors, 244-245; under civilian governor Adamu Atta, 245; and the quest for more local government areas, 245; demand for ranking of baloguns, 246; and Governor Olu Saraki, 246

British residents in Ilorin, David Carnegie, 233; P Dwyer, 233, 238

Ilu chiefs (Ogbomoso)
under British colonial rule, 73-74

Imagbon War, 1892, 31

Jagun/Jagunna Gbonka,
other names for Balogun, 2, 11; Jagunna; Commander in Chief of the Egba army, 144; Egba war chief, 181

Kayokayo festival, 137

Kiriji War
and Awujale Fidipote, 27; and Ogbomoso, 71-72; and Ibadan, 98

Kongi, Balogun (Ibadan), 1914, 99

Kosoko exiled to Epe from Lagos (1851), 115; recalled

to Lagos (1862), 117-118; and slave trade, 170-173

Kuku, Seriki Odueyungbo, 32

Kuku, Chief Akadiri Somori Adefuye--Ijebu-Ode (1927-1950); paramount Balogun under the British, 33, 39-40, 42

Kuku, Chief Bello Odueyungbo (Ijebu-Ode) (1899-1907), 38; para-mount Balogun under the British, 33, 38; wealthy trader, 34-35; appointed Seriki, 34; negotiated a peaceful settlement with British, 35-36; converted to Christianity, 36; became paramount Balogun of Ijebu-Ode (1899), 36; timber magnate, 36-37

Kuku, Chief Gbadamosi Tayo (Ijebu Ode) 1907-1927, 38-39; paramount Balogun under the British, 33

Lafinjin
first Jagun, (Ogbomoso), 58

Lajubu, Balogun (Ibadan),86

Latoosa, Aare (Ibadan)
committed suicide, 92-93; pro traditional war system, 97; prolong-ed Kiriji War, 97

Lisabi, Agbongbolo Akala 144, 145, 149, 157, 163

Egba leader, 141; Egba Olorogun uprising, 141
his unpopularity and demise, 146

Lord Lugard
annexation of Abeokuta, 179; and powerful Baloguns in Ilorin, 232, 238

Oba Adele of Lagos ,158

Odejayi family (Ijebu–Ode) and their claim for the paramount Balogun title, 42, 44-45, 50

Odueyungbo [see Chief Bello Kuku]

Odufopo (1860s)
first Balogun of Ogbomoso, 60, 66, 77

Odunnuga, Chief J.A.B.
contender for Ijebu-Ode paramount Balogun office, 42; appointed Otun Balogun in 1996, 51; became paramount Balogun on the death of Shote, 2001, 51

Odutola, Chief Timothy Adeola, 40-41

INDEX 269

Ogbomoso

origins of, 55-56; emergence of Egbe Alongo, 56-57

19th century frontier town against the Fulani, 66

Soun Olabanjo Ogunlola, head Egbe Alongo, 56; first among equals, 57; the palace chiefs under Soun Ogunlola, 59-61

Aareago, head of Soun's bodyguards, 59-60, 61

Aolu Agoro, 58, 61

Alapo, 60; duties of, 65; Jagun, (war general) 58, 60, 61; Bara, 60; Abese, 60; Alapo, 61; Ikolaba, 60; Are Ona Kakanfo, 61-62

war with Ilorin, 63

Akanni, Baale Toyeje, 63

Soun, 63; walled the city in 1797, 63

Oluwusi, Baale (1826-1840), 63; prominent warriors under, 63; Oyelekan seizes power from 64

five royal families in, 74

kingmaker families, 74

crime in Ogbomoso, 77

Balogun institution 55-77; introduction of Balogun title, 59; installation of, 69 -70; use of the *opagun*, 67, 71; crime control in 75; members of advi-sory council, 78

Ogunmola, Basorun (Ibadan), 1866, 89; also served as a judge, 90; and the reopening of the Egba-Ijebu trade routes, 96

Ojude-Oba Festival, 51, 52

Ola, Balogun (Ibadan) anti-British colonials, 101-102; demoted by British, 102

Olaoye (Orumogege), Baale of Ogbomoso, 1877, 67

Old Oyo Kingdom establishment of *Aare-Ona-Kakanfo* (Balogun), 3 military chief in Old Oyo, 3; Alaafin Obalo-kun, 3; collapse of in 19th century, 3

Olori Ogun, another name for Balogun, 2

Olorogun institution

the Olorogun society (war society);180 under Lisabi, 141, 163; central Olorogun council, 164; became an instrument of political cohesion in Egbaland, 164

Olorogun title, captain, 24, 26; Olorogun chieftaincy titles, 180

Olukongbon
title, commanding general, 24, 26, 53

Olusi, Baale OluwusiAremu (Ogomoso) Soun, 1826 to1840, 63

Onafowokan
first Balogun in Ijebuland, 19, 26; also known *Otutunibon*, 19, 26; and Owu War of 1820, 20; led by Olisa Dipe, 24, 25; and Imagbon war, 1892, 31; under Bri-tish rule, 31-32; ceded his title to Odueyun-gbo (1899), 36; ousts Oba Fidipote (1883), 123

Orowusi, Balogun, pro peaceful trade routes, 96

Otutunibon, (a.k.a. Onafowokan); first Balogun of Ijebu-Ode, 19; removes Awujale in 1883, 28-29

Owota, (war title), 89

Owu War (1820) 20, 26, 139, 146

oye ilu, town chief, 2, 11, 13

seriki, military chief in Old Oyo, 3; junior military officers, 82, 98

Shote, Chief M.O.
Otun Balogun, 48; eulogized by King Sunny Ade, 48; most philan-thropic and wealthy, 49-50; appointed para-mount Balogun in 1996, 50; died in 2001, 51.

slave trade, abolishment supported by Akitoye, 170-173; conflict with Kosoko 70-173; slave trade among Akoko, 208

warlords (19th century)
emergence of, 5; prominent ones, 5, 6; and the rise of private armies, 6; and advent of Christian missions, 8; and the socioeconomic state of Ibadan, 81

wars
Owu war, 139, 146; Ogede-pagbo war between Igbein and Itoku, 146; Agbaje civil war, 147; Itoku and Oba war, 147; Ilugun civil war, 146, 148; Arakanga war of 1835, 161, 162, 181; Owiwi

INDEX

War of 1832, 158, 162, 181; Imag-bon War, 1892, 31

Yisa of Itoko, 150, 169, 181 first Egba man to receive Balogun title, 150; succeeded by Lamodi, 150

INDEX

ABOUT THE EDITORS

Mufutau Oluwasegun Jimoh holds B.A, History and Diplomatic Studies from Olabisi Onabanjo University, Ago- Iwoye and an M.A in History from the University of Ibadan. He is a research fellow of the French Institute of Research in Africa. He is a member of the Society of Social History, USA. He was a research fellow with University of London (Birkbeck college, 2013). He is the author of "Migration and Social Change in the Eastern District of Lagos: The Mahin Factor in Epe History"; "Managing Epidemics: The British approach to 1918-1919 inflluenza in Lagos", 2015; co-authored with Prof. Tajudeen Gbadamosi, Habeeb Sanni, Supo Shasore, SAN, et. al *A History of Lagos State from Earliest Times,* 2015. Co-author with Professor O.A. Lawal "Missile from the 'Kerstine Hall': Macaulay versus Hugh Clifford, 1922-1931". He has attended international confer-ences in UK, France and Israel and Spain.

He is currently a lecturer in history and international studies with the Federal University, Birnin-Kebbi.

Philip Oloruntola holds Bachelor and Master Degrees in History and Anthro-pology, respectively. He is the CEO of Silver Lining Creative and Innovative Concepts, a research and publications advisory firm. H e also examines for the West African Examination Council on Civics.

He is affiliated to the Department of Archaeology and Anthropology, University of Ibadan.

www.ingramcontent.com/pod-product-compliance
Lightning Source LLC
Chambersburg PA
CBHW051351290426
44108CB00015B/1962